Presidential Facts

Presidential Facts

Topical Lists, Comparisons and Statistics

EDWARD S. SKINNER

McFarland & Company, Inc., Publishers
Jefferson, North Carolina, and London

LIBRARY OF CONGRESS CATALOGUING-IN-PUBLICATION DATA

Skinner, Edward S.
    Presidential facts : topical lists, comparisons and statistics /
Edward S. Skinner.
       p.   cm.
    Includes bibliographical references.

    ISBN-13: 978-0-7864-2427-6
    ISBN-10: 0-7864-2427-3 (softcover : 50# alkaline paper)

    1. Presidents—United States—History—Miscellanea.
2. Presidents—United States—Biography—Miscellanea.
I. Title.
E176.1.S614   2006
973.09'9—dc22   2006016743

British Library cataloguing data are available

On the cover: bank note and President Polk portrait ©2005
clipart.com; coins ©2005 PhotoSpin; George Washington
painting ©2005 Pictures Now; Frances Folsom Cleveland
portrait provided by Library of Congress

Manufactured in the United States of America

McFarland & Company, Inc., Publishers
  Box 611, Jefferson, North Carolina 28640
  www.mcfarlandpub.com

IC/REF

Table of Contents

Preface   1

1. The Presidents, Alphabetically   3
2. Presidential Parents   3
3. Date of Birth   6
4. Astrological Signs   8
5. Presidential Full Names   9
6. First Names   10
7. State and Place of Birth   11
8. Order of Birth   12
9. Siblings   13
10. Relatives of Note   15
11. Religious Affiliations   17
12. Height   19
13. Education   20
14. Military Service   21
15. Age at Marriage   23
16. Wives   24
17. Wives' Vital Statistics   27
18. Other Loves   29
19. Children   31
20. Careers Before the Presidency   36
21. Political Party   37
22. Appointed Offices Held   38
23. Elected Offices Held   41
24. Campaign Issues   43

Table of Contents

25.	Popular Vote	47
26.	Percent of Popular Vote	48
27.	Electoral Vote	50
28.	Percent of Electoral Vote	52
29.	States Won	54
30.	Percent of States Won	62
31.	How the States Voted	64
32.	Also-Rans	94
33.	Age at Inauguration	97
34.	Length of Inaugural Address	98
35.	Living Former Presidents at Start of Term	99
36.	Vice Presidents	103
37.	Cabinets	105
38.	Supreme Court Appointees	137
39.	House Composition	141
40.	Senate Composition	146
41.	Presidential Accomplishments and Significant Issues	151
42.	Vetoes	159
43.	States Admitted During Administration	160
44.	Constitutional Amendments	163
45.	Wars	164
46.	Presidential Pardons	166
47.	White House Pets	167
48.	Time Spent in Office	171
49.	Age Upon Leaving Office	172
50.	How the Presidents Relaxed	173
51.	Places of Retirement	176
52.	Years Lived after the Presidency	177
53.	Last Words	178
54.	Date of Death	180
55.	Age at Death	181
56.	Cause of Death	182
57.	Place of Death	184
58.	Burial Places	185
59.	Presidents Who Held No Other Elected Office	186
60.	Post-Presidential Offices	187

61. Vice Presidents Succeeding Presidents Who Died in Office   187
62. Bearded Presidents   187
63. Presidential Firsts, Lasts, and Onlies   188
64. Presidential Salaries   190
65. Calendar of Presidential Events   191
66. Presidential Quotes   218
67. Books by Presidents   225
68. Presidential Historical Sites and Libraries   228

Preface

The United States has had forty-two men serve as Chief Executive. These men have ranged in age from forty-two to seventy-nine when they assumed office. They have hailed from eighteen states. They have been both slave holders and those opposed to the institution.

The nation has elected the temperate and the indulgent; the ultra-liberal and the ultra-conservative. The nation has tried holders of ideas of all stripes in the executive mansion. They have all been sincere in their service to country, some successful and some not so. Some served with eagerness, some with reluctance. But the changes they wrought, the marks they left in history, are with us today.

The purpose of this book is not to judge their efforts or their methods. This book is meant to serve as a comparison tool in different categories. Each chapter will show the differences and the similarities of each President.

This book will show the changing voting patterns of the states. It will show the preference of worship of the Presidents. It will illustrate the ways in which they came to office.

Using this book will aid in research on a particular President or the institution of the Presidency. By going to a particular chapter one can gather the needed information for a particular President or compare all of the Presidents. It is the intent of this work to trace the path each followed from birth to the grave, in an orderly manner. Many interesting facts are contained in the individual chapters. Further illumination is provided in the endnotes.

This is meant to serve as an aid to research, not as an all-inclusive work. There are many good volumes available on the Presidents, and this one is meant as a quick reference guide to supplement those works. It is far easier to reference, for example, the chapter on "Age Upon Entering the Presidency" than to attempt to find the same information in another kind of work. Thus the purpose is to ease the effort of research and to compare the Presidents in an easy to use format for each category.

This is the culmination of years of research on the different aspects of the Presidency, and is offered to the serious student and researcher as well as to the reader who simply wants some information on a particular President or a comparison among two or more.

It is hoped that this work will make it easy for others to answer questions on which President received the highest number of votes and which received the greatest percentage of votes. The Electoral College is also covered by number and by percent.

In the chapter on Supreme Court appointments one can find that President Taft was named Chief Justice by President Harding. There is a chapter dealing with each President's Cabinet.

The original lists were for personal satisfaction, but soon the idea of this book was formed. It is hoped that the reader will find the contents useful and easy to consult.

1. The Presidents, Alphabetically

Of the forty-two men who have served as the nation's Chief Executive, none has a last name beginning with the letters D, I, O, Q, S, U, X, Y, or Z. The other sixteen letters of the alphabet are all represented in the list below. The most-used letter is H, by 5 Presidents. Next are C, J, and T, representing 4 Presidents each.

Adams, John	Grant, Ulysses	Monroe, James
Adams, John Q.	Harding, Warren	Nixon, Richard
Arthur, Chester	Harrison, Benjamin	Pierce, Franklin
Buchanan, James	Harrison, William	Polk, James
Bush, George H. W.	Hayes, Rutherford	Reagan, Ronald
Bush, George W.	Hoover, Herbert	Roosevelt, Franklin
Carter, James	Jackson, Andrew	Roosevelt, Theodore
Cleveland, Grover	Jefferson, Thomas	Taft, William
Clinton, William	Johnson, Andrew	Taylor, Zachary
Coolidge, Calvin	Johnson, Lyndon	Truman, Harry
Eisenhower, Dwight	Kennedy, John	Tyler, John
Fillmore, Millard	Lincoln, Abraham	Van Buren, Martin
Ford, Gerald	McKinley, William	Washington, George
Garfield, James	Madison, James	Wilson, Woodrow

2. Presidential Parents

All Presidents had them. Some helped, some hindered. Teddy Roosevelt's father was the guiding force in his life. Young Teddy was a sickly, asthmatic child and a victim of "smother love" by his mother. Papa Roosevelt took him in hand and told him to build his body and become strong.

Teddy may have gone a bit overboard, but the results clearly showed parental influence.

President	Mother	Father
George Washington	Mary Ball[1]	Augustine Washington[2]
John Adams	Susanna Boylston	John Adams
Thomas Jefferson	Jane Randolph	Col. Peter Jefferson[3]
James Madison	Eleanor Rose Conway	James Madison
James Monroe	Elizabeth Jones	Spence Monroe
John Quincy Adams	Abigail Smith[4]	John Adams[5]
Andrew Jackson	Elizabeth Hutchinson[6]	Andrew Jackson[7]
Martin Van Buren	Maria Hoes Van Alen[8]	Abraham Van Buren
William Henry Harrison	Elizabeth Bassett	Benjamin Harrison V.[9]
John Tyler	Mary Armistead[10]	John Tyler
James Polk	Jane Knox[11]	Samuel Polk
Zachary Taylor	Sarah Dabney Strother	Richard Taylor
Millard Fillmore	Phoebe Millard	Nathaniel Fillmore[12]
Franklin Pierce	Anna Kendrick	Benjamin Pierce[13]
James Buchanan	Elizabeth Speer	James Buchanan Sr.
Abraham Lincoln	Nancy Hanks[14]	Thomas Lincoln
Andrew Johnson	Mary McDonough	Jacob Johnson
Ulysses Grant[15]	Hannah Simpson	Jesse Root Grant
Rutherford Hayes	Sophia Birchard	Rutherford Hayes[16]
James Garfield	Eliza Ballou[17]	Abram Garfield
Chester Arthur	Malvina Stone	Rev. William Arthur[18]
Grover Cleveland	Ann Neal	Rev. Richard Cleveland[19]
Benjamin Harrison	Elizabeth Irwin	John Scott Harrison[20]
William McKinley	Nancy Allison	William McKinley, Sr.
Theodore Roosevelt Jr.	Martha Bulloch[21]	Theodore Roosevelt, Sr.
William Taft	Louisa Maria Torrey	Alphonso Taft[22]
Woodrow Wilson	Janet Woodrow	Joseph R. Wilson[23]
Warren Harding	Dr. Elizabeth Dickerson[24]	George Tryon Harding[25]
Calvin Coolidge	Victoria Moor[26]	John Calvin Coolidge[27]
Herbert Hoover	Huldah Minthorn[28]	Jesse Clark Hoover[29]
Franklin D. Roosevelt	Sara Delano[30]	James Roosevelt[31]
Harry Truman	Martha Ellen Young[32]	John A. Truman
Dwight Eisenhower	Ida Elizabeth Stover	David Eisenhower
John Kennedy	Rose Fitzgerald	Joseph P. Kennedy[33]
Lyndon Johnson	Rebekah Baines	Sam Ealy Johnson[34]
Richard Nixon	Hannah Milhous	Francis A. Nixon
Gerald Ford	Dorothy Ayer Gardner[35]	Leslie Lynch King
Jimmy Carter	Lillian Gordy	James Earl Carter
Ronald Reagan	Nelle Wilson	John Edward Reagan
George H. W. Bush	Dorthy Walker	Prescott Bush[36]
Bill Clinton	Virginia Cassidy[37]	William Blythe
George W. Bush	Barbara Pierce[38]	George H. W. Bush[39]

NOTES

1. Mary's father died when she was 3. At 12 she was orphaned and raised by George Eskridge. She may have been the first First Mother but, by all reports, George spent more time fighting Indians, the French, Redcoats, and congressmen than in her company.

2. He died when George was an infant. George was raised by his half-brother Lawrence.

3. He was a colonel in the local militia, and later a general.

4. The first woman to be wife to one President and mother to another.

5. Second President of the United States. Adams died during his son's Presidency.

6. She raised three boys on her own, in the frontier, as a single mother.

7. He died a few days before Andrew was born.

8. Her first marriage was to Johannes Van Alen.

9. A signer of the Declaration of Independence for the Virginia delegation. A congressman, and the only man to be both father of one President and great-grandfather of a President.

10. She died when Tyler was seven years old.

11. She was the first Presidential mother to outlive her son the President.

12. First father to visit his son the President in the White House.

13. Fought at Lexington and Bunker Hill and was at Valley Forge. Anna was his second wife. Elizabeth Andrews, his first wife, died.

14. She died when Abe was nine.

15. Grant was the first President to have both parents living when he took office.

16. Died eleven weeks prior to his son's birth.

17. First mother to attend her son's inauguration. She survived him by about seven years.

18. He was a Baptist preacher.

19. He first preached as a Congregationalist, then as a Presbyterian.

20. Elizabeth was his second wife. He is the only man to be the son of one President and father of another.

21. She was a Southerner married to a New Yorker during the Civil War. She actively supported the Confederacy during the war.

22. First wife Fanny Phelps died at age 29 of tuberculosis. Alphonso helped found the Republican Party. He served as Grant's Secretary of War in 1876, and as minister to Austria-Hungry and Russia for Arthur.

23. He was a Presbyterian minister and a staunch supporter of the Confederacy.

24. She was a medical doctor. She gained her license in 1896.

25. He married Warren's mother when he was 20. After her death he remarried at age 68, and after her death he again remarried, this time at age 78.

26. She died when Cal was twelve.

27. He married his second wife, Carrie Brown, six years after the death of his first. He was a notary public and justice of the peace. In this capacity he administered the Presidential Oath of Office to his son in the family cabin in Vermont.

28. She died when Herbert was nine.

29. He died when Herbert was six.

30. She was James' second wife and sixth cousin. She opposed FDR entering politics.

31. He died when FDR was starting Harvard.

32. She was raised in Missouri as a Confederate. When she visited her son in the White House she refused to sleep in the Lincoln Room.

33. No, he was not a bootlegger. On the eve of the repeal of Prohibition he formed a company and gained the sole U.S. distribution rights for certain brands of Scotch and gin. He also made money in real estate, movies, and retail merchandising.

34. As a state legislator, Sam co-sponsored a bill to purchase the Alamo.

35. Her first husband fathered her son. The son was named for him. She left her husband because he was reportedly beating her. She took her son to her parents at Grand Rapids, Michigan. There she met and married Gerald R. Ford and renamed her son after him. President Ford was never legally adopted.

36. Served in WWI as a captain. Defeated Abraham Ribicoff in a special election for the U.S. Senate. As senator he co-sponsored the Federal Aid Highway Act of 1956.

37. She married William Jefferson Blythe in 1943. He was killed in an auto accident in 1946 before Bill was born. She then married Roger Clinton in 1950. He adopted young Bill. Virginia and William divorced in 1962, but remarried in the same year. He died in 1967. She then married Jeff Dwire, who died in 1974. In 1982 she married Richard Kelly.

38. Following Abigail Adams, Barbara was married to one President and mother to another.

39. The other father and son President team.

3. Date of Birth

We celebrate Presidents' Day in February. Four presidents were born in that month, but that is also true of January, March and April. By being born in June, George H. W. Bush filled the last open month in the calendar. The only other month with a single representative is September, Taft. November has five presidents, but October leads the pack with six. Two Presidents, Polk and Harding, share November 2 as a birthday; they are the only Presidents with a common birthday. They were born seventy years apart.

Nixon and Ford were both born in 1913; Clinton and G. W. Bush were both born in 1946.

Presidents born 100 years apart:

Jefferson (1743) & McKinley (1843)
Monroe (1758) & T. Roosevelt (1858)
Van Buren (1782) & F. Roosevelt (1882)
Tyler (1790) & Eisenhower (1890)
A. Johnson (1808) & L. Johnson (1908)[1]

3 Presidents were born in years ending in 0
4 Presidents were born in years ending in 1

6 Presidents were born in years ending in 2
6 Presidents were born in years ending in 3
6 Presidents were born in years ending in 4
3 Presidents were born in years ending in 5
3 Presidents were born in years ending in 6
5 Presidents were born in years ending in 7
4 Presidents were born in years ending in 8
2 Presidents were born in a year ending in 9

JANUARY	7 (1800) Fillmore		11 (1767) J. Q. Adams
	9 (1913) Nixon		14 (1913) Ford[4]
	29 (1843) McKinley	AUGUST	
	30 (1882) F. Roosevelt	AUGUST	10 (1874) Hoover
			19 (1946) Clinton
FEBRUARY	6 (1911) Reagan		20 (1833) B. Harrison
	9 (1773) W. H. Harrison[s]		27 (1908) L. Johnson
	12 (1809) Lincoln		
	22 (1732) Washington	SEPTEMBER	15 (1857) Taft
MARCH	15 (1767) Jackson[3]	OCTOBER	1 (1924) Carter[5]
	16 (1751) Madison		4 (1822) Hayes
	18 (1837) Cleveland		5 (1829) Arthur
	29 (1790) Tyler		14 (1890) Eisenhower
			27 (1858) T. Roosevelt
APRIL	13 (1743) Jefferson		30 (1735) Adams
	23 (1791) Buchanan		
	27 (1822) Grant	NOVEMBER	2 (1795) Polk
	28 (1758) Monroe		(1865) Harding
			19 (1831) Garfield
MAY	8 (1884) Truman		23 (1804) Pierce
	29 (1917) Kennedy		24 (1784) Taylor
JUNE	12 (1924) Bush	DECEMBER	5 (1782) Van Buren
JULY	4 (1872) Coolidge		28 (1856) Wilson
	6 (1946) G. W. Bush		29 (1808) A. Johnson

NOTES

1. Andrew Johnson and Lyndon Johnson were the only Presidents to share a last name but not be related. The Adamses and Bushes were father and son, the Harrisons were grandfather and grandson, and the Roosevelts were cousins.

2. William Henry Harrison was the last President who was born a British subject.

3. Some of his political enemies (and their numbers were legion) claimed Jackson was actually born on the ship which brought his parents to this country. If true, Jackson would have been barred by the Constitution from the Presidency.

4. Ford was born Leslie King.

5. Carter was the first of our Presidents to be born in a hospital.

4. Astrological Signs

Many world leaders, dating back to ancient times, have looked to the stars to learn the future. Many battles have been planned around the positions of the stars. There is no magic astrological sign for Presidents. No sign has given us fewer than two Presidents. Scorpio and Aquarius have each provided us with five Presidents, while Aries and Gemini have each given us two. Starting with Aries (the first sign of the Zodiac), the Presidents are listed below by sign and in order of service.

ARIES (March 21–April 19)
Jefferson
Tyler

TAURUS (April 20–May 20)
Monroe
Buchanan
Grant
Truman

GEMINI (May 21–June 21)
Kennedy
Bush, G.H.W.

CANCER (June 22–July 22)
Adams, J. Q.
Coolidge
Ford
Bush, G. W.

LEO (Jul 23–Aug 22)
B. Harrison
Hoover
Clinton

VIRGO (Aug 23–Sept 22)
Taft
L. Johnson

LIBRA (Sept 23–Oct 23)
Hayes
Arthur
Eisenhower
Carter

SCORPIO (Oct 24–Nov 21)
Adams
Polk
Garfield
T. Roosevelt
Harding

SAGITTARIUS (Nov 22–Dec 21)
Van Buren
Taylor
Pierce

CAPRICORN (Dec 22–Jan 19)
Fillmore
A. Johnson
Wilson
Nixon

AQUARIUS (Jan 20–Feb 18)
W. H. Harrison
Lincoln
McKinley
F. Roosevelt
Reagan

PISCES (Feb 19–March 20)
Washington
Madison
Jackson
Cleveland

5. Presidential Full Names

We've known them as "Zach," "Bill," "Jimmy," and "Ike." They have served us with their middle names, nicknames and, on occasion, their formal monikers. Here is how they were named by their families.

George Washington
John Adams
Thomas Jefferson
James Madison, Jr.
James Monroe
John Quincy Adams
Andrew Jackson
Martin Van Buren
William Henry Harrison
John Tyler
James Knox Polk
Zachary Taylor
Millard Fillmore
Franklin Pierce
James Buchanan
Abraham Lincoln
Andrew Johnson
Ulysses Simpson Grant[1]
Rutherford Birchard Hayes
James Abram Garfield
Chester Alan Arthur

Stephen Grover Cleveland
Benjamin Harrison
William McKinley, Jr.
Theodore Roosevelt, Jr.
William Howard Taft
Thomas Woodrow Wilson
Warren Gamaliel Harding
John Calvin Coolidge
Herbert Clark Hoover
Franklin Delano Roosevelt
Harry S Truman[2]
David Dwight Eisenhower[3]
John Fitzgerald Kennedy
Lyndon Baines Johnson
Richard Milhous Nixon
Gerald Rudolph Ford, Jr.[4]
James Earl Carter, Jr.
Ronald Wilson Reagan
George Herbert Walker Bush
William Jefferson Clinton[5]
George Walker Bush

NOTES

1. Originally named Hiram Ulysses Grant. A clerical error at West Point changed his name to Ulysses Simpson Grant. He considered how the initials USG vs. his given name would look on his footlocker and kept the new name.
2. That's it. "S" was his middle name.
3. There is a story that his mother was frustrated because everyone called his two older brothers, Arthur and Edgar, Art and Ed. Thus she named her third son Dwight, reasoning that the name could not be shortened. It worked. People called him "Ike." (His first and middle names were eventually reversed.)
4. He was born Leslie Lynch King, Jr. His stepfather renamed him.
5. Born William Jefferson Blythe, he was adopted by his mother's second husband.

6. First Names

What is in a name? We have had Presidents whose names reflected their times, such as Rutherford and Calvin. We have had an Abraham and a Zachary. In between we've had Presidents with more common names, such as James (with six, it is the most used name among the Presidents) and Ronald. In this chapter we are dealing with the name used (James), not nicknames or other variations (Jim or Jimmy).

Given	Last	Given	Last
Abraham	Lincoln		Carter
Andrew	Jackson	John	Adams
	Johnson		Adams (Q.)
Benjamin	Harrison		Tyler
Calvin	Coolidge		Kennedy
Chester	Arthur	Lyndon	Johnson
Dwight	Eisenhower	Martin	Van Buren
Franklin	Pierce	Millard	Fillmore
	Roosevelt	Richard	Nixon
George	Washington	Ronald	Reagan
	Bush	Rutherford	Hayes
	Bush (W.)	Theodore	Roosevelt
Gerald[1]	Ford	Thomas	Jefferson
Grover	Cleveland	Ulysses[2]	Grant
Harry	Truman	Warren	Harding
Herbert	Hoover	William	Harrison
James	Madison		McKinley
	Monroe		Taft
	Polk		Clinton
	Buchanan	Woodrow	Wilson
	Garfield	Zachary	Taylor

NOTES

1. Born Leslie Lynch King, Jr. Ford was adopted by Gerald Rudolf Ford, Sr. and renamed for him. Ford later changed the spelling of his middle name to Rudolph.
2. Born Hiram Ulysses Grant. When he went to West Point, in order to avoid the initials HUG on his trunk, he changed his name to Ulysses Hiram Grant. Through error, he was enrolled as Ulysses Simpson Grant. He liked it and never changed it.

7. State and Place of Birth

Eighteen states have given us our forty-two Presidents. Virginia has given us the most Presidents (eight), but Ohio is close behind with seven. Here are the states which have been the birthplace of our chief executives, alphabetically by state, and then in order served for states producing two or more Presidents.

State	President	Birth Place
Arkansas	Clinton	Hope
California	Nixon	Yorba Linda
Connecticut	G. W. Bush	New Haven
Georgia	Carter[1]	Plains
Illinois	Reagan	Tampico
Iowa	Hoover	West Branch
Kentucky	Lincoln	Hardin (Larue) County
Massachusetts	J. Adams	Braintree (Quincy)
	J. Q. Adams	Braintree (Quincy)
	Kennedy	Brookline
	G. H. W. Bush	Milton
Missouri	Truman	Lamar
Nebraska	Ford	Omaha
New Hampshire	Pierce	Hillsborough
New Jersey	Cleveland	Caldwell
New York	Van Buren	Kinderhook
	Fillmore	Locke Township
	T. Roosevelt	New York City
	F. Roosevelt	Hyde Park
North Carolina	Polk	Mecklenburg County
	A. Johnson	Raleigh
Ohio	Grant	Point Pleasant
	Hayes	Delaware
	Garfield	Orange
	B. Harrison	North Bend
	McKinley	Niles
	Taft	Cincinnati
	Harding	Corsica
Pennsylvania	Buchanan	Cove Gap
South Carolina	Jackson[2]	Waxhaw Region
Texas	Eisenhower	Denison
	L. Johnson	Johnson City

State	*President*	*Birth Place*
Vermont	Arthur	North Fairfield
	Coolidge	Plymouth Notch
Virginia	Washington	Westmoreland County
	Jefferson	Shadwell (Albermarle County)
	Madison	Port Conway
	Monroe	Westmoreland County
	W. H. Harrison[3]	Charles City County
	Tyler	Charles City County
	Taylor	Orange County
	Wilson	Staunton

NOTES

1. Carter was the first President born in a hospital.
2. There is some dispute as to Jackson's actual birthplace. Both North and South Carolina claim to be the birth place of the seventh president. In order to settle the dispute, albeit on a temporary basis, the high schools of Union County in North Carolina, and Lancaster County in South Carolina, square off in an annual gridiron contest known as the *Old Hickory Football Classic*. The winner has the right to claim itself as "Old Hickory's" birthplace for the following year.
3. William Harrison was the last President to be born a British subject.

---

8. Order of Birth

The oldest? The youngest? The middle child? Which is most likely to become President? In the United States 12 of our 43 Presidents were first born children, and 20 were born somewhere between first and last. Seven were last born, and three have been only children.

In order of birth and then by order served. In parentheses is the number of children in the family. For the middle children the second figure is where they fit into the birth order.

First Born

George Washington	(5)[1]		Warren Harding	(6)
John Adams	(3)		Calvin Coolidge	(2)
James Madison	(7)		Harry Truman	(3)
James Polk	(10)		Lyndon Johnson	(5)
James Buchanan	(8)		Jimmy Carter	(4)
Ulysses Grant	(6)		George W. Bush	(5)

Middle Born

Thomas Jefferson*	(8)	(3rd)	John Q. Adams*	(4)	(2nd)	
James Monroe	(5)	(2nd)*	Martin Van Buren	(5)[2]	(3rd)	
Benjamin Harrison	(6)[3]	(2nd)	William McKinley	(8)	(7th)	
John Tyler	(8)	(6th)	William Taft	(4)	(2nd)	
Zachary Taylor	(8)	(3rd)	Woodrow Wilson*	(4)	(3rd)	
Millard Fillmore	(9)	(2nd)	Herbert Hoover	(3)	(2nd)	
Franklin Pierce	(7)	(6th)	Dwight Eisenhower	(6)	(3rd)	
Chester Arthur	(8)	(5th)	John Kennedy	(9)	(2nd)	
Grover Cleveland	(9)	(5th)	Richard Nixon	(5)	(2nd)	
Theodore Roosevelt	(4)	(2nd)	George H.W. Bush	(5)	(2nd)	

Last Born

Andrew Jackson	(3)	Rutherford Hayes*	(2)
William Harrison	(7)	James Garfield	(4)
Abraham Lincoln	(2)	Ronald Reagan	(2)
Andrew Johnson	(2)		

Presidents who were the only child:

Franklin Roosevelt (Older half-brother)
Gerald Ford (4 younger half-brothers and 2 younger half-sisters)
Bill Clinton (younger half-brother)

*Denotes first born male. (20 of our 42 presidents were first born male.)

NOTES

1. Washington had 2 older half brothers.
2. Van Buren had 2 half brothers, and 1 half sister.
3. Harrison had 2 half sisters.

9. Siblings

Our Presidents have come from families of all sizes, from large ones to simple a mother and her son. Family seems neither to help nor hinder in reaching the nation's highest office. No President was raised an only child. Each President has had at least one sibling, although some were half sister or brother. Listed here in order of total siblings, and order served as a secondary category, are all 42 men who served as Presidents.

Total	Bros.	Sis.	President
9	5	4	James Polk
8	5	3	Millard Fillmore
	3	5	Grover Cleveland
	3	5	John Kennedy
7	1	6	Thomas Jefferson
	2	5	John Tyler
	4	3	Zachary Taylor
	3	4	James Buchanan
	1	6	Chester Arthur
	3	4	William McKinley
6	3	3	James Madison
	2	4	William Harrison
	4	2	Franklin Pierce
5	3	2	George Washington
	2	3	Ulysses Grant
	3	2	Benjamin Harrison
	1	4	Warren Harding
	5	0	Dwight Eisenhower
4	3	1	James Monroe

Total	Bros.	Sis.	President
	2	2	Martin Van Buren
	1	3	Lyndon Johnson
	4	0	Richard Nixon
	3	1	George H. W. Bush
	3	1[1]	George W. Bush
3	2	1	John Q. Adams
	1	2	James Garfield
	2	1	Theodore Roosevelt
	2	1	William Taft
	1	2	Woodrow Wilson
	1	2	Jimmy Carter
2	2	0	John Adams
	2	0	Andrew Jackson
	1	1	Herbert Hoover
	1	1	Harry Truman
1	0	1	Abraham Lincoln
	1	0	Andrew Johnson
	0	1	Rutherford Hayes
	0	1	Calvin Coolidge
	1	0	Ronald Reagan

Half brothers and sisters

Total	Bros.	Sis.	President
6	4	2	Gerald Ford
3	2	1	Martin Van Buren
2	2	0	George Washington
	0	2	Benjamin Harrison
	2	0	William Taft
1	0	1	Franklin Pierce
	1	0	Franklin Roosevelt
	1	0	Bill Clinton

NOTES

1. George W. Bush's sister is said to be the first person publicly baptized in Communist China.

10. Relatives of Note

Many of the Presidents have been related to other Presidents, or to other well-known people. Here is a list of the Presidents and their relatives who also were famous.

GEORGE WASHINGTON   James Madison (half first cousin, twice removed); Queen Elizabeth II (2nd cousin, seven times removed); Robert E. Lee (3rd cousin, twice removed); Winston Churchill (8th cousin, six times removed).

JOHN ADAMS   John Q. Adams (son); Samuel Adams (2nd cousin); Abigail Smith Adams[1] (3rd cousin).

THOMAS JEFFERSON   Chief Justice John Marshall[2] (2nd cousin, once removed).

JAMES MADISON   George Washington (half first cousin, twice removed); Zachary Taylor (2nd cousin).

JAMES MONROE   none

JOHN Q. ADAMS   John Adams (father); Samuel Adams (2nd cousin, once removed); Abigail Adams[3] (3rd cousin once removed).

ANDREW JACKSON   None of note.

MARTIN VAN BUREN   Theodore Roosevelt (3rd cousin, twice removed).

WILLIAM HENRY HARRISON   Benjamin Harrison (grandson).

JOHN TYLER   Harry S Truman (great-nephew).

JAMES K. POLK   None

ZACHARY TAYLOR   None

MILLARD FILLMORE   None

FRANKLIN PIERCE   None

JAMES BUCHANAN   None

ABRAHAM LINCOLN   Robert Todd Lincoln[4] (son).

ANDREW JOHNSON   None

ULYSSES GRANT   Franklin Roosevelt (4th cousin, once removed); Grover Cleveland (6th cousin, once removed); Judy Garland (1st cousin, three times removed).

RUTHERFORD HAYES   None

JAMES GARFIELD   None

CHESTER ARTHUR   None

GROVER CLEVELAND   Ulysses Grant (6th cousin, once removed).

BENJAMIN HARRISON   William Henry Harrison (grandfather); William Harrison[5] (grandson).

WILLIAM McKINLEY   None

THEODORE ROOSEVELT   Martin Van Buren (3rd cousin, twice removed); Franklin D. Roosevelt (5th cousin); Eleanor Roosevelt (niece); Joseph Alsop (great-nephew); Stewart Alsop (great-nephew).

WILLIAM TAFT   Richard Nixon (7th cousin, twice removed); Ralph Waldo Emerson (distant relative).

WOODROW WILSON   None

WARREN HARDING   None

CALVIN COOLIDGE   None

HERBERT HOOVER   Richard Nixon (8th cousin, once removed).

FRANKLIN D. ROOSEVELT   Ulysses Grant (4th cousin, once removed); Zachary Taylor (4th cousin, three times removed); Theodore Roosevelt (5th cousin); Eleanor Roosevelt[6] (5th cousin, once removed); Winston Churchill (7th cousin, once removed).

HARRY TRUMAN   John Tyler (great-uncle).

DWIGHT EISENHOWER   None

JOHN F. KENNEDY   None

LYNDON B. JOHNSON   None

RICHARD NIXON   Jessamyn West[7] (2nd cousin); William H. Taft (7th cousin, twice removed); Herbert Hoover (8th cousin, once removed).

GERALD FORD   George H. W. Bush (11th cousin, once removed); George W. Bush (11th cousin, twice removed).

JIMMY CARTER   None

RONALD REAGAN   None

GEORGE H. W. BUSH   Benedict Arnold (4th cousin, seven times removed); Franklin Pierce (5th cousin, four times removed); Theodore Roosevelt (7th cousin, three times removed); Abraham Lincoln (7th cousin, four times removed); Winston Churchill (8th cousin, once removed); Marilyn Monroe (9th cousin, twice removed); Dan Quayle[8] (10th cousin, once removed); Gerald Ford[9] (11th cousin, once removed); George W. Bush (son); J. E. B. Bush[10] (son).

WILLIAM CLINTON   None

GEORGE W. BUSH[11]   Barbara Bush (mother)

NOTES

    1. She was Adams' wife.
    2. Marshall was Chief Justice of the United States Supreme Court.
    3. Abigail was also John Quincy Adams' mother.
    4. He was the only Lincoln child to live to maturity. He served as Secretary of War for President Garfield and President Arthur. He was minister to Great Britain (1889–1893). He also served as president of the Pullman Company.
    5. Wyoming representative in Congress: 1951–1955; 1961–1965; 1967–1969.
    6. Eleanore was FDR's wife.
    7. Author, best known for *The Friendly Persuasion*.
    8. Dan Quayle served as G. H. W. Bush's Vice President.
    9. Bush served as chief U.S. liaison in China for President Ford.
    10. "JEB" is the governor of Florida.
    11. Refer to George H. W. Bush for additional family connections.

11. Religious Affiliations

All of our Presidents were raised in the Christian faith. Some practiced it, some did not. Eleven were Episcopalian, six were Presbyterian. Hoover and Nixon were members of the Society of Friends, or Quakers. Even the Presidents who practiced no faith held a belief, if not in God, in some higher power. Lincoln was most definitely a believer. Many were not members of any denomination simply because of a lack of organized churches in their areas. Here are our Presidents and their chosen forms of worship.

President	Practiced	President	Practiced
Washington	Episcopalian[1]	Cleveland	Presbyterian
Adams	Unitarian	B. Harrison	Presbyterian
Jefferson	None[2]	McKinley	Methodist
Madison	Episcopalian	T. Roosevelt	Dutch Reform
Monroe	Episcopalian	Taft	Unitarian
J. Q. Adams	Unitarian[3]	Wilson	Presbyterian
Jackson	Presbyterian[4]	Harding	Baptist
Van Buren	Dutch Reformed[5]	Coolidge[13]	Congregationalist
W. H. Harrison	Episcopalian	Hoover	Quaker
Tyler	Episcopalian	F. Roosevelt	Episcopalian
Polk	Methodist[6]	Truman	Baptist
Taylor	Episcopalian[7]	Eisenhower[14]	Presbyterian
Fillmore	Unitarian	Kennedy[15]	Roman Catholic
Pierce	Episcopalian[8]	L. Johnson[16]	Disciples of Christ
Buchanan	Presbyterian[9]	Nixon	Quaker
Lincoln[10]	None	Ford	Episcopalian
A. Johnson	None	Carter	Baptist
Grant[11]	Methodist	Reagan	Disciples of Christ
Hayes[12]	Methodist	Bush	Episcopalian
Garfield	Disciples of Christ	Clinton	Southern Baptist
Arthur	Episcopalian	G. W. Bush[17]	Methodist

NOTES

1. Washington was raised as an Episcopalian, but in his speeches and writings he referred to Providence in lieu of a deity.

2. Jefferson was raised in the Anglican faith. In early adulthood he left organized religion and relied on reason rather than religion. He never lost his belief in the teachings of Jesus, and believed that mankind would come to the logical conclusion that these teachings showed the path to a better way of interacting with one another.

3. Although a devout Christian all his life, J. Q. did not formally join the Unitarian Church until he became President.

4. Although Jackson did not formally join a church until after his retirement from public life, he was deeply religious. His manners and language caused many to doubt his commitment to faith, but his writings show a deep religious tendency.

5. President Van Buren attended services at St. John's Episcopal Church since there was no Dutch Reformed Church in the Capital City.

6. Polk's mother tried to have him baptized as a Presbyterian. His father refused to profess faith in the Presbyterian Church, and the Reverend refused to perform the baptism. Polk was still raised as a Presbyterian and practiced the faith until 1833, when he converted to the Methodist point of view after being moved by a sermon by a Methodist preacher.

7. Taylor attended Episcopal services, but never joined a church.

8. Pierce was not baptized into the church until after he left the White House. Much of his faith seems to have stemmed from the death of his son.

9. Buchanan found his faith at the end of his Presidency. He postponed joining the church until he left office.

10. Lincoln was born Baptist and later attended Presbyterian services. He never joined any church.

11. Grant was never baptized into the church, but he did attend services regularly.

12. As a youth Hayes was baptized a Presbyterian. He attended the Methodist Church out of deference to his wife. He never formally joined.

13. While a regular at Sunday Services, Coolidge did not join the church until after becoming President.

14. Although raised in a strict religious environment, Ike was not baptized into the church until 1953.

15. Kennedy is the only Roman Catholic President.

16. LBJ was the first incumbent President to meet with the Pope.

17. With an Episcopalian father and a Presbyterian mother, "W" set his own course and joined his wife's church.

12. Height

Lincoln, of course, was the tallest President. James Madison was the shortest. Between them were forty others. Here they are, tall and short.

6'4"

Abraham Lincoln

6'3"

Lyndon Johnson

6'2½"

Thomas Jefferson
William Clinton

6'2"

George Washington
Chester A. Arthur
William H. Taft
George Bush

6'1"

Andrew Jackson
Franklin D. Roosevelt
Ronald Reagan

6'½"

John F. Kennedy

6'

James Monroe
John Tyler
James Buchanan
James Garfield
Grover Cleveland
Warren G. Harding
Gerald Frod
George W. Bush

5'11½"

Dwight Eisenhower
Richard Nixon

5'11"

Woodrow Wilson
Herbert Hoover

5'10"

Franklin Pierce
Andrew Johnson
Calvin Coolidge
Harry S Truman

5'9½"

James E. Carter

5'9"

Millard Fillmore

5'8½"

Rutherford B. Hayes

5'8"

James K. Polk
William H. Harrison
Zachary Taylor
Theodore Roosevelt

5'7"   *5'6"*   *5'4"*

John Q. Adams   John Adams   James Madison
Ulysses S. Grant   Martin Van Buren
William McKinley   Benjamin Harrison

13. Education

Seven Presidents attended Harvard. Four went to Yale. George W. Bush went to both.

They have also attended Bowdoin College, Union College, or taught themselves. Though there is no constitutional requirement that the President even be able to read or write, all of them possessed at least a rudimentary education. Andrew Johnson was taught to read and write by his wife. For our purposes, "self educated" means little to no formal education. The listing is in order each man served.

President	Education
Washington	Self Educated
Adams	Harvard
Jefferson	College of William and Mary
Madison	College of New Jersey (Princeton)
Monroe	College of William and Mary
J. Q. Adams	Harvard
Jackson	Self Educated
Van Buren	Self Educated
W. H. Harrison	Hampden-Sydney College; Pennsylvania Medical School
Tyler	College of William and Mary
Polk	University of North Carolina
Taylor	Self Educated
Fillmore	Self Educated
Pierce	Bowdoin College
Buchanan	Dickenson College
Lincoln	Self Educated
A. Johnson[1]	Self Educated
Grant	U.S. Military Academy at West Point
Hayes	Kenyon College; Harvard Law School
Garfield	Williams College
Arthur	Union College

President	Education
Cleveland	Self Educated[2]
B. Harrison	Miami University (Ohio)
McKinley	Allegheny College; Albany Law School[3]
T. Roosevelt	Harvard
Taft	Yale; Cincinnati Law School
Wilson	College of New Jersey (Princeton); Johns Hopkins University
Harding	Ohio Central College
Coolidge	Amherst
Hoover	Stanford University
F. Roosevelt	Harvard
Truman	Kansas City Law School[4]
Eisenhower	U.S. Military Academy at West Point; U.S. Army Command General Staff School; Army War College; Industrial College of the Armed Forces
Kennedy	Harvard
L. Johnson	Southwest Texas State Teachers College
Nixon	Whittier College; Duke University School of Law
Ford	University of Michigan; Yale Law School
Carter	U.S. Naval Academy at Annapolis
Reagan	Eureka College
G. H. W. Bush	Yale
Clinton	Georgetown University; Oxford University;[5] Yale
G. W. Bush	Yale; Harvard Business School

NOTES

1. Johnson never set foot inside a classroom as a student. Almost all of his education was from his wife, Eliza.
2. Cleveland was our last President who did not receive a formal education.
3. Attended. Did not graduate.
4. Truman was the last President who did not graduate college. His tenure at Kansas City Law School was two years.
5. Clinton attended Oxford for two years, as a Rhodes Scholar.

14. Military Service

Some Presidents served in the military, some didn't. Our tradition would seem to require military service in order to be Commander-in-Chief. Washington, Jackson, Grant, Teddy Roosevelt, and Eisenhower were all war heroes. But, out of our forty-two Presidents, thirteen had no military background. Of the remaining twenty-five, Tyler, Lincoln, and T. Roosevelt served in a very limited capacity. Lincoln never saw action in the Blackhawk War. Six consecutive Presidents, Taft to FDR (1909–1945) had no military background. The next nine Presidents, Truman to Bush, all had military background, Truman in WWI and Carter in peacetime. The rest served in WWII. Until Kennedy, all Presidents with a service background had come from the Army. Kennedy was the first Navy man elected. Four of the five Presidents who followed him were also Navy men. Of those five only Reagan served in the Army. Jackson was the first President to serve in the U.S. Armed Forces. The following is but a recap of the Presidents' military backgrounds. Some were civilian soldiers; others, Ike for one, had military careers. In order of Presidential service.

President	*Service*
Washington	Colonel (Virginia Militia), French and Indian War; Commander of Continental Army, Revolutionary War
Adams	None
Jefferson	None
Madison	Colonel (Virginia Militia), Revolutionary War
Monroe	Major (Continental Army), Revolutionary War
J. Q. Adams	None
Jackson[1]	Revolutionary War Militia Member; 1st Seminole War; Major General (U.S. Army), War of 1812
Van Buren	None
W. H. Harrison	General, Shawnee Indian War; Brigadier General, War of 1812
Tyler	Militia Captain, War of 1812
Polk	Colonel, War of 1812
Taylor	War of 1812; Blackhawk War; 2nd Seminole War; Major General, Mexican War
Fillmore	None
Pierce	Brigadier General, Mexican War
Buchanan	Served in War of 1812
Lincoln	Militia Captain,[2] Blackhawk Indian War
A. Johnson	Brigadier General, Civil War (Military Governor of Tennessee)
Grant	Captain, Mexican War; General of the Armies, Civil War
Hayes	Major General, Civil War
Garfield	Major General, Civil War
Arthur	Quartermaster General (New York Militia), Civil War
Cleveland	None
B. Harrison	Brigadier General, Civil War
McKinley	Major, Civil War[3]
T. Roosevelt	Colonel, Spanish-American War
Taft	None
Wilson	None
Harding	None

President	Service
Coolidge	None
Hoover	None
F. Roosevelt	None
Truman	Brevet Major, WWI[4]
Eisenhower	Supreme Commander (Five Star General), Allied Expeditionary Forces in Europe, WWII
Kennedy	Lieutenant (U.S. Navy), WWII
L. Johnson	Lt. Commander (U.S. Navy), WWII
Nixon	Lt. Commander (U.S. Navy), WWII
Ford	Lieutenant (U.S. Navy), WWII
Carter	Lieutenant, U.S. Navy[5]
Reagan	Captain (U.S. Army), WWII[1]
G.H.W. Bush	Lieutenant (U.S. Navy), WWII
Clinton	None
G.W. Bush	Lieutenant, Texas Air National Guard

NOTES

1. Jackson was the last of the Revolutionary War Presidents. He is the only President to have been a prisoner of war.

2. Lincoln was elected captain of his company. It is reported that this honor meant more to him than the Presidential nomination of 1860.

3. McKinley was the last of the Civil War Presidents.

4. Truman is the only president to have served in WWI. He is generally thought of as a captain. The brevet rank is a temporary promotion given in wartime. He reverted to captain when he left the Army.

5. Carter was in the Navy during the Korean War, but saw no fighting. He is the only President to have served on submarines, and the only one to serve during the Korean War.

6. Reagan was barred from combat due to poor eyesight. He spent WWII stateside attending war bond rallies, and narrating training films.

15. Age at Marriage

We can't have a first lady without a marriage. Forty-one of our forty-two Presidents were married. Here they are listed by age at the time of marriage. The only bachelor President, Buchanan, does not appear in this list. In cases of two marriages the name of the first wife is shown in parentheses. When the age at marriage is the same, the first to have served is listed first.

Age	President	Age	President
18	A. Johnson		Polk
20	B. Harrison (Caroline[1])		T. Roosevelt (Edith)
	G. Bush		Taft
21	Carter		Wilson (Ellen[5])
22	W. H. Harrison		Reagan (Jane[6])
	T. Roosevelt (Alice[3])	29	Pierce
23	Tyler (Letitia[4])		Clinton
	F. Roosevelt	30	J. Q. Adams
24	Jackson		Hayes
	Van Buren		Arthur
	Hoover	31	G. W. Bush
25	Taylor	33	Lincoln
	Harding		Coolidge
	Eisenhower	35	Truman
26	Washington		Ford
	Fillmore (Abigail[2])	36	Kennedy
	Garfield	43	Madison
	Grant	41	Reagan (Nancy)
	L. Johnson	49	Cleveland
27	Monroe	54	Tyler (Julia)
	Nixon	58	Fillmore (Caroline)
	McKinley		Wilson (Edith)
28	Jefferson	62	B. Harrison (Mary)
	J. Adams		

NOTES

1. Caroline Harrison died of tuberculosis 25 Oct. 1892, just two weeks before her husband was defeated for reelection.

2. Abigail Fillmore died 30 March 1853. She caught a cold at the inauguration of Franklin Pierce. The cold turned to pneumonia.

3. Alice Roosevelt died of Bright's disease and childbirth complications 14 Feb. 1884, the same day and in the same house as Roosevelt's mother.

4. Letitia Tyler died of a stroke 10 Sept. 1842.

5. Ellen Wilson died of Bright's disease 6 Aug. 1914.

6. Jane Wyman divorced Ronald Reagan. The divorce was finalized 18 July 1949.

16. Wives

"I desire you would remember the ladies," Abigail Adams wrote in a letter to her husband, John Adams, as the Continental Congress debated independence.

The "First Lady" is an unofficial official of the United States government. She is hostess of the White House and a goodwill ambassador at home and abroad.

The office of the First Lady, as we know it today, is credited to Eleanor Roosevelt. But prior to her, "Lemonade Lucy" Hayes banned liquor from use in the White House. Edith Wilson was active in her husband's administration to the point that she was referred to as Mrs. President. Not all who served as first lady were wives, nor were all wives First Ladies. Some who served as First Lady were daughters, and even a niece served.

Alphabetically, by President's last name.

Presidents	*Wives*
Adams, J.	Abigail Smith Adams[1]
Adams, J. Q.	Louisa Catherine Johnson Adams[2]
Arthur	Ellen Lewis Herndon[3]
Buchanan	Harriet Lane[4]
Bush, G.H.W.	Barbara Pierce
Bush, G. W.	Laura Welch
Carter	Rosalynn Smith
Cleveland	Francis Folsom
Clinton	Hillary Rodham
Coolidge	Grace Anna Goodhue
Eisenhower	Marie (Mamie) Geneva Doud
Fillmore	Abigail Powers
Ford	Elizabeth Anne Bloomer[5]
Garfield	Lucretia Rudolph
Grant	Julia Boggs Dent
Harding	Florence Mabel Kling
B. Harrison	Caroline Lavinia Scott[6]
	Mary Scott Lord Dimmick[7]
W. H. Harrison	Anna Tuthill Symes[8]
Hayes	Lucy Wares Webb[9]
Hoover	Lou Henry
Jackson	Rachel Donelson Robards[10]
Jefferson	Martha Wayles Skelton[11]
A. Johnson	Eliza McCardle
L. Johnson	Claudia Alta Taylor
Kennedy	Jacqueline Lee Bouvier
Lincoln	Mary Todd
Madison	Dolley Payne Todd[12]
McKinley	Ida Saxon
Monroe	Elizabeth Kortright
Nixon	Thelma Catherine (Patricia) Ryan
Pierce	Jane Means Appleton
Polk	Sarah Childress

Presidents	Wives
Reagan	Jane Wyman
	Nancy Davis[13]
F. Roosevelt	Anna Eleanor Roosevelt[15]
T. Roosevelt	Alice Hathaway Lee
	Edith Kermit Carow[14]
Taft	Helen Herron
Taylor	Margaret (Peggy) Mackall Smith[16]
Truman	Elizabeth (Bess) Virginia Wallace
Tyler[17]	Letitia Christian[18]
	Julia Gardiner[19]
Van Buren	Hanna Hoes[20]
Washington	Martha Dandridge Custis[21]
Wilson[22]	Ellen Louise Axson[23]
	Edith Bolling Galt[24]

Notes

1. Abigail Adams and Barbara Bush are the only two First Ladies to also be mothers of Presidents.

2. Louisa was born in London, England. She is the only foreign-born First Lady.

3. Ellen died a year and a half prior to Arthur's becoming President. The duties of White House hostess were performed by his sister, Mary Arthur McElroy.

4. Harriet was Buchanan's niece. Buchanan was our only bachelor President.

5. Ford was the second husband of Betty. Her first marriage ended in divorce.

6. Caroline served as First Lady. She died 25 Oct. 1892 of tuberculosis.

7. Harrison married Mary four years after leaving office.

8. Due to illness, Mrs. Harrison never saw the White House. Their daughter-in-law, Jane Irwin Harrison, served as hostess for the single month of the Harrison Presidency.

9. Lucy Rudolph Hayes became known as "Lemonade Lucy" because of her absolute devotion to the temperance movement. During the Hayes Administration she forbade intoxicating beverages of any type in the White House.

10. Jackson's beloved Rachel died 22 Dec. 1828, less than 3 months before Jackson's inauguration. The hostess duties were carried out by Jackson's niece, Emily Jackson.

11. Martha died 6 Sept. 1782. Hostess duties were carried out by Dolly Madison and Jefferson's daughter Martha (Patsy) Randolph. Although no portrait exists of Mrs. Jefferson, she was said to have been a very lovely lady.

12. Born Dolley Payne. She married John Todd, Jr. in 1790. Todd died three years later.

13. Nancy was Reagan's second wife. He divorced Jane Wyman (born Sarah Jane Fulks) in 1948.

14. Edith was Roosevelt's second wife. His first wife, Alice Hathaway Lee, died of Bright's disease, and childbirth complications, 14 Feb. 1884, the same day his mother died.

15. Franklin and Eleanor were fifth cousins. The happy couple were married 17

March 1905. The bride was given away by her uncle, Teddy Roosevelt, the President of the United States.

16. Mrs. Taylor was a semi-invalid. She remained in the family quarters of the White House. The Taylors' daughter, Betty Bliss, acted as hostess.

17. Both of Tyler's wives served as First Lady.

18. Letitia died 10 Sept. 1842. She is the first First Lady to die in the White House.

19. Julia and John were the first Presidential couple to wed in the White House, 26 June 1844.

20. Hannah succumbed to tuberculosis 5 Feb. 1819. Van Buren never remarried.

21. Martha was a widow when she married Washington. She was first married to a wealthy planter Daniel Parke Custis. When he died she inherited his estate and by all accounts became the catch of the county.

22. Both wives served as First Lady.

23. Ellen died 6 Aug. 1914, during Wilson's first term in office.

24. Born Edith Bolling, she married Norman Galt in 1896. He died in 1908. Wilson married Edith 18 Dec. 1915.

---

17. Wives' Vital Statistics

Eliza Johnson married at the youngest age. She was only 16 when she married Andrew Johnson.

Bess Truman lived longer than any other Presidential wife. She died at the age of 97.

Here are birth dates; age at marriage; date of death; and years lived for all Presidential wives whether or not they were First Ladies.

Currently we have seven living First Ladies. They are listed at the end in the order their husbands served as President. Otherwise, the wives are listed in descending order by age at death.

Wife	President	DOB	Age Wed	DOD	Age
Elizabeth Wallace	Harry Truman	02/13/1895	34	10/18/1982	97
Mary Lord	Benjamin Harrison[1]	04/30/1858	37	01/05/1948	89
Edith Galt[2]	Woodrow Wilson	10/15/1872	43	12/29/1961	89
Sarah Childress	James Polk	09/04/1803	24	07/10/1891	87
Edith Carrow	Theodore Roosevelt	08/06/1861	25	09/30/1948	87
Lucretia Rudolph	James Garfield	04/19/1852	26	03/14/1918	85
Frances Folsom	Grover Cleveland	07/21/1864	21	10/29/1947	83
Marie Doud	Dwight Eisenhower	11/14/1896	19	11/11/1979	83
Helen Folsom	William Taft	06/02/1861	25	05/22/1943	81
Dolly Todd	James Madison	05/29/1748	26	07/12/1849	81
Catherine Ryan	Richard Nixon	03/16/1912	28	06/22/1993	81

17. Wives' Vital Statistics

Wife	President	DOB	Age Wed	DOD	Age
Grace Goodhue	Calvin Coolidge	01/3/1879	26	07/08/1957	78
Eleanor Roosevelt	Franklin Roosevelt	10/18/1884	20	11/07/1962	78
Louisa Johnson[3]	John Q. Adams	02/12/1775	22	05/15/1852	77
Julia Dent	Ulysses Grant	01/26/1826	22	12/14/1902	75
Abigail Smith	John Adams	11/23/1744	19	10/28/1818	73
Margaret Smith	Zachary Taylor	09/21/1788	21	08/14/1852	73
Caroline McIntosh	Millard Fillmore	10/21/1813	44	08/11/1881	73
Martha Custis	George Washington	06/21/1731	27	05/22/1802	70
Lou Henry	Herbert Hoover	03/29/1874	24	01/07/1944	69
Anna Symmes	W. H. Harrison	07/25/1795	20	02/25/1864	68
Lucy Webb	Rutherford Hayes	08/28/1831	22	06/25/1889	67
Eliza McCardle	Andrew Johnson	10/04/1810	16	01/15/1876	66
Julia Gardiner[4]	John Tyler	05/04/1824	24[5]	07/10/1889	65
Jacqueline Bouvier	John Kennedy	07/28/1929	24	05/19/1994	64
Mary Todd	Abraham Lincoln	12/13/1818	23	07/16/1882	63
Elizabeth Kortright	James Monroe	06/30/1768	17	09/23/1830	62
Rachel Robards	Andrew Jackson	02/12/1775	26[6]	12/22/1828	61
Florence Kling	Warren Harding	08/15/1860	25	08/06/1924	61
Caroline Scott[7]	Benjamin Harrison	10/01/1832	21	10/25/1892	60
Ida Saxton	William McKinley	06/08/1847	23	05/23/1907	60
Jane Appleton	Franklin Pierce	03/12/1806	28	12/02/1863	57
Abigail Powers	Millard Fillmore	03/13/1798[8]	27	03/30/1853	55
Ellen Axson	Woodrow Wilson	05/15/1860	25	08/06/1914	54
Letitia Christian	John Tyler	11/12/1790	22	09/10/1842[9]	51
Ellen Herndon	Chester Arthur	08/30/1837	22	01/10/1880[10]	42
Hannah Hoes[11]	Martin Van Buren	03/08/1783	23	02/05/1819	35
Martha Skelton	Thomas Jefferson	10/30/1748	23	09/06/1782[12]	34
Alice Lee	Theodore Roosevelt	07/29/1861	19	02/14/1884[13]	22
Claudia Alta	Lyndon Johnson	12/22/1912	21		
Elizabeth Bloomer	Gerald Ford	04/08/1918	30		
Rosalyn Smith	Jimmy Carter	08/18/1927	18		
Jane Faulks[14]	Ronald Reagan	01/04/1914	26		
Anne Robbins[15]	Ronald Reagan	07/06/1923[16]	30		
Barbara Pierce	George Bush	06/08/1925	20		
Hillary Rodham	William Clinton	10/26/1947	27		
Laura Welch	George W. Bush	11/04/1946	31		

NOTES

1. Harrison was 62 when he and Mary wed.
2. Edith Bolling was her name at birth. She was a widow when she married Wilson, who was 58 and President of the United States.
3. Louisa Johnson is the only foreign-born First Lady. She was born in London, England.
4. Julia Gardiner also served as First Lady.

5. Tyler was 54 when he married Julia.
6. Rachel and Andrew Jackson were both 22 when they first married. The marriage was declared invalid because Rachel's divorce from Lewis Robards was not final. They remarried four years later.
7. Caroline Scott was Harrison's first wife. She served as First Lady, but died during his re-election campaign.
8. Abigail Fillmore was the last First Lady born in the 18th century.
9. Letitia Tyler died in the White House.
10. Ellen died of pneumonia. Although she never served as First Lady, Arthur had fresh flowers placed before her picture every day of his Presidency.
11. Hannah Van Buren died of tuberculosis. She never served as First Lady, having died 17 years before Van Buren became President. Van Buren never remarried.
12. Martha Jefferson was never first lady. She died 19 years before Jefferson became President and died four months after giving birth to a daughter. The daughter died at age two. Jefferson promised her that he would never remarry when she was dying.
13. Alice Roosevelt died of Bright's disease. In a tragic twist of fate she died on the same day in the same house as TR's mother.
14. Her stage name is Jane Wyman.
15. Nancy was a nickname for Anne Frances Robbins. We know her as Nancy Davis due to her adoption by her mother's second husband.
16. Nancy lists her year of birth as 1923. Other records put it at 1921.

---

18. Other Loves

Some Presidents fell in love, were married and never had an interest in anyone other than their wives. The bachelor President, Buchanan, loved Anne Coleman but she died abruptly, and he never loved another. Other Presidents loved more than once, some before marriage, some after, some before, after, and during.

In order served.

President	*Romantic Interest*
Washington[1]	Betsy Fauntleroy; Mary Philipse; Sally Fairfax
Adams, John	Hannah Quincy
Jefferson	Rebecca Burwell; Betsey Walker; Maria Cosway[2]; Sally Hemmings[3]
Madison	Kitty Floyd
Monroe	Nannie Brown
Adams, John Q.	Nancy Hazen; Mary Frazier
Jackson	Mary Crawford[4]
Van Buren[5]	Ellen Randolph; Margaret Sylvester

President	Romantic Interest
Harrison, William H.	"Miss M"[6]
Tyler	None
Polk	None
Taylor	None
Fillmore	None
Pierce	None
Buchanan	Anne Coleman[7]
Lincoln	Ann Rutledge; Mary Owens
Johnson, Andrew	Sara Wood
Grant	None
Hayes	Fanny Perkins
Garfield	Mary Hubell; Rebecca Selleck
Arthur	None
Cleveland	Maria Halpin[8]
Harrison, Benjamin	None
McKinley	None
Roosevelt, Theodore	None
Taft	None
Wilson	None
Harding	Carrie Phillips[9]; Nan Britton[10]
Coolidge	None
Hoover	None
Roosevelt, Franklin	Lucy Page Mercer[11]
Truman	None
Eisenhower	Kay Summersby[12]
Kennedy[13]	Frances Cannon; Charlotte McDonnell; Harriet Price; Inga Arvad
Johnson[14]	Alice Glass[15]
Nixon	Ola Florence Welch
Ford	Phyllis Brown
Carter	None
Reagan	Margaret Cleaver
Bush	None
Clinton[16]	Gennifer Flowers; Paula Jones;[17] Monica Lewinsky
Bush, G. W.	None

NOTES

1. These three were all prior to Washington's marriage to Martha.
2. The affairs with Maria Cosway and Sally Hemmings came after his wife's death. Jefferson promised Martha he would never remarry.
3. Sally was one of Jefferson's slaves. Their affair lasted 38 years, and Jefferson is rumored to have fathered at least one child with her.
4. Mary Crawford was Andrew's cousin.

5. Van Buren's wife died after 10 years of marriage. His two affairs took place after her death.

6. A Presidential mystery. Harrison met and seems to have fallen in love with "Miss M" while in Philadelphia. He referred to her in a letter to his brother, but precious few details exist as to her identity.

7. Anne Coleman broke off the engagement for unknown reasons. She died, possibly of suicide, while visiting relatives in Philadelphia. Buchanan never loved again.

8. Maria Halpin was a widow with two children. She moved to Buffalo, alone, and was keeping company with Cleveland and others. She became pregnant and named Cleveland as the father. He denied it, but paid to support the child, since he was a bachelor and all other potential fathers were married.

9. Carrie Phillips was the wife of Harding's friend James Phillips. The affair was unknown until 1963, when several love letters were discovered. The affair seems to have begun around 1905, and continued on and off for several years.

10. Harding fathered a daughter with Nan Britton. This affair started around 1917 and ran concurrent with the Carrie Phillips affair.

11. Lucy Mercer was Eleanor's social secretary.

12. Kay Summersby was Ike's driver in London. The certainty of the affair is in question. Ike and Kay did spend time in each other's company, but no concrete evidence exists to support a love affair.

13. There is no hard evidence that Jack cheated on Jackie. It was after his assassination that rumors of affairs began. They include Blaze Starr (stripper), Mary Pinchot Meyer, Judith Exner, and Marilyn Monroe.

14. Johnson's brother claims that LBJ was engaged to the daughter of a KKK leader. No name is available. He allegedly broke the engagement when her father made scurrilous remarks about his family.

15. This romance is said to have run from the late 1930s into the 1960s, when Alice broke it off due to her opposition to the war in Viet Nam.

16. All affairs were after marriage.

17. Paula Jones claims to have had sex with then Arkansas Governor Bill Clinton. Clinton denies the liaison and it has never been proven.

---

19. Children

The father of our country fathered no children of which we are aware. Thus there are no known, direct descendants of George Washington. Others with no progeny are Madison, Jackson, Polk and Buchanan. Pierce and McKinley both had children who died in their youth. Tyler was the most productive with fourteen offspring. Unless otherwise noted, children shown are those who lived to maturity.

Here the Presidents are listed by order of progeny produced, and the order served.

19. Children

President	Wife	Children
Tyler (14)	Letitia	Mary
		Robert
		John, Jr.
		Letitia
		Elizabeth[1]
		Alice
		Tazewell
Julia[2]	David Gardiner	("Gardie")
		John Alexander ("Alex")
		Julia Gardiner
		Lachian
		Lyon Gardiner
		Robert Fitzwater ("Fitz")
		Pearl[3]
Harrison, W. H. (9)	Anna	Elizabeth "Betty" Bassett
		John Cleves Symmes
		Lucy Singleton
		William Henry, Jr.
		John Scott[4]
		Benjamin
		Mary Symmes
		Carter Bassett
		Anna Tuthill
Roosevelt, T. (6)	Alice	Alice
	Edith	Theodore, Jr.
		Kermit
		Ethel Crow
		Archibald Bulloch
		Quentin[5]
Johnson, A. (5)	Eliza	Martha[6]
		Charles[7]
		Mary
		Robert
		Andrew, Jr.
Hayes (5)	Lucy	Sardis Birchard
		James Webb[8]
		Rutherford Platt
		Francis ("Fanny")
		Scott Russell
Garfield (5)	Lucretia	Harry Augustus
		James Rudolph
		Mary ("Mollie")
		Irvin McDowell
		Abram
Cleveland (5)	Frances	Ruth

President	Wife	Children
		Esther[9]
		Marion
		Richard Folsom
		Francis Grover
Roosevelt, F. (5)	Eleanor	Anna Eleanor
		James
		Elliot
		Franklin Delano, Jr.
		John Aspin Wall
Bush, G. H. W. (5)	Barbara	George W.[10]
		John (Jeb)
		Neil
		Marvin
		Dorothy
Adams, John (4)	Abigail	Abigail (Nabby)
		John Quincy[11]
		Charles
		Thomas Boylston
Van Buren (4)	Hannah	Abraham
		John
		Martin, Jr.
		Smith Thompson
Taylor (4)	Margaret	Ann Mackall
		Sarah Knox[12]
		Mary Elizabeth ("Betty")[13]
		Richard ("Dick")
Grant (4)	Julia	Frederick Dent
		Ulysses ("Buck")
		Ellen "Nellie" Wrenshall
		Jesse Root
Ford (4)	Elizabeth	Michael Gerald
		John "Jack" Gardner
		Steven Meigs
		Susan Elizabeth
Carter (4)	Rosalynn	John "Jack" William
		James Earl ("Chip")
		Jeffrey
		Amy
Reagan (4)	Jane	Maureen
	Nancy	Michael[14]
		Patti
		Ronald Prescott
Adams, J. Q. (3)	Louisa	George Washington
		John II
		Charles Francis

President	Wife	Children
Pierce (3)	Jane	Franklin, Jr.[15]
		Frank Robert[16]
		Benjamin ("Bennie")[17]
Lincoln (3)	Mary	Robert Todd
		William "Willie" Wallace[18]
		Thomas ("Tad")
Harrison, B. (3)	Caroline	Russell Benjamin
		Mary Scott ("Mamie")[19]
	Mary[20]	Elizabeth
Taft (3)	Helen	Robert Alphonso
		Helen Herron
		Charles Phelps
Wilson (3)	Ellen	Margaret Woodrow
		Jessie Woodrow[21]
		Eleanor Randolph[22]
	Edith	No Issue
Jefferson (2)	Martha	Martha ("Patsy")[23]
		Mary ("Polly")
Monroe (2)	Elizabeth	Eliza[24]
		Maria Hester[25]
Fillmore (2)	Abigail	Millard Powers
		Mary Abigail[26]
Arthur (2)	Ellen	Chester Alan Jr.
		Ellen ("Nell")
McKinley (2)	Ida	Katherine ("Katie")[27]
		Ida[28]
Coolidge (2)	Grace	John
		Calvin, Jr.
Hoover (2)	Lou	Herbert, Jr.
		Allan
Eisenhower (2)	Mamie	Dwight D. II ("Icky")[29]
		John Sheldon Doud
Kennedy (2)	Jacqueline	Caroline
		John, Jr.
Johnson, L. (2)	Claudia	Lynda Bird[30]
		Luci Baines
Nixon (2)	Thelma Catherine	Patricia[31]
		Julie[32]
Bush, G. W. (2)	Laura	Barbara Pierce[33]
		Jenna Welch
Truman (1)	Bess	Margaret
Clinton (1)	Hillary	Chelsea
Washington[34]	Martha	No Issue
Madison	Dolley	No Issue
Jackson[35]	Rachel	No Issue

President	Wife	Children
Polk	Sarah	No Issue
Buchanan	No Wife	No Issue
Harding[36]	Florence	No Issue

NOTES

1. Elizabeth had a White House wedding.
2. All of Julia's children were born after the Tylers left the White House.
3. Tyler was 70 when Pearl was born.
4. Father of future President Benjamin Harrison.
5. Killed in action in WWI.
6. Served as White House hostess for her invalid mother.
7. Died in the Civil War fighting for the Union.
8. Served as his father's Presidential secretary. Founded Union Carbide. Served in the Spanish-American War and was awarded the Congressional Medal of Honor.
9. The only child of a President to be born in the White House.
10. Future President.
11. Future President.
12. Against the wishes of her father, she married Jefferson Davis, future president of the Confederate States of America.
13. Elizabeth served as White House hostess. Her mother was chronically ill.
14. Michael was adopted.
15. Died in infancy.
16. Died at age 4 of typhus.
17. Bennie was killed in a railroad accident, perhaps the most tragic loss the Pierces had. Bennie was traveling with his parents, just two months prior to his father's inauguration. They were to attend the funeral of a family friend. The train derailed and the only fatality was Bennie.
18. Only child to die in the White House.
19. Co-founder and vice president of General Electric. Assisted as White House hostess.
20. Married Harrison after his Presidency.
21. White House wedding, 1913.
22. Eleanore married William G. McAdoo, Wilson's Secretary of the Treasury, in May 1914. She was 25.
23. White House hostess.
24. White House hostess.
25. Hers was the first White House wedding.
26. Mary served as White House hostess.
27. Died in infancy.
28. Died in infancy.
29. "Icky" died at age 3 of scarlet fever. For the rest of his life, Ike sent Mamie flowers on Icky's birthday.
30. Married Charles Robb in a White House wedding.
31. Married Edward Cox in the only outdoor wedding ceremony at the White House.
32. Married David Eisenhower, grandson of former President Dwight Eisenhower.
33. Barbara and Jenna are twin sisters, the only twins fathered by a President.

34. While George and Martha Washington had no children, Washington did adopt Martha's two children from her marriage to Daniel Parke Custis.

35. Jackson and Rachel adopted one of her nephews and named him Andrew Jackson, Jr.

36. There is some evidence that Harding fathered a daughter with his lover, Nan Britton.

---

20. Careers Before the Presidency

The office of Chief Executive was to be filled by the people choosing one of their own to lead them. To this end, the intent of the Founding Fathers has worked very well indeed. We have had Presidents from the very rich to the very poor, from the well-educated to the self-educated. They have had careers in the military, politics and trades.

In order served, by their major careers.

President	*Career*
Washington	Surveyor; Farmer; Military
Adams	Surveyor; Lawyer; Diplomat; Politician
Jefferson	Lawyer; Politician; Farmer; Scientist
Madison	Politician
Monroe	Politician
Adams, J. Q.	Lawyer; Diplomat; Politician
Jackson	Lawyer; Politician: Military
Van Buren	Lawyer; Politician
Harrison, W. H.	Military; Politician
Tyler	Politician
Polk	Politician
Taylor	Military
Fillmore	Lawyer; Politician
Pierce	Lawyer; Politician
Buchanan	Lawyer; Politician
Lincoln	Storekeeper; Postmaster; Lawyer; Politician
Johnson, A.	Tailor; Politician; Military Governor of Tennessee
Grant	Military; Farmer; Merchant
Hayes	Lawyer; Politician; Military
Garfield	Educator; Lawyer; Politician; Military
Arthur	Educator; Lawyer; Political Appointee
Cleveland	Lawyer; Politician
Harrison, B.	Lawyer; Politician

McKinley	Lawyer; Politician
Roosevelt, T.	Politician; Rancher
Taft	Lawyer; Judge; Educator
Wilson	Educator; President of Princeton; Politician
Harding	Newspaper Publisher; Politician
Coolidge	Lawyer; Politician
Hoover	Engineer; Head of American Relief Efforts (Europe Post-WWI); Secretary of Commerce
Roosevelt, F.	Politician
Truman	Clerk; Farmer; Store Owner; Politician
Eisenhower	Military; President of Columbia University
Kennedy	Journalist; Politician
Johnson, L.	Educator; Politician
Nixon	Lawyer; Politician
Ford	Lawyer; Politician
Carter	Farmer; Politician
Reagan	Broadcaster; Actor; Politician
Bush	Businessman; Politician
Clinton	Educator; Politician
Bush, G. W.	Businessman; Politician

21. Political Party

In the 55 Presidential elections held in the United States, the winner has come from five parties. Include the five Vice Presidents who succeeded to the office, but were not elected in their own right, and the total does not change. The Federalist Party gave us our first two Presidents and was never to elect another. The Democrat-Republican Party elected four, including Monroe during the "Era of Good Feeling" when he ran virtually unopposed for a second term. The Whigs provided us four Presidents. Today's two major political parties have given us a total of 32 of our 42 Presidents, the Democrats 14 and the Republicans 18. Lincoln was twice elected by the same party, but in 1864 the Republican Party became the National Union Party. Lincoln's second Vice President, Andrew Johnson, was a Democrat.

Federalist

George Washington (1789–1797)
J. Adams (1797–1801)

Democrat Republican

Thomas Jefferson (1801–1809)
James Madison (1809–1817)
James Monroe (1817–1825)

None[1]

J. Q. Adams (1825–1829)

Whig

W. H. Harrison (1841)
John Tyler (1841–1845)
Zachary Taylor (1849–1850)
Millard Fillmore (1850–1853)

Democrat

Andrew Jackson (1829–1837)
Martin Van Buren (1837–1841)
James Polk (1845–1849)
Franklin Pierce (1853–1857)
James Buchanan (1857–1861
Andrew Johnson (1865–1869)
Grover Cleveland (1885–1889);
   (1893–1897)
Woodrow Wilson (1913–1921)
Franklin Roosevelt (1933–1945)
Harry Truman (1945–1951)
John Kennedy (1961–1963)

Lyndon Johnson (1963–1969)
Jimmy Carter (1977–1981)
Bill Clinton (1993–2001)

Republican

Abraham Lincoln (1861–1865)
Ulysses Grant (1869–1877)
Rutherford Hayes (1877–1881)
James Garfield (1881)
Chester Arthur (1881–1885)
Benjamin Harrison (1889–1893)
William McKinley (1897–1901)
Theodore Roosevelt (1901–1909)
William Taft (1909–1913)
Warren Harding (1921–1923)
Calvin Coolidge 1923–1929)
Herbert Hoover (1929–1933)
Dwight Eisenhower (1953–1961)
Richard Nixon 1969–1974)
Gerald Ford (1974–1977)
Ronald Reagan (1981–1989)
George Bush (1989–1993)
George W. Bush (2001 to present)

NOTE

1. No parties were active for the 1825 election.

---

22. Appointed Offices Held

Some Chief Executives were appointed by their predecessors, or by other politicians, to military or bureaucratic positions. Hoover ran only for President; all the other government positions he held were by appointment. Only Taft held an appointed office after being President. President Warren Harding appointed him Chief Justice of the United States. Taft is the only President to hold this office. In this work senators who served prior to the 17th Amendment are treated as appointed.

President	*Office*	*Dates*
George Washington	Washington held no appointed positions	
John Adams	Diplomat	1778–1788

President	Office	Dates
Thomas Jefferson	Minister to France	1785–1789
	Secretary of State	1790–1793
James Madison	Secretary of State	1801–1809
James Monroe	United States Senator (Virginia)	1790–1794
	Minister to France	1794–1796
	Special Envoy to France	1803
	Minister to England	1803–1807
	Secretary of State	1811–1817
	Secretary of War	1814–1815
John Q. Adams	Minister to Netherlands	1794–1797
	U.S. Senator (Massachusetts)	1803–1808
	Minister to Prussia	1809–1811
	Chief Negotiator, Treaty of Ghent[1]	1814
	Minister to Great Britain	1815–1817
	Secretary of State	1817–1825
Andrew Jackson	United States Senator (Tennessee)	1797–1798
	Governor, Florida Territory	1821
	United States Senator (Tennessee)	1823–1825
Martin Van Buren	United States Senator (New York)	1821–1828
	Secretary of State	1829–1831
W. H. Harrison	Secretary, Northwest Territory	1798–1799
	Territorial Delegate to Congress	1799–1800
	Territorial Governor, Indiana	1800–1812
	United States Senator (Ohio)	1825–1828
	Minister to Colombia	1828–1829
John Tyler	United States Senator (Virginia)	1827–1836
James Polk	Polk held no appointed positions	
Zachary Taylor	Taylor held no appointed positions	
Millard Fillmore	Fillmore held no appointed positions	
Franklin Pierce	United States Senator (New Hampshire)	1837–1842
James Buchanan	Minister to Russia	1832–1833
	United States Senator (Pennsylvania)	1834–1845
	Secretary of State	1845–1849
	Minister to Great Britain	1853–1856
Abraham Lincoln	Postmaster, New Salem, Ill.	1833–1836
Andrew Johnson	United States Senator[2] (Tennessee)	1857–1862
	Military Governor of Tennessee	1862–1864
	United States Senator (Tennessee)	1875[3]
Ulysses Grant	Secretary of War[4]	1867–1868
Rutherford Hayes	Cincinnati City Solicitor	1858–1861
James Garfield	Garfield held no appointed positions	
Chester Arthur	Collector, Port of New York	1871–1878
Grover Cleveland	Cleveland held no appointed positions	
Benjamin Harrison	United States Senator (Ohio)	1881–1887
William McKinley	McKinley held no appointed positions	

              23. Elected Offices Held

President	Office	Dates
Theodore Roosevelt	Civil Service Commission	1889–1895
	New York City Police Commissioner	1895–1897
	Assistant Secretary of Navy	1897–1898
William Taft	Commissioner of Philippines	1900–1901
	Governor-General of Philippines	1901–1904
	Secretary of War	1904–1908
	Chief Justice of the United States[5]	1921–1930
Woodrow Wilson	Wilson held no appointed positions	
Warren Harding	Harding held no appointed positions	
Calvin Coolidge	Coolidge held no appointed offices	
Herbert Hoover	American Relief Committee[6]	1914
	Head of Commission Relief of Belgium	1914–1919
	U.S. Food Administrator	1917–1918
	War Trade Council	1917–1920
	Chairman, Sugar Equalization Board	1918–1919
	European Coal Council	1919
	Supreme Economic Council[7]	
	Secretary of Commerce	1921–1928
Franklin Roosevelt	Assistant Secretary Navy	1913–1920
Harry Truman	Truman held no appointed offices	
Dwight Eisenhower	Supreme Commander, NATO	1951–1952
John Kennedy	Kennedy held no appointed offices	
Lyndon Johnson	Director National Youth Admin., Texas	1935–1937
Richard Nixon	Nixon held no appointed offices	
Gerald Ford	Vice President[8]	1973–1974
Jimmy Carter	Carter held no appointed offices	
Ronald Reagan	Reagan held no appointed offices	
George Bush	Ambassador, United Nations	1971–1973
	Chairman, Republican National Committee	1973–1974
	Chief Liaison in China	1974–1975
	CIA Director	1976–1977
Bill Clinton	Clinton held no appointed offices	
George W. Bush	Bush held no appointed offices	

NOTES

    1. This treaty ended the War of 1812.

    2. Johnson was the only Southern senator to remain loyal to the Union.

    3. The only President to serve in the United States Senate both before and after being President. He died in office in 1875.

    4. Grant served as interim during Johnson's impeachment. Johnson dismissed Secretary of War Stanton. Stanton refused to leave his office until Johnson was acquitted. Grant served during this period. After he was acquitted, Johnson appointed John Schofield to finish the term of office.

5. Appointed by President Harding in 1921. This was the office that Taft had always wanted, and he is the only President to serve on the nation's highest court.

6. In this capacity Hoover aided American citizens stranded in Europe at the beginning of WWI hostilities.

7. Hoover served as director. He also served as economic advisor to President Wilson during the Versailles Peace Conference.

8. Ford was the first appointed Vice President. He was appointed by Nixon, upon the resignation of Vice President Spiro Agnew, under the provisions of the 25th Amendment. He, in turn, appointed Nelson Rockefeller to be his Vice President.

23. Elected Offices Held

Some Presidents held several political offices, but others won their first elections running for the Presidency. This list starts with Vice President and works down from there. Senators who served before 1913 (the year the 17th Amendment was passed) are considered appointed by their state legislatures, and are noted in the chapter Appointed Offices Held. Those who served in offices before the creation of the Union are not included. This list is in order served as President.

Presidents Who Were Vice President

John Adams	1789–1797	Calvin Coolidge	1821–1923
Thomas Jefferson	1797–1801	Harry Truman	1945
Martin Van Buren	1833–1837	Lyndon Johnson	1961–1963
John Tyler	1841	Richard Nixon	1953–1961
Millard Fillmore	1849–1850	Gerald Ford	1973–1974
Andrew Johnson	1865	George Bush	1981–1989
Chester Arthur	1881		
Theodore Roosevelt	1901		

Presidents Who Were United States Senators

Warren Harding	1915–1921	Lyndon Johnson	1949–1961
Harry Truman	1935–1945	Richard Nixon	1951–1953
John Kennedy[1]	1953–1961		

Presidents Who Served as Members of Congress

James Madison	1789–1797	John Tyler	1823–1825
John Quincy Adams[2]	1831–1848	James Polk	1825–1839
Andrew Jackson	1796–1797	Millard Fillmore	1833–1835
William H. Harrison	1816–1819		& 1837–1843

Franklin Pierce	1833–1837	William McKinley	1877–1883
James Buchanan	1821–1831		& 1885–1891
Abraham Lincoln	1847–1849	John Kennedy	1947–1953
Andrew Johnson	1843–1853	Lyndon Johnson	1937–1949
Rutherford Hayes	1865–1867	Richard Nixon	1947–1950
James Garfield	1863–1880	Gerald Ford	1949–1973
		George Bush	1967–1971

Presidents Who Were State Governors

James Monroe (VA)	1799–1802	William McKinley (OH)	1892–1896
	& Jan. to	Theodore Roosevelt (NY)	1898–1900
	March 1811	Woodrow Wilson (NJ)	1911–1913
Martin Van Buren (NY)	1829	Calvin Coolidge (MA)	1919–1920
John Tyler (VA)	1825–1827	Franklin Roosevelt (NY)	1929–1933
James Polk (TN)	1838–1841	Jimmy Carter (GA)	1971–1975
Andrew Johnson (TN)	1853–1857	Ronald Reagan (CA)	1967–1975
Rutherford Hayes (OH)	1868–1872	Bill Clinton (AK)	1979–1981
	& 1876–1877		& 1983–1992
Grover Cleveland (NY)	1883–1885	George W. Bush (TX)	1994–2001

Presidents Who Held State Offices

James Madison	VA House of Delegates	1799–1800
John Q. Adams	MA State Senator	1802
Martin Van Buren	NY State Senator	1812–1820
William Harrison	OH State Senator	1819–1821
John Tyler	VA House of Delegates	1811–1816;
		& 1838–1840
James Polk	TN House of Representatives	1823–1825
Millard Fillmore	NY State Assemblyman	1829–1831
	NY State Comptroller	1848–1849
Franklin Pierce	NH Legislature	1829–1832
James Buchanan	PA House of Representatives	1815–1816
Abraham Lincoln	IL Legislature	1834–1842
Andrew Johnson	TN House of Representatives	1835–1837
		& 1839–1841
	TN State Senator	1841–1843
James Garfield	OH State Senator	1853–1861
Teddy Roosevelt	NY State Assemblyman	1882–1884
Warren Harding	OH State Senator	1899–1903
	OH Lieutenant Governor	1903–1905
Calvin Coolidge	MA State Legislator	1907–1908
	MA State Senator	1912–1915
	MA Lieutenant Governor	1916–1918
Franklin Roosevelt	NY State Senator	1911–1913
Jimmy Carter	GA State Senator	1963–1967
Bill Clinton	AK Attorney General	1977–1979

Presidents Who Held Minor Elected Offices

Andrew Jackson	Justice, TN Supreme Court	1798–1804
Andrew Johnson	Alderman, Greenville, TN	1828–1830
Rutherford B. Hayes	Cincinnati City Solicitor[3]	1858–1861
Grover Cleveland	Sheriff of Erie County, NY[4]	1871–1873
	Mayor of Buffalo	1882
William McKinley	Stark County Prosecutor, OH	1869–1871
Calvin Coolidge	Mayor, Northampton, MA	1910–1911
Harry Truman	Judge, Jackson County, MO	1922–1924

NOTES

1. Kennedy and Johnson were both senators when elected President and Vice President. They are the only team of sitting U.S. Senators ever elected President and Vice President.

2. John Quincy Adams was elected to the House two years after serving as President. He is the only President to serve in the House after being President.

3. Hayes was originally appointed to this post to fill a vacancy. He then ran for and won a term in his own right.

4. As sheriff, Cleveland also served as public executioner.

24. Campaign Issues

Presidential campaigns have been everything from mundane to dirty, and from simple to complicated. Many Presidents of days gone by would be astounded at the expense of the present day Presidential campaigns. In the past the candidates sometimes stayed home and let their supporters do the actual campaigning and speaking. Here are some important and some lackluster campaign issues, along with a few slogans.

Washington v. Adams 1789 —There were no real issues in this election. The public liked Washington.

Washington v. Adams 1792 —Again, no issues.

Adams v. Jefferson 1796 —The major flavor of the campaign was elitist v. popular government, with Adams representing the elitist viewpoint. The other issue of note was the French Revolution.

Jefferson v. Adams 1800 —States' rights. Alien & Sedition Act. Voters were urged to choose "God and a religious President, over Jefferson and no God."[1]

Jefferson v. Pinckney 1804 — At this point the Federalist Party was dying. Pinckney ran a successful campaign in only 3 states: Connecticut, Delaware and Maryland.

Madison v. Pickney 1808 — Trade embargo

Madison v. Clinton 1812 — War of 1812. At this point the U.S. had suffered defeats in the West.

Monroe v. King 1816 — The major issue of this campaign was foreign affairs, but the opposition was token.

Monroe v. None 1820 — Monroe was virtually unopposed.

John Q. Adams v. Jackson 1824 — Protective tariffs & infrastructure

Jackson v. John Q. Adams 1828 — Tariffs & infrastructure. This campaign also focused on the candidates' personalities.

Jackson v. Clay 1832 — Bank of the United States[2]; the spoils system[3]; veto usage

Van Buren v. W. H. Harrison[4] 1836 — Economy; slavery; Bank of the United States; infrastructure

W. H. Harrison v. Van Buren 1840 — Depression; Panic of 1833; Whig campaign slogan: "Tippecanoe and Tyler too!"

Polk v. Clay 1844 — Annexation of Texas[5]; slavery

Taylor v. Cass 1848 — Slavery

Pierce v. Scott 1852 — Slavery; citizenship for immigrants[6]; War records.[7] Democrats' campaign slogan: "We Polked you in 1844; we shall Pierce you in 1852"; "54'40 or Fight"[8]

Buchanan v. Fremont 1856 — Impending Civil War; slavery; "Bleeding Kansas"; religion[9]; Republican slogan: "Free speech, free press, free soil, free men, Fremont and victory"

Lincoln v. Douglas[10]; Breckinridge & Bell 1860 — Slavery; states' right to secede from the Union.

Lincoln v. McClellan 1864 — Civil War.; Democrats' campaign slogan: "Mac will win the Union back"; Republican campaign slogan: "Don't swap horses in the middle of the stream"

Grant[11] v. Seymour 1868 — Reconstruction

Grant v. Greeley 1872 — Scandals of Grant's administration; Reconstruction

Hayes v. Tilden 1876 — Corruption; Reconstruction

Garfield v. Hancock 1880 — Tariff; Credit Mobilier scandal

Cleveland v. Blaine 1884 — Personal attacks; Republican slogan: "Ma, Ma, where's my Pa? Gone to the White House, Ha, Ha, Ha!"[12]; Democrats' slogan: "Blaine! Blaine! James G. Blaine! Continental liar from the state of Maine!"

B. Harrison v. Cleveland 1888 — Tariff

Cleveland v. B. Harrison 1892 — Tariff; monetary system

McKinley v. Bryan 1896 — Currency[13]; tariffs

McKinley v. Bryan 1900 — Imperialism; Republican campaign slogan: "Four more years of the full dinner pail."

T. Roosevelt v. Parker 1904 — Personalities[14]

Taft v. Bryan 1908 — Business[15]

Wilson v. T. Roosevelt & Taft 1912 — Monopolies; labor

Wilson v. Hughes 1916 — War in Europe; Democratic campaign slogan: "He kept us out of war!"

Harding v. Cox 1920 — League of Nations; Prohibition; education; poverty

Coolidge v. Davis & LaFollette 1924 — Prosperity; League of Nations; Republican campaign slogan: "Keep cool with Coolidge!"

Hoover v. Smith 1928 — Religion[16]; Prohibition; corruption of Harding presidency; Republican campaign slogans: "Let's keep what we've got," and "A chicken in every pot and a car in every garage."

Roosevelt v. Hoover 1932 — The Great Depression; Roosevelt's record as governor of New York; Republican campaign slogan: "Play safe with Hoover"; Democratic campaign slogan: "Kick out Depression with a Democratic vote."

Roosevelt v. Landon 1936 — Economic recovery; Democratic campaign slogan: "Follow through with Roosevelt."; Republican campaign slogans: "Life, liberty, and Landon." "Off the rocks with Landon and Knox."[17]

Roosevelt v. Willkie 1940 — War in Europe; Third term

Roosevelt v. Dewey 1944 — Roosevelt's health; government waste[18]; Democratic campaign slogan: "Don't change horses in midstream."

Truman v. Dewey[19] v. Thurmond 1948 — Republican control of Congress;[20] The Taft-Hartley Act.

Eisenhower v. Stevenson 1952 — Korean War; Republican campaign slogan: "I like Ike."

Eisenhower v. Stevenson 1956 — Eisenhower's health; foreign affairs

Kennedy v. Nixon 1960 — Economy; communism; civil rights

Johnson v. Goldwater 1964 — Foreign affairs; civil rights; Vietnam; Democratic campaign slogan: "All the way with LBJ"; Republican campaign slogan: "In your heart you know he's right."[21]

Nixon v. Humphrey v. Wallace 1968 — Vietnam; law & order; drug trade; civil rights

Nixon v. McGovern 1972[22] — Vietnam; tax reform; government spending

Carter v. Ford 1976 — Nixon pardon; Watergate

Reagan v. Carter 1980 — Inflation; fuel shortages; Iran hostage crisis; Equal Rights Amendment[23]

Reagan v. Mondale 1984[24] — Balanced budget; defense spending; tariffs; Reagan's age

Bush v. Dukakis 1988 — Personal attacks; government spending
Clinton v. Bush 1992 — Inflation; personal attacks; government spending; taxes; government health insurance; welfare
Clinton v. Dole 1996 — Personalities
G. W. Bush v. Gore 2000 — Tax cuts; Social Security; Medicare; abortion; environment
G. W. Bush v. Kerry 2004 — Personal attacks; war in Iraq & Afghanistan; national security; Social Security

NOTES

1. See chapter on Religious Affiliations.
2. Jackson vehemently opposed the Bank of the United States on the grounds that it was unconstitutional and elitist.
3. Clay accused Jackson of abusing the system — a common practice.
4. Harrison was the major candidate. The Whig Party was formed in opposition to Jackson and his policies. The opposition was not united on a candidate; thus several ran and divided the vote.
5. Texas was Polk's main goal. He wanted Texas in the Union while Clay opposed annexation.
6. Pierce supported citizenship for the Irish and German immigrants who completed one year of military service.
7. General Franklin Pierce served under General Winfield Scott in the Mexican War.
8. This was a reference to the northern boundary of the Oregon Territory. The final settlement was the 49th parallel. The 54th parallel would have taken the northern boundary of the United States into British Columbia, roughly at Prince Rupert.
9. Democrats accused Fremont of being Catholic. His wife and adopted daughter were; Fremont was Episcopalian.
10. Douglas was the only candidate to actively campaign. He carried only one state, Missouri.
11. Grant did not participate in the campaign. He sent a letter of acceptance to the Republican convention.
12. This referred to Cleveland's affair with Maria Halpin. See chapter Other Loves.
13. It was during this campaign that William Jennings Bryan made his famous "Cross of Gold" speech. The main issue was the gold standard vs. silver.
14. Roosevelt and Parker differed little on the issues.
15. While the campaign centered on which candidate could best carry the Roosevelt policies, Bryan did propose establishing a Federal Deposit Insurance program. This was an idea that would be adopted by FDR.
16. Alfred Smith was Catholic.
17. Fred Knox, Illinois newspaper publisher, was the Vice Presidential candidate.
18. Republicans charged that Roosevelt dispatched a Navy destroyer to the Aleutian Islands to retrieve his dog Fala. Roosevelt responded: "I don't resent these attacks, and my family doesn't resent attacks, but Fala does resent them."
19. This is the campaign from which the saying "Give you a Dewey button" sprang. It was a result of Dewey's loss to Truman in a race everyone thought Dewey would win.

20. Truman complained that the 80th Congress, controlled by the Republicans, was the "Do Nothing 80th Congress."

21. The Democrats had two underground slogans to counter this. "In your heart you know he might" (referring to Goldwater's apparent readiness to use nuclear weapons); and "In your guts you know he's nuts."

22. First election opened to 18–20 year olds.

23. This amendment was designed to guarantee equal rights for women. It failed to gain adequate support from the states.

24. This was the first time a woman was on a major party ticket. Geraldine Ferraro was the Vice Presidential candidate for the Democrats.

25. Popular Vote

To be President it helps to be loved by the voters. That's the key to winning. In order to win the electoral vote the candidate needs to win the popular vote, although not always does the race go to the winner of the popular vote. Cleveland won the popular vote three times but the Presidency only twice. Clinton, in two tries, never won a majority of the popular vote. Wilson was also elected and re-elected without winning a majority of the popular vote. (No vote records are available from the first nine elections of the new republic.)

President	Year	Popular Vote
George W. Bush	2004	59,668,261
Ronald Reagan	1984	54,450,603
George W. Bush	2000	50,456,167
George Bush	1988	47,946,422
Richard Nixon	1972	47,170,179
Bill Clinton	1996	45,628,667
Bill Clinton	1992	44,908,233
Ronald Reagan	1980	43,904,153
Lyndon Johnson	1964	43,129,566
James E. Carter	1976	41,426,405
Dwight D. Eisenhower	1956	35,590,472
John F. Kennedy	1960	34,227,096
Dwight D. Eisenhower	1952	33,936,234
Richard M. Nixon	1968	31,785,480
Franklin D. Roosevelt	1936	27,752,869
Franklin D. Roosevelt	1944	27,307,819
Franklin D. Roosevelt	1940	25,606,585

President	Year	Popular Vote
Harry S Truman	1948	24,179,345
Franklin D. Roosevelt	1932	22,809,638
Herbert Hoover	1928	21,391,993
Warren G. Harding	1920	16,143,407
Calvin Coolidge	1924	15,718,211
Woodrow Wilson	1916	9,127,695
William H. Taft	1908	7,628,320
Theodore Roosevelt	1904	7,628,461
William McKinley	1900	7,218,491
William McKinley	1896	7,102,246
Woodrow Wilson	1912	6,296,547
Grover Cleveland	1892	5,555,426
Benjamin Harrison	1888	5,447,129
Grover Cleveland	1884	4,879,129
James Garfield	1880	4,453,295
Rutherford Hayes	1876	4,036,572
Ulysses Grant	1872	3,597,070
Ulysses Grant	1868	3,012,833
Abraham Lincoln	1864	2,206,938
Abraham Lincoln	1860	1,832,955
James Buchanan	1856	1,832,955
Franklin Pierce	1852	1,601,117
Zachary Taylor	1848	1,601,117
James Polk	1844	1,338,464
William Harrison	1840	1,274,624
Martin Van Buren	1836	765,483
Andrew Jackson	1832	687,502
Andrew Jackson	1828	647,286
John Q. Adams	1824	108,740

26. Percent of Popular Vote

No records exist for the popular vote of the first nine Presidential elections, from 1789 through 1820. We do know that Jefferson had a very close call in 1800. This was the first election decided by the House of Representatives, and resulted in the famous duel between Aaron Burr and Alexander Hamilton. Burr believed, correctly, that Hamilton had made a deal, with Jefferson, to throw his support to Jefferson. It also brought about the Twelfth Amendment, which provides for the direct election of the Vice President.

Here are the results, by percent, of the other 46 elections, highest to lowest percent. Three Presidents, Cleveland, Wilson and Clinton, were elected and reelected without ever receiving a majority of the popular vote. Of those Presidents reelected only Jackson was reelected with a lower percent after four years. FDR's percentage dropped for his third and fourth terms, but rose after the initial term. The percents are rounded off to two digits. In cases of ties, the first President elected by that figure appears first. (No data exist for the popular vote prior to 1824.)

President	Election Year	Percent of Vote
Warren G. Harding	1920	62%
Franklin D. Roosevelt	1936	62%
Lyndon Johnson	1964	61%
Richard M. Nixon	1972	61%
Herbert Hoover	1928	59%
Franklin D. Roosevelt	1932	59%
Ronald Reagan	1984	59%
Dwight D. Eisenhower	1956	58%
Andrew Jackson	1828	56%
Ulysses S. Grant	1872	56%
Teddy Roosevelt	1904	56%
Andrew Jackson	1832	55%
Abraham Lincoln	1864	55%
Franklin D. Roosevelt	1940	55%
Dwight D. Eisenhower	1952	55%
Calvin Coolidge	1924	54%
George Bush	1988	54%
W. H. Harrison	1840	53%
Ulysses Grant	1868	53%
Franklin D. Roosevelt	1944	53%
William McKinley	1900	53%
William H. Taft	1908	52%
Martin Van Buren	1836	51%
Franklin Pierce	1852	51%
William McKinley	1896	51%
Ronald Reagan	1980	51%
George W. Bush	2004	51%
James Polk	1844	50%
Harry S Truman	1948	50%
John F. Kennedy	1960	50%
James E. Carter	1976	50%
Grover Cleveland	1884	49%
Woodrow Wilson	1916	49%
William J. Clinton	1996	49%
Rutherford B. Hayes	1876	48%

President	Election Year	Percent of Vote
James Garfield	1880	48%
Benjamin Harrison	1888	48%
George W. Bush	2000	48%
Zachary Taylor	1848	47%
Grover Cleveland	1892	46%
James Buchanan	1856	45%
Richard M. Nixon	1968	43%
William J. Clinton	1992	43%
Woodrow Wilson	1912	42%
Abraham Lincoln	1860	40%
J. Q. Adams	1824	32%

27. Electoral Vote

To be President of the United States, the candidate must win the electoral vote. Only twice in our history has the Presidency been decided by the House of Representatives, in 1800 and 1824. Other than those two exceptions, the Electoral College has decided the outcome of the election for President. The power of the electoral vote can be seen in the elections of as recently as 1992, 1996 and 2000 when Bill Clinton and George W. Bush won the White House without winning the popular vote. Below are the winners beginning with the most electoral votes in descending order.

President	Year	Electoral Votes
Ronald Reagan	1984	525
Franklin D. Roosevelt	1936	523
Richard M. Nixon	1972	520
Ronald Reagan	1980	489
Lyndon B. Johnson	1964	486
Franklin D. Roosevelt	1932	472
Dwight D. Eisenhower	1952	457
Franklin D. Roosevelt	1940	449
Herbert Hoover	1928	444
Dwight D. Eisenhower	1952	442
Woodrow Wilson	1912	435
Franklin D. Roosevelt	1944	432
George Bush	1972	426
Warren G. Harding	1920	404
Calvin Coolidge	1924	382

President	Year	Electoral Votes
Bill Clinton	1996	379
Bill Clinton	1992	370
Theodore Roosevelt	1904	336
William H. Taft	1908	321
Harry S Truman	1948	303
John F. Kennedy	1960	303
Richard M. Nixon	1968	301
Jimmy Carter	1976	297
William McKinley	1900	292
Ulysses S. Grant	1872	286
George W. Bush	2004	286
Grover Cleveland	1892	277
Woodrow Wilson	1916	277
William McKinley	1896	271
George W. Bush[1]	2000	271
Franklin Pierce	1852	254
William H. Harrison	1840	234
Benjamin Harrison	1888	233
James Monroe	1820	231
Andrew Jackson	1832	219
Grover Cleveland	1884	219
Ulysses S. Grant	1868	214
James A. Garfield	1880	214
Abraham Lincoln	1864	212
Rutherford B. Hayes[2]	1876	185
James Monroe	1816	183
Abraham Lincoln	1860	180
Andrew Jackson	1828	178
James C. Buchanan	1856	174
Martin Van Buren	1836	170
James K. Polk	1844	170
Zachary Taylor	1848	163
Thomas Jefferson	1804	162
George Washington	1792	132
James Madison	1812	128
James Madison	1808	122
John Q. Adams	1824	84[3]
Thomas Jefferson	1800[4]	73
John Adams	1796	71
George Washington	1789	69

NOTES

1. In 2000 George W. Bush appeared to have won the vote in Florida. The critical electoral votes were needed by both candidates to win the Presidency. Vice President Al

Gore, Bush's opponent, challenged the results of the vote. The case went to the courts, and after several court battles, the Supreme Court awarded Florida's electoral votes to Bush.

2. In 1876, because of disputed voting practices in some Southern states, the election was decided, not by the Electoral College, nor the House, but by a congressionally appointed commission. The commission, composed of eight Republicans and seven Democrats, gave the electoral votes from the disputed states to Hayes.

3. Because no candidate won a majority of the electoral vote, the election was decided by the House of Representatives in favor of Adams.

4. This was the fourth Presidential election and the first to be decided by the House of Representatives.

28. Percent of Electoral Vote

The presidents are actually elected by the electoral college. This is a group of electors pledged, by popular vote to a particular candidate. Each state has a number of electors based on the population of the state. Thus California has the most, while Alaska; Delaware; The District of Columbia; Montana; North Dakota; South Dakota; Vermont and Wyoming have the fewest.

Washington is the only president to receive 100% of the electoral vote, 1789 & 1792. James Monroe won 100% of the electoral vote in the election of 1820, but he was denied the vote of William Plumer, Governor of New Hampshire, so that Washington would remain the only president to receive a unanimity of the electors. Thus, Monroe's figure for the 1820 is shown with a decimal, all others are rounded off.

President	Year	Percent	President	Year	Percent
Washington	1789	100%	Eisenhower	1956	86%
Washington	1792	100%	F. Roosevelt	1940	85%
Monroe	1820	99.6%	Monroe	1816	84%
F. Roosevelt	1936	98%	Hoover	1928	84%
Reagan	1984	98%	Eisenhower	1952	83%
Nixon	1972	97%	Wilson	1912	82%
Jefferson	1804	92%	W. H. Harrison	1840	81%
Lincoln	1864	91%	Grant	1872	81%
Reagan	1980	91%	F. Roosevelt	1944	81%
L. Johnson	1964	90%	Jackson	1832	77%
F. Roosevelt	1932	89%	Bush	1988	79%
Pierce	1852	86%	Harding	1920	76%

President	Year	Percent	President	Year	Percent
Grant	1868	73%	B. Harrison	1888	58%
Coolidge	1924	72%	Van Buren	1836	57%
T. Roosevelt	1904	71%	Truman	1948	57%
Madison	1808	70%	Taylor	1848	56%
Clinton	1996	70%	Kennedy	1960	56%
Clinton	1992	69%	Nixon	1968	56%
Jackson	1828	68%	Cleveland	1892	55%
Taft	1908	66%	Carter	1976	55%
McKinley	1900	65%	Bush, G. W.	2004	53%
Polk	1844	62%	Wilson	1916	52%
Cleveland	1892	62%	Adams	1796	51%
McKinley	1896	61%	Hayes[1]	1876	50%
Madison	1812	59%	Bush, G. W.[2]	2000	50%
Lincoln	1860	60%	Jefferson[3]	1800	35%
Buchanan	1856	58%	J. Q. Adams[4]	1824	32%
Garfield	1880	58%			

NOTES

1. In the aftermath of the Civil War, and during Reconstruction, Tilden appeared to have won the election. Three states, however, were disputed by the Republicans: South Carolina, Louisiana, and Florida. In addition to these there was one disputed electoral vote in Oregon. All three of the Southern states were controlled by the Republicans. Tilden led in the popular vote and was one vote shy of winning a majority of the electoral vote. At this point Republican officials in all three Southern states stepped in and ruled some of Tilden's votes invalid. A commission was appointed to rule on the votes. The commission consisted of eight Republicans and seven Democrats. The commission voted eight to seven in favor of Hayes.

2. In a repeat of 1876, Florida's votes were again contested. The candidates disputed Florida's voting methods. The votes were recounted and recounted again. Finally the matter went to the courts. The Supreme Court decided that Bush was the winner in Florida. This gave him enough electoral votes to become President.

3. Jefferson and Burr each had 73 electoral votes. John Adams held 65. The election went to the House of Representatives for a decision. After 36 ballots over an eight day period the house decided in Jefferson's favor. This election had two aftermaths. The Hamilton-Burr duel, in which Alexander Hamilton was mortally wounded, and the passage of the 12th Amendment, calling for Presidential and Vice Presidential candidates.

4. Jackson won a plurality of the electoral votes, 99 out of 261. Adams won 84. A majority is needed. The election went to the House of Representatives, with each state casting one vote. Two other candidates had electoral votes, Crawford (41) and Clay (37). The house chose from the top three, eliminating Clay, who gave his support to Adams. When the house voted on Feb. 9, 1825, Adams won the Presidency with no votes to spare. Jackson went back to the Hermitage determined to win in 1828.

29. States Won

Winning the electoral vote means winning enough states to gain a majority of the Electoral College. Currently that means winning enough states to have a total of 270 electoral votes. Candidates have employed different strategies throughout the years in order to accomplish this. In 1968 Nixon used his Southern Strategy to defeat Hubert Humphrey. Today the Republicans still rely on Southern votes to win the White House.

Since 1968 only two Democrats have won the Presidency. Both Jimmy Carter and Bill Clinton were Southerners.

Here are the Presidents and the states they won. The total number of states participating in the election follows the election year. The figures in parentheses show the electoral votes won and the number of electoral votes cast.

Washington 1789 10 States (69/69)—Connecticut; Delaware; Georgia; Maryland; Massachusetts; New Hampshire; New Jersey; Pennsylvania; South Carolina; Virginia.

Washington 1792 15 States (132/132)—Connecticut; Delaware; Georgia; Kentucky; Maryland; Massachusetts; New Hampshire; New Jersey; New York; North Carolina; Pennsylvania; Rhode Island; South Carolina; Vermont; Virginia.

Adams, J. 1796 16 States (71/139)—Connecticut; Delaware; Maryland; Massachusetts; New Hampshire; New Jersey; New York; Rhode Island; Vermont.

Jefferson 1800 16 States (73^1/139)—Georgia; Kentucky; New York; North Carolina; Pennsylvania; Tennessee; Virginia.

Jefferson 1804 17 States (162/176)—Georgia; Kentucky; Maryland; Massachusetts; New Hampshire; New Jersey; New York; North Carolina; Ohio; Pennsylvania; Rhode Island; South Carolina; Tennessee; Vermont; Virginia.

Madison 1808 17 States (122/176)—Georgia; Kentucky; Maryland; New Jersey; New York; North Carolina; Ohio; Pennsylvania; South Carolina; Tennessee; Vermont; Virginia.

Madison 1812 18 States (128/218)—Georgia; Kentucky; Louisiana; Maryland; North Carolina; Ohio; Pennsylvania; South Carolina; Tennessee; Vermont; Virginia.

Monroe 1816 19 States (183/221)—Georgia; Indiana; Kentucky; Louisiana;

Maryland; New Hampshire; New Jersey; New York; North Carolina; Ohio; Pennsylvania; Rhode Island; South Carolina; Tennessee; Vermont; Virginia.

Monroe 1820 24 States (231^2/235)—Alabama; Connecticut; Delaware; Georgia; Illinois; Indiana; Kentucky; Louisiana; Maine; Maryland; Massachusetts; Mississippi; Missouri; New Hampshire; New Jersey; New York; North Carolina; Ohio; Pennsylvania; Rhode Island; South Carolina; Tennessee; Vermont; Virginia.

Adams, J. Q. 1824 24 States (84^3/261)—Connecticut; Maine; Massachusetts; New Hampshire; New York; Rhode Island; Vermont.

Jackson 1828 24 States (178/261)—Alabama; Georgia; Illinois; Indiana; Kentucky; Louisiana; Mississippi; Missouri; New York; North Carolina; Ohio; Pennsylvania; South Carolina; Tennessee; Virginia.

Jackson[4] 1832 24 States (219/288)—Alabama; Georgia; Illinois; Indiana; Louisiana; Maine; Mississippi; Missouri; New Hampshire; New Jersey; New York; North Carolina; Ohio; Pennsylvania; Tennessee; Virginia.

Van Buren 1836 26 States (170/294)—Alabama; Arkansas; Connecticut; Illinois; Louisiana; Maine; Michigan; Mississippi; Missouri; New Hampshire; New York; North Carolina; Pennsylvania; Rhode Island; Virginia.

Harrison, W. H.[5] 1840 26 States (234/294)—Connecticut; Delaware; Georgia; Indiana; Kentucky; Louisiana; Maine; Maryland; Massachusetts; Michigan; Mississippi; New Jersey; New York; North Carolina; Ohio; Pennsylvania; Rhode Island; Tennessee; Vermont.

Polk[6] 1844 26 States (170/275)—Alabama; Arkansas; Georgia; Illinois; Indiana; Louisiana; Maine; Michigan; Mississippi; Missouri; New Hampshire; New York; Pennsylvania; South Carolina; Virginia.

Taylor 1848[7] 30 States (163/290)—Connecticut; Delaware; Florida; Georgia; Kentucky; Louisiana; Maryland; Massachusetts; New Jersey; New York; North Carolina; Pennsylvania; Rhode Island; Tennessee; Vermont.

Pierce 1852 31 States (254/296)—Alabama; Arkansas; California; Connecticut; Delaware; Florida; Georgia; Illinois; Indiana; Iowa; Louisiana; Maine; Maryland; Michigan; Mississippi; Missouri; New Hampshire; New Jersey; New York; North Carolina; Ohio; Pennsylvania; Rhode Island; South Carolina; Texas; Virginia; Wisconsin.

Buchanan 1856 31 States (174/296)—Alabama; Arkansas; California; Delaware; Florida; Georgia; Illinois; Indiana; Kentucky; Louisiana; Mississippi; Missouri; New Jersey; North Carolina; Pennsylvania; South Carolina; Tennessee; Texas; Virginia

Lincoln[8] 1860 33 States (180/303)—California; Connecticut; Illinois; Indiana; Iowa; Maine; Massachusetts; Michigan; Minnesota; New Hampshire; New Jersey; New York; Ohio; Oregon; Pennsylvania; Rhode Island; Vermont; Wisconsin.

Lincoln 1864 25 States[9] (212/233)—California; Connecticut; Illinois; Indiana; Iowa; Kansas; Maine; Maryland; Massachusetts; Michigan; Minnesota; Missouri; Nevada; New Hampshire; New York; Ohio; Oregon; Pennsylvania; Rhode Island; Vermont; West Virginia; Wisconsin.

Grant 1868 34 States[10] (214/317[11])—Alabama; Arkansas; California; Connecticut; Florida; Illinois; Indiana; Iowa; Kansas; Maine; Massachusetts; Michigan; Minnesota; Missouri; Nebraska; Nevada; New Hampshire; North Carolina; Ohio; Pennsylvania; Rhode Island; South Carolina; Tennessee; Vermont; West Virginia; Wisconsin.

Grant 1872 37 States (286/366[12])—Alabama; California; Connecticut; Delaware; Florida; Illinois; Indiana; Iowa; Kansas; Maine; Massachusetts; Michigan; Minnesota; Mississippi; Nebraska; Nevada; New Hampshire; New Jersey; New York; North Carolina; Ohio; Oregon; Pennsylvania; Rhode Island; South Carolina; Vermont; Virginia; West Virginia; Wisconsin.

Hayes[13] **1876 38 States** (185/369)—California; Colorado; Florida; Illinois; Iowa; Kansas; Louisiana; Maine; Massachusetts; Michigan; Minnesota; Nebraska; Nevada; New Hampshire; Ohio; Oregon; Pennsylvania; Rhode Island; South Carolina; Vermont; Wisconsin.

Garfield 1880 38 States (214/369)—Colorado; Connecticut; Illinois; Indiana; Iowa; Kansas; Maine; Massachusetts; Michigan; Minnesota; Nebraska; New Hampshire; New York; Ohio; Oregon; Pennsylvania; Rhode Island; Vermont; Wisconsin.

Cleveland 1884 38 States (219/401)—Alabama; Arkansas; Connecticut; Delaware; Florida; Georgia; Indiana; Kentucky; Louisiana; Maryland; Mississippi; Missouri; New Jersey; New York; North Carolina; South Carolina; Tennessee; Texas; Virginia; West Virginia.

Harrison, B. 1888 38 States (233/401)—California; Colorado; Illinois; Indiana; Iowa; Kansas; Maine; Massachusetts; Michigan; Minnesota; Nebraska; Nevada; New Hampshire; New York Ohio; Oregon; Pennsylvania; Rhode Island; Vermont; Wisconsin.

Cleveland 1892 43 States (277/145)—Alabama; Arkansas; California; Connecticut; Delaware; Florida; Georgia; Illinois; Indiana; Kentucky; Louisiana; Maryland; Mississippi; Missouri; New Jersey; New York; North Carolina; South Carolina; Tennessee; Texas; Virginia; West Virginia; Wisconsin.

McKinley 1896 45 States (271/447)—California; Connecticut; Delaware; Illinois; Indiana; Iowa; Kentucky; Maine; Maryland; Massachusetts; Michigan; Minnesota; New Hampshire; New Jersey; New York; North Dakota; Ohio; Oregon; Pennsylvania; Rhode Island; Vermont; West Virginia; Wisconsin.

McKinley 1900 45 States (292/447)—California; Connecticut; Delaware;

Illinois; Indiana; Iowa; Kansas; Maine; Maryland; Massachusetts; Michigan; Minnesota; Nebraska; New Hampshire; New Jersey; New York; North Dakota; Ohio; Oregon; Pennsylvania; Rhode Island; South Dakota; Utah; Vermont; Washington; West Virginia; Wisconsin; Wyoming.

Roosevelt, T. 1904 **45 States (336/476)**—California; Colorado; Connecticut; Delaware; Idaho; Illinois; Indiana; Iowa; Kansas; Maine; Massachusetts; Michigan; Minnesota; Missouri; Montana; Nebraska; Nevada; New Hampshire; New Jersey; New York; North Dakota; Ohio; Oregon; Pennsylvania; Rhode Island; South Dakota; Utah; Vermont; Washington; West Virginia; Wisconsin; Wyoming.

Taft 1908 46 States (321/483)—California; Connecticut; Delaware; Idaho; Illinois; Indiana; Iowa; Kansas; Maine; Massachusetts; Michigan; Minnesota; Missouri; Montana; New Hampshire; New Jersey; New York; North Dakota; Ohio; Oregon; Pennsylvania; Rhode Island; South Dakota; Utah; Vermont; Washington; West Virginia; Wisconsin; Wyoming.

Wilson 1912 48 States (435/531)—Alabama; Arizona; Arkansas; Colorado; Connecticut; Delaware; Florida; Georgia; Idaho; Illinois; Indiana; Iowa; Kansas; Kentucky; Louisiana; Maine; Maryland; Massachusetts; Mississippi; Missouri; Montana; Nebraska; Nevada; New Hampshire; New Jersey; New Mexico; New York; North Carolina; North Dakota; Ohio; Oklahoma; Oregon; Rhode Island; South Carolina; Tennessee; Texas; Virginia; West Virginia; Wisconsin; Wyoming.

Wilson 1916[14] **48 States (277/531)**—Alabama; Arizona; Arkansas; California; Colorado; Florida; Georgia; Idaho; Kansas; Kentucky; Louisiana; Maryland; Mississippi; Missouri; Montana; Nebraska; Nevada; New Hampshire; New Mexico; North Carolina; North Dakota; Ohio; Oklahoma; South Carolina; Tennessee; Texas; Utah; Virginia; Washington; Wyoming.

Harding 1920 48 States (404/531)—Arizona; California; Colorado; Connecticut; Delaware; Idaho; Illinois; Indiana; Iowa; Kansas; Maine; Maryland; Massachusetts; Michigan; Minnesota; Missouri; Montana; Nebraska; Nevada; New Hampshire; New Jersey; New Mexico; New York; North Dakota; Ohio; Oklahoma; Oregon; Pennsylvania; Rhode Island; South Dakota; Tennessee; Utah; Vermont; Washington; West Virginia; Wisconsin; Wyoming.

Coolidge 1924 48 States (382/531)—Arizona; California; Colorado; Connecticut; Delaware; Idaho; Illinois; Indiana; Iowa; Kansas; Kentucky; Maine; Maryland; Massachusetts; Michigan; Minnesota; Missouri; Montana; Nebraska; Nevada; New Hampshire; New Jersey; New Mexico; New York; North Dakota; Ohio; Oregon; Pennsylvania; Rhode Island; South Dakota; Utah; Vermont; Washington; West Virginia; Wyoming.

Hoover 1928 48 States (444/531)—Arizona; California; Colorado; Connecticut; Delaware; Florida; Idaho; Illinois; Indiana; Iowa; Kansas; Kentucky; Maine; Maryland; Michigan; Minnesota; Missouri; Montana; Nebraska; Nevada; New Hampshire; New Jersey; New Mexico; New York; North Carolina; North Dakota; Ohio; Oklahoma; Oregon; Pennsylvania; South Dakota; Tennessee; Texas; Utah; Vermont; Virginia; Washington; West Virginia; Wisconsin; Wyoming.

Roosevelt, F. 1932 48 States (472/531)—Alabama; Arizona; Arkansas; California; Colorado; Florida; Georgia; Idaho; Illinois; Indiana; Iowa; Kansas; Kentucky; Louisiana; Maryland; Massachusetts; Michigan; Minnesota; Mississippi; Missouri; Montana; Nebraska; Nevada; New Jersey; New Mexico; New York; North Carolina; North Dakota; Ohio; Oklahoma; Oregon; Rhode Island; South Carolina; South Dakota; Tennessee; Texas; Utah; Virginia; Washington; West Virginia; Wisconsin; Wyoming.

Roosevelt, F. 1936 48 States (523/531)—Alabama; Arizona; Arkansas; California; Colorado; Connecticut; Delaware; Florida; Georgia; Idaho; Illinois; Indiana; Iowa; Kansas; Kentucky; Louisiana; Maryland; Massachusetts; Michigan; Minnesota; Mississippi; Missouri; Montana; Nebraska; Nevada; New Hampshire; New Jersey; New Mexico; New York; North Carolina; North Dakota; Ohio; Oklahoma; Oregon; Pennsylvania; Rhode Island; South Carolina; South Dakota; Tennessee; Texas; Utah; Virginia; Washington; West Virginia; Wisconsin; Wyoming.

Roosevelt, F. 1940 48 States (449/531)—Alabama; Arizona; Arkansas; California; Connecticut; Delaware; Florida; Georgia; Idaho; Illinois; Kentucky; Louisiana; Maryland; Massachusetts; Minnesota; Mississippi; Missouri; Montana; Nevada; New Hampshire; New Jersey; New Mexico; New York; North Carolina; Ohio; Oklahoma; Oregon; Pennsylvania; Rhode Island; South Carolina; Tennessee; Texas; Utah; Virginia; Washington; West Virginia; Wisconsin; Wyoming.

Roosevelt, F. 1944 48 States (432/531)—Alabama; Arizona; Arkansas; California; Connecticut; Delaware; Florida; Georgia; Idaho; Illinois; Kentucky; Louisiana; Maryland; Massachusetts; Michigan; Minnesota; Mississippi; Missouri; Montana; Nevada; New Hampshire; New Jersey; New Mexico; New York; North Carolina; Oklahoma; Oregon; Pennsylvania; Rhode Island; South Carolina; Tennessee; Texas; Utah; Virginia; Washington; West Virginia.

Truman 1948 48 States (303/531)—Arizona; Arkansas; California; Colorado; Florida; Georgia; Idaho; Illinois; Iowa; Kentucky; Massachusetts; Minnesota; Missouri; Montana; Nevada; New Mexico; North Carolina; Ohio; Oklahoma; Rhode Island; Tennessee; Texas; Utah; Virginia; Washington; West Virginia; Wisconsin; Wyoming.

Eisenhower 1952 48 States (442/531)—Arizona; California; Colorado; Connecticut; Delaware; Florida; Idaho; Illinois; Indiana; Iowa; Kansas; Maine; Maryland; Massachusetts; Michigan; Minnesota; Missouri; Montana; Nebraska; Nevada; New Hampshire; New Jersey; New Mexico; New York; North Dakota; Ohio; Oklahoma; Oregon; Pennsylvania; Rhode Island; South Dakota; Tennessee; Texas; Utah; Vermont; Virginia; Washington; Wisconsin; Wyoming.

Eisenhower 1956 48 States (457/531)—Arizona; California; Colorado; Connecticut; Delaware; Florida; Idaho; Illinois; Indiana; Iowa; Kansas; Kentucky; Louisiana; Maine; Maryland; Massachusetts; Michigan; Minnesota; Montana; Nebraska; Nevada; New Hampshire; New Jersey; New Mexico; New York; North Dakota; Ohio; Oklahoma; Oregon; Pennsylvania; Rhode Island; South Dakota; Tennessee; Texas; Utah; Vermont; Virginia; Washington; West Virginia; Wisconsin; Wyoming.

Kennedy 1960 50 States (303/537)—Arkansas; Connecticut; Delaware; Georgia; Hawaii; Illinois; Louisiana; Maryland; Massachusetts; Michigan; Minnesota; Missouri; Nevada; New Jersey; New Mexico; New York; North Carolina; Pennsylvania; Rhode Island; South Carolina; Texas; West Virginia.

Johnson, L. 1964 50 States (486/538)—Alaska; Arkansas; California; Colorado; Connecticut; Delaware; Florida; Hawaii; Idaho; Illinois; Indiana; Iowa; Kansas; Kentucky; Maine; Maryland; Massachusetts; Michigan; Minnesota; Missouri; Montana; Nebraska; Nevada; New Hampshire; New Jersey; New Mexico; New York; North Carolina; North Dakota; Ohio; Oklahoma; Oregon; Pennsylvania; Rhode Island; South Dakota; Tennessee; Texas; Utah; Vermont; Virginia; Washington; West Virginia; Wisconsin; Wyoming; District of Columbia.

Nixon 1968 50 States (301/538)—Alaska; Arizona; California; Colorado; Delaware; Florida; Idaho; Illinois; Indiana; Iowa; Kansas; Kentucky; Missouri; Montana; Nebraska; Nevada; New Hampshire; New Jersey; New Mexico; North Carolina; North Dakota; Ohio; Oklahoma; Oregon; South Carolina; South Dakota; Tennessee; Utah; Vermont; Virginia; Wisconsin; Wyoming.

Nixon 1972 50 States (520/537)—Alabama; Alaska; Arizona; Arkansas; California; Colorado; Connecticut; Delaware; Florida; Georgia; Hawaii;[15] Idaho; Illinois; Indiana; Iowa; Kansas; Kentucky; Louisiana; Maine; Maryland; Michigan; Minnesota; Mississippi; Missouri; Montana; Nebraska; Nevada; New Hampshire; New Jersey; New Mexico; New York; North Carolina; North Dakota; Ohio; Oklahoma; Oregon; Pennsylvania; Rhode Island; South Carolina; South Dakota; Tennessee; Texas; Utah; Vermont; Virginia; Washington; West Virginia; Wisconsin; Wyoming.

Carter 1976 50 States (297/537)—Alabama; Arkansas; Delaware; Florida; Georgia; Hawaii; Kentucky; Louisiana; Maryland; Massachusetts; Minnesota; Mississippi; Missouri; New York; North Carolina; Ohio; Pennsylvania; Rhode Island; South Carolina; Tennessee; Texas; West Virginia; Wisconsin; District of Columbia.

Reagan 1980 50 States (489/538)—Alabama; Alaska; Arizona; Arkansas; California; Colorado; Connecticut; Delaware; Florida; Idaho; Illinois; Indiana; Iowa; Kansas; Kentucky; Louisiana; Maine; Massachusetts; Michigan; Mississippi; Missouri; Montana; Nebraska; Nevada; New Hampshire; New Jersey; New Mexico; New York; North Carolina; North Dakota; Ohio; Oklahoma; Oregon; Pennsylvania; South Carolina; South Dakota; Tennessee; Texas; Utah; Vermont; Virginia; Washington; Wisconsin; Wyoming.

Reagan 1984 50 States (525/538)—Alabama; Alaska; Arizona; Arkansas; California; Colorado; Connecticut; Delaware; Florida; Georgia; Hawaii; Idaho; Illinois; Indiana; Iowa; Kansas; Kentucky; Louisiana; Maine; Maryland; Massachusetts; Michigan; Mississippi; Missouri; Montana; Nebraska; Nevada; New Hampshire; New Jersey; New Mexico; New York; North Carolina; North Dakota; Ohio; Oklahoma; Oregon; Pennsylvania; Rhode Island; South Carolina; South Dakota; Tennessee; Texas; Utah; Vermont; Virginia; Washington; West Virginia; Wisconsin; Wyoming.

Bush, G. H. W.[16] **1988 50 States** (426/538)—Alabama; Alaska; Arizona; Arkansas; California; Colorado; Connecticut; Delaware; Florida; Georgia; Idaho; Illinois; Indiana; Kansas; Kentucky; Louisiana; Maine; Maryland; Michigan; Mississippi; Missouri; Montana; Nebraska; Nevada; New Hampshire; New Jersey; New Mexico; North Carolina; North Dakota; Ohio; Oklahoma; Pennsylvania; South Carolina; South Dakota; Tennessee; Texas; Utah; Vermont; Virginia; Wyoming.

Clinton 1992 50 States (370/538)—Arkansas; California; Colorado; Connecticut; Delaware; Georgia; Hawaii; Illinois; Iowa; Kentucky; Louisiana; Maine; Maryland; Massachusetts; Michigan; Minnesota; Missouri; Montana; Nevada; New Hampshire; New Jersey; New Mexico; New York; Ohio; Oregon; Pennsylvania; Rhode Island; Tennessee; Vermont; Washington; West Virginia; Wisconsin; District of Columbia.

Clinton 1996 50 States (379/538)—Arizona; Arkansas; California; Colorado; Connecticut; Delaware; Georgia; Florida; Hawaii; Illinois; Iowa; Kentucky; Louisiana; Maine; Maryland; Massachusetts; Michigan; Minnesota; Missouri; Montana; Nevada; New Hampshire; New Jersey; New Mexico; New York; Ohio; Oregon; Pennsylvania; Rhode Island; Tennessee; Vermont; Washington; West Virginia; Wisconsin; District of Columbia.

Bush, G. W.[17] **2000 50 States (271/538)** — Alabama; Alaska; Arizona; Arkansas; Colorado; Florida; Georgia; Idaho; Indiana; Kansas; Kentucky; Louisiana; Mississippi; Missouri; Montana; Nebraska; Nevada; New Hampshire; North Carolina; North Dakota; Ohio; Oklahoma; South Carolina; South Dakota; Tennessee; Texas; Utah; Virginia; West Virginia; Wyoming.

Bush, G. W. 2004 50 States (286/538) — Alabama; Alaska; Arizona; Arkansas; Colorado; Florida; Georgia; Idaho; Indiana; Iowa; Kansas; Kentucky; Louisiana; Mississippi; Missouri; Montana; Nebraska; Nevada; New Mexico; North Carolina; North Dakota; Ohio; Oklahoma; South Carolina; South Dakota; Tennessee; Texas; Utah; Virginia; West Virginia; Wyoming.

NOTES

1. These electors were pledged to Jefferson for President and Burr for Vice President. Burr refused to accept the Vice Presidency, and this forced the issue into the House of Representatives. Maryland's votes were split between Jefferson and Adams. Each state had one vote in the House. After 36 ballots Jefferson added Maryland, New Jersey and Vermont.

2. One vote was cast for John Quincy Adams. The purpose was to deny Monroe a unanimous electoral vote. There were three abstentions.

3. No candidate won a majority of electoral votes. In accordance with the 12th Amendment, the election was decided by the House of Representatives. The House decided among the top three candidates. Clay gave his support to Adams, who was then elected as President.

4. Jackson was born in either North Carolina or South Carolina. In 1832 he carried North Carolina but not South Carolina. His home state was Tennessee, which he carried in both 1828 and 1832.

5. W. H. Harrison was Virginia born. He failed to carry his birth state but did carry his home state of Ohio.

6. Polk was born in North Carolina; his home state was Tennessee. He failed to carry either in his election to the White House.

7. Taylor failed to carry Virginia, his birth state, but did win his home state of Kentucky. The 1848 election is the first Presidential election held on the same day nationwide.

8. Lincoln carried his home state of Illinois in both 1860 and 1864. His birth state, Kentucky, never supported him.

9. The eleven states of the Confederacy did not participate in the 1864 election. West Virginia (1863) and Nevada (1864) had been admitted to the Union.

10. The Civil War was over and eight of the eleven Confederate States had been readmitted to the Union. Only Mississippi, Texas, and Virginia had not rejoined.

11. Twenty-three electoral votes from Southern states were excluded from the count.

12. Horace Greeley, candidate for the Democrats, died prior to the convening of the Electoral College. Votes which he would have won were divided amongst other candidates.

13. This may be the most controversial election in our history. Tilden was a clear winner in the popular vote, but lacked one electoral vote. Republicans contested the vote in four states: Florida, Louisiana, Oregon and South Carolina. Each of the four returned two sets of votes. A special commission was set up to decide the matter. The commission consisted of 8 Republicans and 7 Democrats. All votes were on strict party lines and Hayes was named President.

14. In his first election to the White House Wilson won both his home state, New Jersey, and his birth state, Virginia. In his 1916 reelection he failed to carry New Jersey.

15. Nixon was the first Republican, and one of only two, to win Hawaii. The other was Reagan in 1984.

16. Bush did not carry his birth state, Massachusetts, but did carry Texas, his home state.

17. Following in his father's footsteps, Bush carried his home state of Texas twice, but never carried his birth state, Connecticut. He also carried Clinton's home state, Arkansas, and Gore's home state of Tennessee.

30. Percent of States Won

Washington is the only President to be elected and reelected by 100 percent of the states. Though the Union was much smaller, consisting of only 10 and 15 states when he was President, the support he enjoyed is remarkable.

Here are the 55 elections by percent of states won beginning with Washington and continuing in order of percent, and then year of election. Washington, D.C. is counted as a state beginning 1964.

President	Year	Number of States	States Won	Percent Won
Washington	1789	10	10	100%
Washington	1792	15	15	100%
Monroe[1]	1820	24	24	100%
Nixon	1972	51	49	96.08%
Reagan	1984	51	49	96.08%
Roosevelt, F.	1936	48	46	95.83%
Jefferson	1804	17	15	88.24%
Johnson, L.	1964	51[2]	45	88.24%
Lincoln	1864	25[3]	22	88%
Roosevelt, F.	1932	48	42	87.50%
Pierce	1852	31	27	87.10%

President	Year	Number of States	States Won	Percent Won
Reagan	1980	51	44	86.27%
Eisenhower	1956	48	41	85.42%
Monroe	1816	19	16	84.21%
Wilson	1912	48	40	83.33%
Hoover	1928	48	40	83.33%
Grant	1872	37	29	83.86%
Eisenhower	1952	48	39	81.25%
Roosevelt, F.	1940	48	38	79.17%
Bush, G. H. W.	1988	40	51	78.43%
Harding	1920	48	37	77.08%
Grant	1868	34[4]	26	76.47%
Roosevelt, F.	1944	48	36	75%
Harrison, W. H.	1840	26	19	73.08%
Coolidge	1924	48	35	72.92%
Roosevelt, T.	1904	45	32	71.11%
Madison	1808	17	12	70.59%
Jackson	1832	24	16	66.67%
Clinton	1992	51	33	64.71%
Taft	1908	46	29	63.04%
Nixon	1968	51	32	62.75%
Clinton	1996	51	32	62.75%
Jefferson	1800	16	10[5]	62.50%
Jackson	1828	24	15	62.50%
Wilson	1916	48	30	62.50%
McKinley	1900	45	28	62.22%
Buchanan	1856	31	19	61.29%
Madison	1812	18	11	61.11%
Bush, G. W.	2004	51	31	60.78%
Bush, G. W.	2000	51	30	58.82%
Truman	1948	48	28	58.33%
Van Buren	1836	26	15	57.69%
Polk	1844	26	15	57.69%
Adams, J.	1796	16	9	56.25%
Hayes	1876	38	21	55.26%
Lincoln	1860	33	18	54.55%
Cleveland	1884	38	20	52.63%
Harrison, B.	1888	38	20	52.63%
Adams, J. Q.	1824	21	11[6]	52.38%
Cleveland	1892	44	23	52.27%
McKinley	1896	45	23	51.11%
Taylor	1848	30	15	50%
Garfield	1880	38	19	50%
Carter	1976	51	24	47.06%
Kennedy	1960	50	22	44%

NOTES

1. Monroe won all of the states and all of the electoral votes. He was denied one vote in order to maintain Washington as the only President to win unanimously.

2. The District of Columbia gained access to the Electoral College. From the 1964 election forward it would be counted as a state.

3. Eleven states had left the Union to form the Confederate States of America.

4. Mississippi, Texas, and Virginia had not yet rejoined the Union.

5. Jefferson had won 8 states. When the matter went to Congress he added the additional 2 to his count.

6. In the popular vote, Adams won 7 states. The four additional were awarded by Congress when the Electoral College was unable to elect a President.

---

31. How the States Voted

To be President the candidate needs to win the electoral vote, and that means winning states with large chunks of electoral votes. Here are the states and the Presidents for whom they voted. The years in parentheses show the Presidential election year after admission, for those other than the original 13. The next number is the current number of electors. The figures under the states are the number of votes for winning candidates, divided by the number of elections, through 2004, and the resulting percentage. The figures beneath that show the number of times the states voted for Democrat, Republican, and Other.

No Republican has ever won the White House without Ohio. Every Buckeye elected to the Presidency has been a Republican. The winner is in **bold print**, and the loser in regular print.

And no, Maine doesn't always vote for the winner. The best bellwether state is New Mexico.

Alabama (1820)[1] (9)
24/46=52.17%
D-30; R-11; O-5

James Monroe	1820	Martin Van Buren	1840
Andrew Jackson	1824	**James Polk**	1844
Andrew Jackson	1828	Lewis Cass	1848
Andrew Jackson	1832	**Franklin Pierce**	1852
Martin Van Buren	1836	**James Buchanan**	1856

Alabama (cont.)

John Breckinridge	1860	**Franklin D. Roosevelt**	**1936**
Ulysses S. Grant	**1868**	**Franklin D. Roosevelt**	**1940**
Ulysses S. Grant	**1872**	**Franklin D. Roosevelt**	**1944**
Samuel Tilden	1876	Strom Thurmond	1948
Winfield Hancock	1880	Adlai Stevenson	1952
Grover Cleveland	**1884**	Adlai Stevenson	1956
Grover Cleveland	1888	Harry Byrd	1960
Grover Cleveland	**1892**	Barry Goldwater	1964
William Bryan	1896	George Wallace	1968
William Bryan	1900	**Richard Nixon**	**1972**
Alton Parker	1904	**Jimmy Carter**	**1976**
William Bryan	1908	**Ronald Reagan**	**1980**
Woodrow Wilson	**1912**	**Ronald Reagan**	**1984**
Woodrow Wilson	**1916**	**George Bush**	**1988**
James Cox	1920	George Bush	1992
John Davis	1924	Bob Dole	1996
Alfred Smith	1928	**George W. Bush**	**2000**
Franklin D. Roosevelt	**1932**	**George W. Bush**	**2004**

Alaska (1960) (3)
8/12=66.66%
D-1; R-11; O-0

Richard Nixon	1960	**Ronald Reagan**	**1984**
Lyndon Johnson	**1964**	**George Bush**	**1988**
Richard Nixon	**1968**	George Bush	1992
Richard Nixon	**1972**	Bob Dole	1996
Gerald Ford	1976	**George W. Bush**	**2000**
Ronald Reagan	**1980**	**George W. Bush**	**2004**

Arizona (1912) (10)
20/24=83.33%
D-8; R-16; O-0

Woodrow Wilson	**1912**	Richard Nixon	1960
Woodrow Wilson	**1916**	Barry Goldwater	1964
Warren Harding	**1920**	**Richard Nixon**	**1968**
Calvin Coolidge	**1924**	**Richard Nixon**	**1972**
Herbert Hoover	**1928**	Gerald Ford	1976
Franklin Roosevelt	**1932**	**Ronald Reagan**	**1980**
Franklin Roosevelt	**1936**	**Ronald Reagan**	**1984**
Franklin Roosevelt	**1940**	**George Bush**	**1988**
Franklin Roosevelt	**1944**	George Bush	1992
Harry Truman	**1948**	**Bill Clinton**	**1996**
Dwight Eisenhower	**1952**	**George W. Bush**	**2000**
Dwight Eisenhower	**1956**	**George W. Bush**	**2004**

Arkansas (1836)[2] (3)
25/42=59.52%
D-34; R-7; O-1

Martin Van Buren	1836	John Davis	1924
Martin Van Buren	1840	Alfred Smith	1928
James Polk	1844	Franklin Roosevelt	1932
Lewis Cass	1848	Franklin Roosevelt	1936
Franklin Pierce	1852	Franklin Roosevelt	1940
James Buchanan	1856	Franklin Roosevelt	1944
John Breckinridge	1860	Harry Truman	1948
Ulysses Grant	1868	Adlai Stevenson	1952
Horace Greeley	1872	Adlai Stevenson	1956
Samuel Tilden	1876	John Kennedy	1960
Winfield Hancock	1880	Lyndon Johnson	1964
Grover Cleveland	1884	George Wallace	1968
Grover Cleveland	1888	Richard Nixon	1972
Grover Cleveland	1892	Jimmy Carter	1976
William Bryan	1896	Ronald Reagan	1980
William Bryan	1900	Ronald Reagan	1984
Alton Parker	1904	George Bush	1988
William Bryan	1908	Bill Clinton	1992
Woodrow Wilson	1912	Bill Clinton	1996
Woodrow Wilson	1916	George W. Bush	2000
James Cox	1920	George W. Bush	2004

California (1852) (55)
32/39=82.05%
D-16; R-22; O-1

Franklin Pierce	1852	Warren Harding	1920
James Buchanan	1856	Calvin Coolidge	1924
Abraham Lincoln	1860	Herbert Hoover	1928
Abraham Lincoln	1864	Franklin Roosevelt	1932
Ulysses Grant	1868	Franklin Roosevelt	1936
Ulysses Grant	1872	Franklin Roosevelt	1940
Rutherford Hayes	1876	Franklin Roosevelt	1944
Winfield Hancock	1880	Harry Truman	1948
James Blaine	1884	Dwight Eisenhower	1952
Benjamin Harrison	1888	Dwight Eisenhower	1956
Grover Cleveland	1892	Richard Nixon	1960
William McKinley	1896	Lyndon Johnson	1964
William McKinley	1900	Richard Nixon	1968
Theodore Roosevelt	1904	Richard Nixon	1972
William Taft	1908	Gerald Ford	1976
Theodore Roosevelt	1912	Ronald Reagan	1980
Woodrow Wilson	1916	Ronald Reagan	1984

California (cont.)

George Bush	1988	Al Gore	2000
Bill Clinton	1992	John Kerry	2004
Bill Clinton	1996		

Colorado (1876) (9)
23/33=69.70%
D-10; R-22; O-1

Rutherford Hayes	1876	Thomas Dewey	1944
James Garfield	1880	Harry Truman	1948
James Blain	1884	Dwight Eisenhower	1952
Benjamin Harrison	1888	Dwight Eisenhower	1956
James Weaver	1892	Richard Nixon	1960
William Bryan	1896	Lyndon Johnson	1964
William Bryan	1900	Richard Nixon	1968
Theodore Roosevelt	1904	Richard Nixon	1972
William Bryan	1908	Gerald Ford	1976
Woodrow Wilson	1912	Ronald Reagan	1980
Woodrow Wilson	1916	Ronald Reagan	1984
Warren Harding	1920	George Bush	1988
Calvin Coolidge	1924	Bill Clinton	1992
Herbert Hoover	1928	Bob Dole	1996
Franklin Roosevelt	1932	George W. Bush	2000
Franklin Roosevelt	1936	George W. Bush	2004
Wendell Willkie	1940		

Connecticut (7)
37/55=67.27%
D-17; R-23; O-15

George Washington	1789	Zachary Taylor	1848
George Washington	1792	Franklin Pierce	1852
John Adams	1796	John Fremont	1856
John Adams	1800	Abraham Lincoln	1860
Charles Pinckney	1804	Abraham Lincoln	1864
Charles Pinckney	1808	Ulysses Grant	1868
DeWitt Clinton	1812	Ulysses Grant	1872
Rufus King	1816	Samuel Tilden	1876
James Monroe	1820	James Garfield	1880
John Q. Adams	1824	Grover Cleveland	1884
John Q. Adams	1828	Grover Cleveland	1888
Henry Clay	1832	Grover Cleveland	1892
Martin Van Buren	1836	William McKinley	1896
William Harrison	1840	William McKinley	1900
Henry Clay	1844	Theodore Roosevelt	1904

Connecticut (cont.)

William Taft	1908	John Kennedy	1960
Thomas Dewey	1948	Lyndon Johnson	1964
Woodrow Wilson	1912	Hubert Humphrey	1968
Charles Hughes	1916	Richard Nixon	1972
Warren Harding	1920	Gerald Ford	1976
Calvin Coolidge	1924	Ronald Reagan	1980
Herbert Hoover	1928	Ronald Reagan	1984
Herbert Hoover	1932	George Bush	1988
Franklin Roosevelt	1936	Bill Clinton	1992
Franklin Roosevelt	1940	Bill Clinton	1996
Franklin Roosevelt	1944	Al Gore	2000
Dwight Eisenhower	1952	John Kerry	2004
Dwight Eisenhower	1956		

Delaware (3)
35/55=63.63%
D-20; R-18; O-17

George Washington	1789	William McKinley	1900
George Washington	1792	Theodore Roosevelt	1904
John Adams	1796	William Taft	1908
John Adams	1800[3]	Woodrow Wilson	1912
Charles Pinckney	1804	Woodrow Wilson	1916
Charles Pinckney	1808	Warren Harding	1920
DeWitt Clinton	1812	Calvin Coolidge	1924
Rufus King	1816	Herbert Hoover	1928
James Monroe	1820	Herbert Hoover	1932
William Crawford	1824	Franklin Roosevelt	1936
John Q. Adams	1828	Franklin Roosevelt	1940
Henry Clay	1832	Franklin Roosevelt	1944
William Harrison	1836	Thomas Dewey	1948
William Harrison	1840	Dwight Eisenhower	1952
Henry Clay	1844	Dwight Eisenhower	1956
Zachary Taylor	1848	John Kennedy	1960
Franklin Pierce	1852	Lyndon Johnson	1964
James Buchanan	1856	Richard Nixon	1968
John Breckinridge	1860	Richard Nixon	1972
George McCellan	1864	Jimmy Carter	1976
Horatio Seymour	1868	Ronald Reagan	1980
Ulysses Grant	1872	Ronald Reagan	1984
Samuel Tilden	1876	George Bush	1988
Winfield Hancock	1880	Bill Clinton	1992
Grover Cleveland	1884	Bill Clinton	1996
Grover Cleveland	1888	Al Gore	2000
Grover Cleveland	1892	John Kerry	2004
William McKinley	1896		

Florida (1848)[4] (27)
28/39=71.79%
D-22; R-15; O-2

Zachary Taylor	1848	Franklin Roosevelt	1932
Franklin Pierce	1852	Franklin Roosevelt	1936
James Buchanan	1856	Franklin Roosevelt	1940
John Breckinridge	1860	Franklin Roosevelt	1944
Ulysses Grant	1868	Harry Truman	1948
Ulysses Grant	1872	Dwight Eisenhower	1952
Rutherford Hayes	1876	Dwight Eisenhower	1956
Winfield Hancock	1880	Richard Nixon	1960
Grover Cleveland	1884	Lyndon Johnson	1964
Grover Cleveland	1888	Richard Nixon	1968
Grover Cleveland	1892	Richard Nixon	1972
William Bryan	1896	Jimmy Carter	1976
William Bryan	1900	Ronald Reagan	1980
Alton Parker	1904	Ronald Reagan	1984
William Bryan	1908	George Bush	1992
Woodrow Wilson	1912	George Bush	1996
Woodrow Wilson	1916	Bill Clinton	1996
James Cox	1920	George W. Bush	2000
John Davis	1924	George W. Bush	2004
Herbert Hoover	1928		

Georgia[5] (15)
32/54=59.26%
D-31; R-7; O-16

George Washington	1789	John Breckinridge	1860
George Washington	1792	Horatio Seymour	1868
Thomas Jefferson	1796	Gratz Brown	1872
Thomas Jefferson	1800	William Bryan	1876
Thomas Jefferson	1804	Winfield Hancock	1880
James Madison	1808	Grover Cleveland	1884
James Madison	1812	Grover Cleveland	1888
James Monroe	1816	Grover Cleveland	1892
James Monroe	1820	William Bryan	1896
William Crawford	1824	William Bryan	1900
Andrew Jackson	1828	Alton Parker	1904
Andrew Jackson	1832	William Bryan	1908
Hugh White	1836	Woodrow Wilson	1912
William Harrison	1840	Woodrow Wilson	1916
James Polk	1844	James Cox	1920
Zachary Taylor	1848	John Davis	1924
Franklin Pierce	1852	Alfred Smith	1928
James Buchanan	1856	Franklin Roosevelt	1932

Georgia (cont.)

Franklin Roosevelt	1936	Richard Nixon	1972
Franklin Roosevelt	1940	Jimmy Carter	1976
Franklin Roosevelt	1944	Jimmy Carter	1980
Harry Truman	1948	Ronald Reagan	1984
Adlai Stevenson	1952	George Bush	1988
Adlai Stevenson	1956	Bill Clinton	1992
John Kennedy	1960	Bob Dole	1996
Barry Goldwater	1964	George W. Bush	2000
George Wallace	1968	George W. Bush	2004

Hawaii (1960)
7/12=58.33%
D-10; R-2

John Kennedy	1960	Ronald Reagan	1984
Lyndon Johnson	1964	Michael Dukakis	1988
Hubert Humphrey	1968	Bill Clinton	1992
Richard Nixon	1972	Bill Clinton	1996
Jimmy Carter	1976	Al Gore	2000
Jimmy Carter	1980	John Kerry	2004

Idaho (1892) (7)
21/29–72.41%
D-10; R-18; O-1

James Weaver	1892	Dwight Eisenhower	1952
William Bryan	1896	Dwight Eisenhower	1956
William Bryan	1900	Richard Nixon	1960
Theodore Roosevelt	1904	Lyndon Johnson	1964
William Taft	1908	Richard Nixon	1968
Woodrow Wilson	1912	Richard Nixon	1972
Woodrow Wilson	1916	Gerald Ford	1976
Warren Harding	1920	Ronald Reagan	1980
Calvin Coolidge	1924	Ronald Reagan	1984
Herbert Hoover	1928	George Bush	1988
Franklin Roosevelt	1932	George Bush	1992
Franklin Roosevelt	1936	Robert Dole	1996
Franklin Roosevelt	1940	George W. Bush	2000
Franklin Roosevelt	1944	George W. Bush	2004
Harry Truman	1948		

Illinois (1820) (21)
39/47=82.98%
D-22; R-24; O-1

James Monroe	1820	Andrew Jackson	1828
Andrew Jackson	1824	Andrew Jackson	1832

Illinois (cont.)

Martin Van Buren	1836	Calvin Coolidge	1924
Martin Van Buren	1840	Herbert Hoover	1928
James Polk	1844	Franklin Roosevelt	1932
Lewis Cass	1848	Franklin Roosevelt	1936
Franklin Pierce	1852	Franklin Roosevelt	1940
James Buchanan	1856	Franklin Roosevelt	1944
Abraham Lincoln	1860	Harry Truman	1948
Abraham Lincoln	1864	Dwight Eisenhower	1952
Ulysses Grant	1868	Dwight Eisenhower	1956
Ulysses Grant	1872	John Kennedy	1960
Rutherford Hayes	1876	Lyndon Johnson	1964
James Garfield	1880	Richard Nixon	1968
James Blaine	1884	Richard Nixon	1972
Benjamin Harrison	1888	Gerald Ford	1976
Grover Cleveland	1892	Ronald Reagan	1980
William McKinley	1896	Ronald Reagan	1984
William McKinley	1900	George Bush	1988
Theodore Roosevelt	1904	Bill Clinton	1992
William Taft	1908	Bill Clinton	1996
Woodrow Wilson	1912	Al Gore	2000
Charles Hughes	1916	John Kerry	2004
Warren Harding	1920		

Indiana (1816) (11)
36/48=75%
D-13; R-32; O-3

James Monroe	1816[6]	Grover Cleveland	1892
James Monroe	1820	William McKinley	1896
Andrew Jackson	1824	William McKinley	1900
Andrew Jackson	1828	Theodore Roosevelt	1904
Andrew Jackson	1832	William Taft	1908
William Harrison	1836	Woodrow Wilson	1912
William Harrison	1840	Charles Hughes	1916
James Polk	1844	Warren Harding	1920
Lewis Cass	1848	Calvin Coolidge	1924
Franklin Pierce	1852	Herbert Hoover	1928
James Buchanan	1856	Franklin Roosevelt	1932
Abraham Lincoln	1860	Franklin Roosevelt	1936
Abraham Lincoln	1864	Wendell Willkie	1940
Ulysses Grant	1868	Thomas Dewey	1944
Ulysses Grant	1872	Thomas Dewey	1948
Samuel Tilden	1876	Dwight Eisenhower	1956
James Garfield	1880	Dwight Eisenhower	1952
Grover Cleveland	1884	Richard Nixon	1960
Benjamin Harrison	1888	Lyndon Johnson	1964

Indiana (cont.)

Richard Nixon	1968	George Bush	1988
Richard Nixon	1972	George Bush	1992
Gerald Ford	1976	Robert Dole	1996
Ronald Reagan	1980	George W. Bush	2000
Ronald Reagan	1984	George W. Bush	2004

Iowa (1848) (7)
28/40=70%
D-12; R-28

Lewis Cass	1848	Herbert Hoover	1928
Franklin Pierce	1852	Franklin Roosevelt	1932
John Fremont	1856	Franklin Roosevelt	1936
Abraham Lincoln	1860	Wendell Willkie	1940
Abraham Lincoln	1864	Thomas Dewey	1944
Ulysses Grant	1868	Harry Truman	1948
Ulysses Grant	1872	Dwight Eisenhower	1952
Rutherford Hayes	1876	Dwight Eisenhower	1956
James Garfield	1880	Richard Nixon	1960
James Blaine	1884	Lyndon Johnson	1964
Benjamin Harrison	1888	Richard Nixon	1968
Benjamin Harrison	1892	Richard Nixon	1972
William McKinley	1896	Gerald Ford	1976
William McKinley	1900	Ronald Reagan	1980
Theodore Roosevelt	1904	Ronald Reagan	1984
William Taft	1908	Michael Dukakis	1988
Woodrow Wilson	1912	Bill Clinton	1992
Charles Hughes	1916	Bill Clinton	1996
Warren Harding	1920	Al Gore	2000
Calvin Coolidge	1924	John Kerry	2004

Kansas (1864) (6)
26/36=73.22%
D-6; R-29; O-1

Abraham Lincoln	1864	Theodore Roosevelt	1904
Ulysses Grant	1868	William Taft	1908
Ulysses Grant	1872	Woodrow Wilson	1912
Rutherford Hayes	1876	Woodrow Wilson	1916
James Garfield	1880	Warren Harding	1920
James Blaine	1884	Calvin Coolidge	1924
Benjamin Harrison	1888	Herbert Hoover	1928
James Weaver	1892	Franklin Roosevelt	1932
William Bryan	1896	Franklin Roosevelt	1936
William McKinley	1900	Wendell Willkie	1940

Kansas (cont.)

Thomas Dewey	1944	Gerald Ford	1976
Thomas Dewey	1948	**Ronald Reagan**	**1980**
Dwight Eisenhower	**1952**	**Ronald Reagan**	**1984**
Dwight Eisenhower	**1956**	**George Bush**	**1988**
Richard Nixon	1960	George Bush	1992
Lyndon Johnson	**1964**	Robert Dole	1996
Richard Nixon	**1968**	**George W. Bush**	**2000**
Richard Nixon	**1972**	**George W. Bush**	**2004**

Kentucky (1792) (8)
35/54=64.81%
D-26; R-12; O-16

George Washington	1792	William Bryan	1900
Thomas Jefferson	1796	Alton Parker	1904
Thomas Jefferson	**1800**	William Bryan	1908
Thomas Jefferson	**1804**	**Woodrow Wilson**	**1912**
James Madison	**1808**	**Woodrow Wilson**	**1916**
James Madison	**1812**	James Cox	1920
James Monroe	**1816**	**Calvin Coolidge**	**1924**
James Monroe	**1820**	**Herbert Hoover**	**1928**
Henry Clay	1824	**Franklin Roosevelt**	**1932**
Andrew Jackson	**1828**	**Franklin Roosevelt**	**1936**
Henry Clay	1832	**Franklin Roosevelt**	**1940**
William Harrison	1836	**Franklin Roosevelt**	**1944**
William Harrison	**1840**	**Harry Truman**	**1948**
Henry Clay	1844	Adlai Stevenson	1952
Zachary Taylor	**1848**	**Dwight Eisenhower**	**1956**
Winfield Scott	1852	Richard Nixon	1960
James Buchanan	**1856**	**Lyndon Johnson**	**1964**
John Bell	1860	**Richard Nixon**	**1968**
George McClellan	1864	**Richard Nixon**	**1972**
Horatio Seymour	1868	**Jimmy Carter**	**1976**
Thomas Hendricks	1872	**Ronald Reagan**	**1980**
Samuel Tilden	1876	**Ronald Reagan**	**1984**
Winfield Hancock	1880	**George Bush**	**1988**
Grover Cleveland	**1884**	**Bill Clinton**	**1992**
Grover Cleveland	1888	**Bill Clinton**	**1996**
Grover Cleveland	**1892**	**George W. Bush**	**2000**
William McKinley	**1896**	**George W. Bush**	**2004**

Louisiana (1812)[7] (9)
31/48=64.59%
D-31; R-7; O-8

James Madison	**1812**	**James Monroe**	**1820**
James Monroe	**1816**	Andrew Jackson	1824

Louisiana (cont.)

Andrew Jackson	**1828**		James Cox	1920
Andrew Jackson	**1832**		John Davis	1924
Martin Van Buren	**1836**		Alfred Smith	1928
William Harrison	**1840**		**Franklin Roosevelt**	**1932**
James Polk	**1844**		**Franklin Roosevelt**	**1936**
Zachary Taylor	**1848**		**Franklin Roosevelt**	**1940**
Franklin Pierce	**1852**		**Franklin Roosevelt**	**1944**
James Buchanan	**1856**		Strom Thurmond	1948
John Breckinridge	1860		Adlai Stevenson	1952
Horatio Seymour	1868		**Dwight Eisenhower**	**1956**
Horace Greeley	1872		**John Kennedy**	**1960**
Benjamin Hayes	**1876**		Barry Goldwater	1964
Winfield Scott	1880		George Wallace	1968
Grover Cleveland	**1884**		**Richard Nixon**	**1972**
Grover Cleveland	1888		**Jimmy Carter**	**1976**
Grover Cleveland	**1892**		**Ronald Reagan**	**1980**
William Bryan	1896		**Ronald Reagan**	**1984**
William Bryan	1900		**George Bush**	**1988**
Alton Parker	1904		**Bill Clinton**	**1992**
William Bryan	1908		**Bill Clinton**	**1996**
Woodrow Wilson	**1912**		**George W. Bush**	**2000**
Woodrow Wilson	**1916**		**George W. Bush**	**2004**

Maine (1820) (4)
31/47=65.96%
D-13; R-30; O-4

James Monroe	**1820**		Benjamin Harrison	1892
John Q. Adams	**1824**		**William McKinley**	**1896**
John Q. Adams	1828		**William McKinley**	**1900**
Andrew Jackson	**1832**		**Theodore Roosevelt**	**1904**
Martin Van Buren	**1836**		**William Taft**	**1908**
William Harrison	**1840**		**Woodrow Wilson**	**1912**
James Polk	**1844**		Charles Hughes	1916
Lewis Cass	1848		**Warren Harding**	**1920**
Franklin Pierce	**1852**		**Calvin Coolidge**	**1924**
John Fremont	1856		**Herbert Hoover**	**1928**
Abraham Lincoln	**1860**		Herbert Hoover	1932
Abraham Lincoln	**1864**		Alfred Landon	1936
Ulysses Grant	**1868**		Wendell Willkie	1940
Ulysses Grant	**1872**		Thomas Dewey	1944
Rutherford Hayes	**1876**		Thomas Dewey	1948
James Garfield	**1880**		**Dwight Eisenhower**	**1952**
James Blaine	1884		**Dwight Eisenhower**	**1956**
Benjamin Harrison	**1888**		Richard Nixon	1960

Maine (cont.)

Lyndon Johnson	1964	George Bush	1988
Hubert Humphrey	1968	Bill Clinton	1992
Richard Nixon	1972	Bill Clinton	1996
Gerald Ford	1976	Al Gore	2000
Ronald Reagan	1980	John Kerry	2004
Ronald Reagan	1984		

Maryland (10)
37/55=67.23%
D-25; R-13; O-17

George Washington	1789	William McKinley	1900
George Washington	1792	Alton Parker	1904
John Adams	1796	William Bryan	1908
Thomas Jefferson	1800[8]	Woodrow Wilson	1912
Thomas Jefferson	1804	Woodrow Wilson	1916
James Madison	1808	Warren Harding	1920
James Madison	1812	Calvin Coolidge	1924
James Monroe	1816	Herbert Hoover	1928
James Monroe	1820	Franklin Roosevelt	1932
Andrew Jackson	1824	Franklin Roosevelt	1936
John Q. Adams	1828	Franklin Roosevelt	1940
Henry Clay	1832	Franklin Roosevelt	1944
William Harrison	1836	Thomas Dewey	1948
William Harrison	1840	Dwight Eisenhower	1952
Henry Clay	1844	Dwight Eisenhower	1956
Zachary Taylor	1848	John Kennedy	1960
Franklin Pierce	1852	Lyndon Johnson	1964
Millard Fillmore	1856	Hubert Humphrey	1968
John Breckinridge	1860	Richard Nixon	1972
Abraham Lincoln	1864	Jimmy Carter	1976
Horatio Seymour	1868	Ronald Reagan	1980
Thomas Hendricks	1872	Ronald Reagan	1984
Samuel Tilden	1876	George Bush	1988
Winfield Hancock	1880	Bill Clinton	1992
Grover Cleveland	1884	Bill Clinton	1996
Grover Cleveland	1888	Al Gore	2000
Grover Cleveland	1892	John Kerry	2004
William McKinley	1896		

Massachusetts (12)
36/55=65.45%)
D-17; R-21; O-17

George Washington	1789	John Adams	1796
George Washington	1792	John Adams	1800

Massachusetts (cont.)

Thomas Jefferson	1804	**William Taft**	**1908**
Charles Pinckney	1808	**Woodrow Wilson**	**1912**
DeWitt Clinton	1812	Charles Hughes	1916
Rufus King	1816	**Warren Harding**	**1920**
James Monroe	1820	**Calvin Coolidge**	**1924**
John Q. Adams	**1824**	Alfred Smith	1928
John Q. Adams	1828	**Franklin Roosevelt**	**1932**
Henry Clay	1832	**Franklin Roosevelt**	**1936**
Daniel Webster	1836[9]	**Franklin Roosevelt**	**1940**
William Harrison	**1840**	**Franklin Roosevelt**	**1944**
Henry Clay	1844	**Harry Truman**	**1948**
Zachary Taylor	**1848**	**Dwight Eisenhower**	**1952**
Winfield Scott	1852	**Dwight Eisenhower**	**1956**
John Fremont	1856	**John Kennedy**	**1960**
Abraham Lincoln	**1860**	**Lyndon Johnson**	**1964**
Abraham Lincoln	**1864**	Hubert Humphrey	1968
Ulysses Grant	**1868**	George McGovern	1972[10]
Ulysses Grant	**1872**	**Jimmy Carter**	**1976**
Rutherford Hayes	**1876**	**Ronald Reagan**	**1980**
James Garfield	**1880**	**Ronald Reagan**	**1984**
James Blain	1884	Michael Dukakis	1988
Benjamin Harrison	**1888**	**Bill Clinton**	**1992**
Benjamin Harrison	1892	**Bill Clinton**	**1996**
William McKinley	**1896**	Al Gore	2000
William McKinley	**1900**	John Kerry	2004
Theodore Roosevelt	**1904**		

Michigan (1840) (17)
30/43=72.09%
D-14; R-27; O-2

Martin Van Buren	**1836**	Benjamin Harrison	1892
William Harrison	**1840**	**William McKinley**	**1896**
James Polk	**1844**	**William McKinley**	**1900**
Lewis Cass	1848	**Theodore Roosevelt**	**1904**
Franklin Pierce	**1852**	**William Taft**	**1908**
John Fremont	1856	Theodore Roosevelt	1912
Abraham Lincoln	**1860**	Charles Hughes	1916
Abraham Lincoln	**1864**	**Warren Harding**	**1920**
Ulysses Grant	**1868**	**Calvin Coolidge**	**1924**
Ulysses Grant	**1872**	**Herbert Hoover**	**1928**
Rutherford Hayes	**1876**	**Franklin Roosevelt**	**1932**
James Garfield	**1880**	**Franklin Roosevelt**	**1936**
James Blaine	1884	Wendell Willkie	1940
Benjamin Harrison	**1888**	**Franklin Roosevelt**	**1944**

Michigan (cont.)

Thomas Dewey	1948	**Ronald Reagan**	**1980**
Dwight Eisenhower	**1952**	**Ronald Reagan**	**1984**
Dwight Eisenhower	**1956**	**George Bush**	**1988**
John Kennedy	**1960**	**Bill Clinton**	**1992**
Lyndon Johnson	**1964**	Bill Clinton	1996
Hubert Humphrey	1968	Al Gore	2000
Richard Nixon	**1972**	John Kerry	2004
Gerald Ford	1976		

Minnesota (1860) (10)
27/37=64.86%
D-16; R-20; O-1

Abraham Lincoln	**1860**	**Franklin Roosevelt**	**1936**
Abraham Lincoln	**1864**	**Franklin Roosevelt**	**1940**
Ulysses Grant	**1868**	**Franklin Roosevelt**	**1944**
Ulysses Grant	**1872**	**Harry Truman**	**1948**
Rutherford Hayes	**1876**	**Dwight Eisenhower**	**1952**
James Garfield	**1880**	**Dwight Eisenhower**	**1956**
James Blaine	1884	**John Kennedy**	**1960**
Benjamin Harrison	**1888**	**Lyndon Johnson**	**1964**
Benjamin Harrison	1892	Hubert Humphrey	1968
William McKinley	**1896**	**Richard Nixon**	**1972**
William McKinley	**1900**	**Jimmy Carter**	**1976**
Theodore Roosevelt	**1904**	Jimmy Carter	1980
William Taft	**1908**	Walter Mondale[11]	1984
Theodore Roosevelt	1912	Michael Dukakis	1988
Charles Hughes	1916	**Bill Clinton**	**1992**
Warren Harding	**1920**	**Bill Clinton**	**1996**
Calvin Coolidge	**1924**	Al Gore	2000
Herbert Hoover	**1928**	John Kerry	2004
Franklin Roosevelt	**1932**		

Mississippi (1820)[12] (6)
23/44=52.27%
D-28; R-10; O-6

James Monroe	**1820**	**Franklin Pierce**	**1852**
Andrew Jackson	1824	**James Buchanan**	**1856**
Andrew Jackson	**1828**	John Breckinridge	1860
Andrew Jackson	**1832**	**Ulysses Grant**	**1872**
Martin Van Buren	**1836**	Samuel Tilden	1876
William Harrison	1840	Winfield Hancock	1880
James Polk	**1844**	**Grover Cleveland**	**1884**
Lewis Cass	1848	Grover Cleveland	1888

Mississippi (cont.)

Grover Cleveland	1892	Adlai Stevenson	1952
William Bryan	1896	Adlai Stevenson	1956
William Bryan	1900	Harry Byrd	1960
Alton Parker	1904	Barry Goldwater	1964
Woodrow Wilson	**1912**	George Wallace	1968
Woodrow Wilson	**1916**	**Richard Nixon**	**1972**
James Cox	1920	**Jimmy Carter**	**1976**
John Davis	1924	**Ronald Reagan**	**1980**
Alfred Smith	1928	**Ronald Reagan**	**1984**
Franklin Roosevelt	**1932**	**George Bush**	**1988**
Franklin Roosevelt	**1936**	George Bush	1992
Franklin Roosevelt	**1940**	Bob Dole	1996
Franklin Roosevelt	**1944**	**George W. Bush**	**2000**
Strom Thurmond	1948	**George W. Bush**	**2004**

Missouri (1820) (11)
36/47=60%
D-30; R-15; O-2

James Monroe[13]	1820	Woodrow Wilson	1916
Henry Clay	1824	**Warren Harding**	**1920**
Andrew Jackson	**1828**	**Calvin Coolidge**	**1924**
Andrew Jackson	**1832**	**Herbert Hoover**	**1928**
Martin Van Buren	**1836**	**Franklin Roosevelt**	**1932**
Martin Van Buren	1840	**Franklin Roosevelt**	**1936**
James Polk	**1844**	**Franklin Roosevelt**	**1940**
Lewis Cass	1848	**Franklin Roosevelt**	**1944**
Franklin Pierce	**1852**	**Harry Truman**	**1948**
James Buchanan	**1856**	**Dwight Eisenhower**	**1952**
Stephen Douglas	1860[14]	Adlai Stevenson	1956
Abraham Lincoln	**1864**	**John Kennedy**	**1960**
Ulysses Grant	**1868**	**Lyndon Johnson**	**1964**
Gratz Brown	1872	**Richard Nixon**	**1968**
Samuel Tilden	1876	**Richard Nixon**	**1972**
Winfield Hancock	1880	**Jimmy Carter**	**1976**
Grover Cleveland	**1884**	**Ronald Reagan**	**1980**
Grover Cleveland	1888	**Ronald Reagan**	**1984**
Grover Cleveland	**1892**	**George Bush**	**1988**
William Bryan	1896	**Bill Clinton**	**1992**
William Bryan	1900	**Bill Clinton**	**1996**
Theodore Roosevelt	**1904**	**George W. Bush**	**2000**
William Taft	**1908**	**George W. Bush**	**2004**
Woodrow Wilson	**1912**		

Montana (1892) (3)
23/29=79.31%
D-11; R-18

Benjamin Harrison	1892	**Dwight Eisenhower**	**1952**
William Bryan	1896	**Dwight Eisenhower**	**1956**
William Bryan	1900	Richard Nixon	1960
Theodore Roosevelt	**1904**	**Lyndon Johnson**	**1964**
William Taft	**1908**	**Richard Nixon**	**1968**
Woodrow Wilson	**1912**	**Richard Nixon**	**1972**
Woodrow Wilson	**1916**	Gerald Ford	1976
Warren Harding	**1920**	**Ronald Reagan**	**1980**
Calvin Coolidge	**1924**	**Ronald Reagan**	**1984**
Herbert Hoover	**1928**	**George Bush**	**1988**
Franklin Roosevelt	**1932**	**Bill Clinton**	**1992**
Franklin Roosevelt	**1936**	Bob Dole	1996
Franklin Roosevelt	**1940**	**George W. Bush**	**2000**
Franklin Roosevelt	**1944**	**George W. Bush**	**2004**
Harry Truman	**1948**		

Nebraska (1868) (5)
24/35=68.57%
D-7; R-28

Ulysses Grant	**1868**	Wendell Willkie	1940
Ulysses Grant	**1872**	Thomas Dewey	1944
Rutherford Hayes	**1876**	Thomas Dewey	1948
James Garfield	**1880**	**Dwight Eisenhower**	**1952**
James Blaine	1884	**Dwight Eisenhower**	**1956**
Benjamin Harrison	**1888**	Richard Nixon	1960
Benjamin Harrison	1892	**Lyndon Johnson**	**1964**
William Bryan	1896	**Richard Nixon**	**1968**
William McKinley	**1900**	**Richard Nixon**	**1972**
Theodore Roosevelt	**1904**	Gerald Ford	1976
William Bryan	1908	**Ronald Reagan**	**1980**
Woodrow Wilson	**1912**	**Ronald Reagan**	**1984**
Woodrow Wilson	**1916**	**George Bush**	**1988**
Warren Harding	**1920**	George Bush	1992
Calvin Coolidge	**1924**	Bob Dole	1996
Herbert Hoover	**1928**	**George W. Bush**	**2000**
Franklin Roosevelt	**1932**	**George W. Bush**	**2004**
Franklin Roosevelt	**1936**		

Nevada (1864) (5)
29/36=80.55%
D-15; R-20; O-1

Abraham Lincoln	**1864**	**Ulysses Grant**	**1872**
Ulysses Grant	**1868**	**Rutherford Hayes**	**1876**

Nevada (cont.)

Winfield Hancock	1880	**Franklin Roosevelt**	**1944**
James Blaine	1884	**Harry Truman**	**1948**
Benjamin Harrison	**1888**	**Dwight Eisenhower**	**1952**
James Weaver	1892	**Dwight Eisenhower**	**1956**
William Bryan	1896	**John Kennedy**	**1960**
William Bryan	1900	**Lyndon Johnson**	**1964**
Theodore Roosevelt	**1904**	**Richard Nixon**	**1968**
William Bryan	1908	**Richard Nixon**	**1972**
Woodrow Wilson	**1912**	Gerald Ford	1976
Woodrow Wilson	**1916**	**Ronald Reagan**	**1980**
Warren Harding	**1920**	**Ronald Reagan**	**1984**
Calvin Coolidge	**1924**	**George Bush**	**1988**
Herbert Hoover	**1928**	**Bill Clinton**	**1992**
Franklin Roosevelt	**1932**	**Bill Clinton**	**1996**
Franklin Roosevelt	**1936**	**George W. Bush**	**2000**
Franklin Roosevelt	**1940**	**George W. Bush**	**2004**

New Hampshire (4)
41/55=74.55%
D-15; R-29; O-11

George Washington	**1789**	James Blaine	1884
George Washington	**1792**	**Benjamin Harrison**	**1888**
John Adams	**1796**	Benjamin Harrison	1892
John Adams	1800	**William McKinley**	**1896**
Thomas Jefferson	**1804**	**William McKinley**	**1900**
Charles Pinckney	1808	**Theodore Roosevelt**	**1904**
DeWitt Clinton	1812	**William Taft**	**1908**
James Monroe	**1816**	**Woodrow Wilson**	**1912**
James Monroe	**1820**	**Woodrow Wilson**	**1916**
John Q. Adams	**1824**	**Warren Harding**	**1920**
John Q. Adams	1828	**Calvin Coolidge**	**1924**
Andrew Jackson	**1832**	**Herbert Hoover**	**1928**
Martin Van Buren	**1836**	Herbert Hoover	1932
Martin Van Buren	1840	**Franklin Roosevelt**	**1936**
James Polk	**1844**	**Franklin Roosevelt**	**1940**
Lewis Cass	1848	**Franklin Roosevelt**	**1944**
Franklin Pierce	**1852**	Thomas Dewey	1948
John Fremont	1856	**Dwight Eisenhower**	**1952**
Abraham Lincoln	**1860**	**Dwight Eisenhower**	**1956**
Abraham Lincoln	**1864**	Richard Nixon	1960
Ulysses Grant	**1868**	**Lyndon Johnson**	**1964**
Ulysses Grant	**1872**	**Richard Nixon**	**1968**
Rutherford Hayes	**1876**	**Richard Nixon**	**1972**
James Garfield	**1880**	Gerald Ford	1976

New Hampshire (cont.)

Ronald Reagan	1980	Bill Clinton	1996
Ronald Reagan	1984	George W. Bush	2000
George Bush	1988	John Kerry	2004
Bill Clinton	1992		

New Jersey (15)
39/55=70.91%
D-22; R-19; O-14

George Washington	1789	William McKinley	1900
George Washington	1792	Theodore Roosevelt	1904
John Adams	1796	William Taft	1908
John Adams	1800	Woodrow Wilson	1912
Thomas Jefferson	1804	Charles Hughes	1916
James Madison	1808	Warren Harding	1920
DeWitt Clinton	1812	Calvin Coolidge	1924
James Monroe	1816	Herbert Hoover	1928
James Monroe	1820	Franklin Roosevelt	1932
Andrew Jackson	1824	Franklin Roosevelt	1936
John Q. Adams	1828	Franklin Roosevelt	1940
Andrew Jackson	1832	Franklin Roosevelt	1944
William Harrison	1836	Thomas Dewey	1948
William Harrison	1840	Dwight Eisenhower	1952
Henry Clay	1844	Dwight Eisenhower	1956
Zachary Taylor	1848	John Kennedy	1960
Franklin Pierce	1852	Lyndon Johnson	1964
James Buchanan	1856	Richard Nixon	1968
Abraham Lincoln	1860	Richard Nixon	1972
George McClellan	1864	Gerald Ford	1976
Horatio Seymour	1868	Ronald Reagan	1980
Ulysses Grant	1872	Ronald Reagan	1984
Samuel Tilden	1876	George Bush	1988
Wilfield Hancock	1880	Bill Clinton	1992
Grover Cleveland	1884	Bill Clinton	1996
Grover Cleveland	1888	Al Gore	2000
Grover Cleveland	1892	John Kerry	2004
William McKinley	1896		

New Mexico (1912) (5)
22/24=91.67%
D-12; R-12

Woodrow Wilson	1912	Calvin Coolidge	1924
Woodrow Wilson	1916	Herbert Hoover	1928
Warren Harding	1920	Franklin Roosevelt	1932

New Mexico (cont.)

Franklin Roosevelt	1936	Richard Nixon	1972
Franklin Roosevelt	1940	Gerald Ford	1976
Franklin Roosevelt	1944	Ronald Reagan	1980
Harry Truman	1948	Ronald Reagan	1984
Dwight Eisenhower	1952	George Bush	1988
Dwight Eisenhower	1956	Bill Clinton	1992
John Kennedy	1960	Bill Clinton	1996
Lyndon Johnson	1964	Al Gore	2000
Richard Nixon	1968	George W. Bush	2004

New York 179215 (31)
44/54=81.48%
D-23; R-20; O-11

George Washington	1792	William McKinley	1900
John Adams	1796	Theodore Roosevelt	1904
Thomas Jefferson	1800	William Taft	1908
Thomas Jefferson	1804	Woodrow Wilson	1912
James Madison	1808	Charles Hughes	1916
DeWitt Clinton	1812	Warren Harding	1920
James Monroe	1816	Calvin Coolidge	1924
James Monroe	1820	Herbert Hoover	1928
John Q. Adams	1824	Franklin Roosevelt	1932
Andrew Jackson	1828	Franklin Roosevelt	1936
Andrew Jackson	1832	Franklin Roosevelt	1940
Martin Van Buren	1836	Franklin Roosevelt	1944
William Harrison	1840	Thomas Dewey	1948
James Polk	1844	Dwight Eisenhower	1952
Zachary Taylor	1848	Dwight Eisenhower	1956
Franklin Pierce	1852	John Kennedy	1960
John Fremont	1856	Lyndon Johnson	1964
Abraham Lincoln	1860	Hubert Humphrey	1968
Abraham Lincoln	1864	Richard Nixon	1972
Horatio Seymour	1868	Jimmy Carter	1976
Ulysses Grant	1872	Ronald Reagan	1980
Samuel Tilden	1876	Ronald Reagan	1984
James Garfield	1880	Michael Dukakis	1988
Grover Cleveland	1884	Bill Clinton	1992
Benjamin Harrison	1888	Bill Clinton	1996
Grover Cleveland	1892	Al Gore	2000
William McKinley	1896	John Kerry	2004

North Carolina (1792)[16]
36/53=67.92%
D-29; R-12; O-12

George Washington	1792	Alton Parker	1904
Thomas Jefferson	1796	William Bryan	1908
Thomas Jefferson	1800	Woodrow Wilson	1912
Thomas Jefferson	1804	Woodrow Wilson	1916
James Madison	1808	James Cox	1920
James Madison	1812	John Davis	1924
James Monroe	1816	Herbert Hoover	1928
James Monroe	1820	Franklin Roosevelt	1932
Andrew Jackson	1824	Franklin Roosevelt	1936
Andrew Jackson	1828	Franklin Roosevelt	1940
Andrew Jackson	1832	Franklin Roosevelt	1944
Martin Van Buren	1836	Harry Truman	1948
William Harrison	1840	Adlai Stevenson	1952
Henry Clay	1844	Adlai Stevenson	1956
Zachary Taylor	1848	John Kennedy	1960
Franklin Pierce	1852	Lyndon Johnson	1964
James Buchanan	1856	Richard Nixon	1968
John Breckinridge	1860	Richard Nixon	1972
Ulysses Grant	1868	Jimmy Carter	1976
Ulysses Grant	1872	Ronald Reagan	1980
Samuel Tilden	1876	Ronald Reagan	1984
Winfield Hancock	1880	George Bush	1988
Grover Cleveland	1884	George Bush	1992
Grover Cleveland	1888	Bob Dole	1996
Grover Cleveland	1892	George W. Bush	2000
William Bryan	1896	George W. Bush	2004
William Bryan	1900		

North Dakota (1892) (3)
21/29=72.41%
D-5; R-23; O-1

James Weaver	1892	Franklin Roosevelt	1936
William McKinley	1896	Wendell Willkie	1940
William McKinley	1900	Thomas Dewey	1944
Theodore Roosevelt	1904	Thomas Dewey	1948
William Taft	1908	Dwight Eisenhower	1952
Woodrow Wilson	1912	Dwight Eisenhower	1956
Woodrow Wilson	1916	Richard Nixon	1960
Warren Harding	1920	Lyndon Johnson	1964
Calvin Coolidge	1924	Richard Nixon	1968
Herbert Hoover	1928	Richard Nixon	1972
Franklin Roosevelt	1932	Gerald Ford	1976

North Dakota (cont.)

Ronald Reagan	1980	Bob Dole	1996
Ronald Reagan	1984	George W. Bush	2000
George Bush	1988	George W. Bush	2004
George Bush	1992		

Ohio (1804) (20)
42/51=82.35%
D-14; R-28; O-9

Thomas Jefferson	1804	William Taft	1908
James Madison	1808	Woodrow Wilson	1912
James Madison	1812	Woodrow Wilson	1916
James Monroe	1816	Warren Harding	1920
James Monroe	1820	Calvin Coolidge	1924
Henry Clay	1824	Herbert Hoover	1928
Andrew Jackson	1828	Franklin Roosevelt	1932
Andrew Jackson	1832	Franklin Roosevelt	1936
William Harrison	1836	Franklin Roosevelt	1940
William Harrison	1840	Thomas Dewey	1944
Henry Clay	1844	Harry Truman	1948
Lewis Cass	1848	Dwight Eisenhower	1952
Franklin Pierce	1852	Dwight Eisenhower	1956
John Fremont	1856	Richard Nixon	1960
Abraham Lincoln	1860	Lyndon Johnson	1964
Abraham Lincoln	1864	Richard Nixon	1968
Ulysses Grant	1868	Richard Nixon	1972
Ulysses Grant	1872	Jimmy Carter	1976
Rutherford Hayes	1876	Ronald Reagan	1980
James Garfield	1880	Ronald Reagan	1984
James Blaine	1884	George Bush	1988
Benjamin Harrison	1888	Bill Clinton	1992
Benjamin Harrison	1892	Bill Clinton	1996
William McKinley	1896	George W. Bush	2000
William McKinley	1900	George W. Bush	2004
Theodore Roosevelt	1904		

Oklahoma (1908) (7)
19/25=76%
D-10; R-15

William Bryan	1908	Franklin Roosevelt	1932
Woodrow Wilson	1912	Franklin Roosevelt	1936
Woodrow Wilson	1916	Franklin Roosevelt	1940
Warren Harding	1920	Franklin Roosevelt	1944
John Davis	1924	Harry Truman	1948
Herbert Hoover	1928	Dwight Eisenhower	1952

Oklahoma (cont.)

Dwight Eisenhower	1956	Ronald Reagan	1984
Richard Nixon	1960	George Bush	1988
Lyndon Johnson	1964	George Bush	1992
Richard Nixon	1968	Bob Dole	1996
Richard Nixon	1972	George W. Bush	2000
Gerald Ford	1976	George W. Bush	2004
Ronald Reagan	1980		

Oregon (1860) (7)
27/37=72.97%
D-12; R-25

Abraham Lincoln	1860	Franklin Roosevelt	1936
Abraham Lincoln	1864	Franklin Roosevelt	1940
Horatio Seymour	1868	Franklin Roosevelt	1944
Ulysses Grant	1872	Thomas Dewey	1948
Rutherford Hayes	1876	Dwight Eisenhower	1952
James Garfield	1880	Dwight Eisenhower	1956
James Blaine	1884	Richard Nixon	1960
Benjamin Harrison	1888	Lyndon Johnson	1964
Benjamin Harrison	1892	Richard Nixon	1968
William McKinley	1896	Richard Nixon	1972
William McKinley	1900	Gerald Ford	1976
Theodore Roosevelt	1904	Ronald Reagan	1980
William Taft	1908	Ronald Reagan	1984
Woodrow Wilson	1912	Michael Dukakis	1988
Charles Hughes	1916	Bill Clinton	1992
Warren Harding	1920	Bill Clinton	1996
Calvin Coolidge	1924	Al Gore	2000
Herbert Hoover	1928	John Kerry	2004
Franklin Roosevelt	1932		

Pennsylvania (21)
44/55=80%
D-18; R-25; O-12

George Washington	1789	Andrew Jackson	1824
George Washington	1792	Andrew Jackson	1828
Thomas Jefferson	1796	Andrew Jackson	1832
Thomas Jefferson	1800	Martin Van Buren	1836
Thomas Jefferson	1804	William Harrison	1840
James Madison	1808	James Polk	1844
James Madison	1812	Zachary Taylor	1848
James Monroe	1816	Franklin Pierce	1852
James Monroe	1820	James Buchanan	1856

Pennsylvania (cont.)

Abraham Lincoln	1860	Franklin Roosevelt	1936
Abraham Lincoln	1864	Franklin Roosevelt	1940
Ulysses Grant	1868	Franklin Roosevelt	1944
Ulysses Grant	1872	Thomas Dewey	1948
Rutherford Hayes	1876	Dwight Eisenhower	1952
James Garfield	1880	Dwight Eisenhower	1956
James Blaine	1884	John Kennedy	1960
Benjamin Harrison	1888	Lyndon Johnson	1964
William McKinley	1896	Hubert Humphrey	1968
Benjamin Harrison	1892	Richard Nixon	1972
William McKinley	1900	Jimmy Carter	1976
Theodore Roosevelt	1904	Ronald Reagan	1980
William Taft	1908	Ronald Reagan	1984
Theodore Roosevelt	1912	George Bush	1988
Charles Hughes	1916	Bill Clinton	1992
Warren Harding	1920	Bill Clinton	1996
Calvin Coolidge	1924	Al Gore	2000
Herbert Hoover	1928	John Kerry	2004
Herbert Hoover	1932		

Rhode Island (1792) (4)
38/54=70.37%
D-19; R-21; O-14

George Washington	1792	Rutherford Hayes	1876
John Adams	1796	James Garfield	1880
John Adams	1800	James Blain	1884
Thomas Jefferson	1804	Benjamin Harrison	1888
Charles Pinckney	1808	Benjamin Harrison	1892
DeWitt Clinton	1812	William McKinley	1896
James Monroe	1816	William McKinley	1900
James Monroe	1820	Theodore Roosevelt	1904
John Q. Adams	1824	William Taft	1908
John Q. Adams	1828	Woodrow Wilson	1912
Henry Clay	1832	Charles Hughes	1916
Martin Van Buren	1836	Warren Harding	1920
William Harrison	1840	Calvin Coolidge	1924
Henry Clay	1844	Alfred Smith	1928
Zachary Taylor	1848	Franklin Roosevelt	1932
Franklin Pierce	1852	Franklin Roosevelt	1936
John Fremont	1856	Franklin Roosevelt	1940
Abraham Lincoln	1860	Franklin Roosevelt	1944
Abraham Lincoln	1864	Harry Truman	1948
Ulysses Grant	1868	Dwight Eisenhower	1952
Ulysses Grant	1872	Dwight Eisenhower	1956

Rhode Island (cont.)

John Kennedy	1960	**Ronald Reagan**	**1984**
Lyndon Johnson	1964	Michael Dukakis	1988
Hubert Humphrey	1968	**Bill Clinton**	**1992**
Richard Nixon	1972	**Bill Clinton**	**1996**
Jimmy Carter	1976	Al Gore	2000
Jimmy Carter	1980	John Kerry	2004

South Carolina[18] (8)
32/54=59.26%
D-27; R-13; O-14

George Washington	1789	William Bryan	1900
George Washington	1792	Alton Parker	1904
Thomas Jefferson	1796	William Bryan	1908
Thomas Jefferson	1800[19]	**Woodrow Wilson**	**1912**
Thomas Jefferson	1804	**Woodrow Wilson**	**1916**
James Madison	1808	James Cox	1920
James Madison	1812	John Davis	1924
James Monroe	1816	Alfred Smith	1928
James Monroe	1820	**Franklin Roosevelt**	**1932**
Andrew Jackson	1824	**Franklin Roosevelt**	**1936**
Andrew Jackson	1828	**Franklin Roosevelt**	**1940**
John Floyd	1832	**Franklin Roosevelt**	**1944**
Willie Mangum	1836	Strom Thurmond	1948
Martin Van Buren	1840	Adlai Stevenson	1952
James Polk	1844	Adlai Stevenson	1956
Lewis Cass	1848	**John Kennedy**	**1960**
Franklin Pierce	1852	Barry Goldwater	1964
James Buchanan	1856	**Richard Nixon**	**1968**
John Breckinridge	1860	**Richard Nixon**	**1972**
Ulysses Grant	1868	**Jimmy Carter**	**1976**
Ulysses Grant	1872	**Ronald Reagan**	**1980**
Rutherford Hayes	1876	**Ronald Reagan**	**1984**
Winfield Hancock	1880	**George Bush**	**1988**
Grover Cleveland	1884	George Bush	1992
Grover Cleveland	1888	Bob Dole	1996
Grover Cleveland	1892	**George W. Bush**	**2000**
William Bryan	1896	**George W. Bush**	**2004**

South Dakota (1892) (3)
18/29=62.07%
D-4; R-24; O-1

Benjamin Harrison	1892	**William McKinley**	**1900**
William Bryan	1896	**Theodore Roosevelt**	**1904**

South Dakota (cont.)

William Taft	1908	Richard Nixon	1960
Theodore Roosevelt	1912	**Lyndon Johnson**	**1964**
Charles Hughes	1916	**Richard Nixon**	**1968**
Warren Harding	**1920**	**Richard Nixon**	**1972**
Calvin Coolidge	**1924**	Gerald Ford	1976
Herbert Hoover	**1928**	**Ronald Reagan**	**1980**
Franklin Roosevelt	**1932**	**Ronald Reagan**	**1984**
Franklin Roosevelt	**1936**	**George Bush**	**1988**
Wendell Willkie	1940	George Bush	1992
Thomas Dewey	1944	Bob Dole	1996
Thomas Dewey	1948	**George W. Bush**	**2000**
Dwight Eisenhower	**1952**	**George W. Bush**	**2004**
Dwight Eisenhower	**1956**		

Tennessee (1796)[20](11)
36/52=69.23%
D-26; R-13; O-13

Thomas Jefferson	1796	Alton Parker	1904
Thomas Jefferson	**1800**	William Bryan	1908
Thomas Jefferson	**1804**	**Woodrow Wilson**	**1912**
James Madison	**1808**	**Woodrow Wilson**	**1916**
James Madison	**1812**	**Warren Harding**	**1920**
James Monroe	**1816**	John Davis	1924
James Monroe	**1820**	**Herbert Hoover**	**1928**
Andrew Jackson	1824	**Franklin Roosevelt**	**1932**
Andrew Jackson	**1828**	**Franklin Roosevelt**	**1936**
Andrew Jackson	**1832**	**Franklin Roosevelt**	**1940**
Hugh White	1836	**Franklin Roosevelt**	**1944**
William Harrison	**1840**	**Harry Truman**	**1948**
Henry Clay	1844	**Dwight Eisenhower**	**1952**
Zachary Taylor	**1848**	**Dwight Eisenhower**	**1956**
Winfield Scott	1852	Richard Nixon	1960
James Buchanan	**1856**	**Lyndon Johnson**	**1964**
John Bell	1860	**Richard Nixon**	**1968**
Ulysses Grant	**1868**	**Richard Nixon**	**1972**
Thomas Hendricks	1872	**Jimmy Carter**	**1976**
Samuel Tilden	1876	**Ronald Reagan**	**1980**
Winfield Hancock	1880	**Ronald Reagan**	**1984**
Grover Cleveland	**1884**	**George Bush**	**1988**
Grover Cleveland	1888	**Bill Clinton**	**1992**
Grover Cleveland	**1892**	**Bill Clinton**	**1996**
William Bryan	1896	**George W. Bush**	**2000**
William Bryan	1900	**George W. Bush**	**2004**

Texas (1848)[21] *(34)*
23–38=60.53%
D-26; R-11; O-1

Lewis Cass	1848	**Franklin Roosevelt**	**1932**
Franklin Pierce	**1852**	**Franklin Roosevelt**	**1936**
James Buchanan	**1856**	**Franklin Roosevelt**	**1940**
John Breckinridge	1860	**Franklin Roosevelt**	**1944**
Thomas Hendricks	1872	**Harry Truman**	**1948**
Samuel Tilden	1876	**Dwight Eisenhower**	**1952**
Winfield Hancock	1880	**Dwight Eisenhower**	**1956**
Grover Cleveland	**1884**	**John Kennedy**	**1960**
Grover Cleveland	1888	**Lyndon Johnson**	**1964**
Grover Cleveland	**1892**	Hubert Humphrey	1968
William Bryan	1896	**Richard Nixon**	**1972**
William Bryan	1900	**Jimmy Carter**	**1976**
Alton Parker	1904	**Ronald Reagan**	**1980**
William Bryan	1908	**Ronald Reagan**	**1984**
Woodrow Wilson	**1912**	**George Bush**	**1988**
Woodrow Wilson	**1916**	George Bush	1992
James Cox	1920	Bob Dole	1996
John Davis	1924	**George W. Bush**	**2000**
Herbert Hoover	**1928**	**George W. Bush**	**2004**

Utah (1896) (5)
22/28=78.57%
D-8; R-20

William Bryan	1896	**Dwight Eisenhower**	**1952**
William McKinley	**1900**	**Dwight Eisenhower**	**1956**
Theodore Roosevelt	**1904**	Richard Nixon	1960
William Taft	**1908**	**Lyndon Johnson**	**1964**
William Taft	1912	**Richard Nixon**	**1968**
Woodrow Wilson	**1916**	**Richard Nixon**	**1972**
Warren Harding	**1920**	Gerald Ford	1976
Calvin Coolidge	**1924**	**Ronald Reagan**	**1980**
Herbert Hoover	**1928**	**Ronald Reagan**	**1984**
Franklin Roosevelt	**1932**	**George Bush**	**1988**
Franklin Roosevelt	**1936**	George Bush	1992
Franklin Roosevelt	**1940**	Bob Dole	1996
Franklin Roosevelt	**1944**	**George W. Bush**	**2000**
Harry Truman	1948	**George W. Bush**	**2004**

Vermont (1792) (3)
35/54=64.81%
D-5; R-33; O-16

George Washington	**1792**	**Thomas Jefferson**	**1800**
John Adams	**1796**	**Thomas Jefferson**	**1804**

Vermont (cont.)

James Madison	1808	**William Taft**	**1908**
James Madison	1812	William Taft	1912
James Monroe	1816	Charles Hughes	1916
James Monroe	1820	**Warren Harding**	**1920**
John Q. Adams	1824	**Calvin Coolidge**	**1924**
John Q. Adams	1828	**Herbert Hoover**	**1928**
William Wirt	1832	Herbert Hoover	1932
William Harrison	1836	Alf Landon	1936
William Harrison	**1840**	Wendell Willkie	1940
Henry Clay	1844	Thomas Dewey	1944
Zachary Taylor	**1848**	Thomas Dewey	1948
Winfield Scott	1852	**Dwight Eisenhower**	**1952**
John Fremont	1856	**Dwight Eisenhower**	**1956**
Abraham Lincoln	**1860**	Richard Nixon	1960
Abraham Lincoln	**1864**	**Lyndon Johnson**	**1964**
Ulysses Grant	**1868**	**Richard Nixon**	**1968**
Ulysses Grant	**1872**	**Richard Nixon**	**1972**
Rutherford Hayes	**1876**	Gerald Ford	1976
James Garfield	**1880**	**Ronald Reagan**	**1980**
James Blaine	1884	**Ronald Reagan**	**1984**
Benjamin Harrison	**1888**	**George Bush**	**1988**
Benjamin Harrison	1892	**Bill Clinton**	**1992**
William McKinley	**1896**	**Bill Clinton**	**1996**
William McKinley	**1900**	Al Gore	2000
Theodore Roosevelt	**1904**	John Kerry	2004

Virginia[22] (13)
35/53=66.04%
D-27; R-15; O-11

George Washington	**1789**	Lewis Cass	1848
George Washington	**1792**	**Franklin Pierce**	**1852**
Thomas Jefferson	1796	**James Buchanan**	**1856**
Thomas Jefferson	**1800**	John Bell	1860
Thomas Jefferson	**1804**	**Ulysses Grant**	**1872**
James Madison	**1808**	Samuel Tilden	1876
James Madison	**1812**	Winfield Hancock	1880
James Monroe	**1816**	**Grover Cleveland**	**1884**
James Monroe	**1820**	Grover Cleveland	1888
William Crawford	1824	**Grover Cleveland**	**1892**
Andrew Jackson	**1828**	William Bryan	1896
Andrew Jackson	**1832**	William Bryan	1900
Martin Van Buren	**1836**	Alton Parker	1904
Martin Van Buren	1840	William Bryan	1908
James Polk	**1844**	**Woodrow Wilson**	**1912**

Virginia (cont.)

Woodrow Wilson	1916	Lyndon Johnson	1964
James Cox	1920	Richard Nixon	1968
John Davis	1924	Richard Nixon	1972
Herbert Hoover	1928	Gerald Ford	1976
Franklin Roosevelt	1932	Ronald Reagan	1980
Franklin Roosevelt	1936	Ronald Reagan	1984
Franklin Roosevelt	1940	George Bush	1988
Franklin Roosevelt	1944	George Bush	1992
Harry Truman	1948	Bob Dole	1996
Dwight Eisenhower	1952	George W. Bush	2000
Dwight Eisenhower	1956	George W. Bush	2004
Richard Nixon	1960		

Washington (1892)(11)
20/29=68.97%
D-14; R-14; O-1

Benjamin Harrison	1892	Dwight Eisenhower	1952
William Bryan	1896	Dwight Eisenhower	1956
William McKinley	1900	Richard Nixon	1960
Theodore Roosevelt	1904	Lyndon Johnson	1964
William Taft	1908	Hubert Humphrey	1968
Theodore Roosevelt	1912	Richard Nixon	1972
Woodrow Wilson	1916	Gerald Ford	1976
Warren Harding	1920	Ronald Reagan	1980
Calvin Coolidge	1924	Ronald Reagan	1984
Herbert Hoover	1928	Michael Dukakis	1988
Franklin Roosevelt	1932	Bill Clinton	1992
Franklin Roosevelt	1936	Bill Clinton	1996
Franklin Roosevelt	1940	Al Gore	2000
Franklin Roosevelt	1944	John Kerry	2004
Harry Truman	1948		

West Virginia (1864)(5)
28/36=77.78%
D-20; R-16

Abraham Lincoln	1864	William McKinley	1896
Ulysses Grant	1868	William McKinley	1900
Ulysses Grant	1872	Theodore Roosevelt	1904
Samuel Tilden	1876	William Taft	1908
Winfield Hancock	1880	Woodrow Wilson	1912
Grover Cleveland	1884	Charles Hughes	1916
Grover Cleveland	1888	Warren Harding	1920
Grover Cleveland	1892	Calvin Coolidge	1924

West Virginia (cont.)

Herbert Hoover	1928	Hubert Humphrey	1968
Franklin Roosevelt	1932	Richard Nixon	1972
Franklin Roosevelt	1936	Jimmy Carter	1976
Franklin Roosevelt	1940	Jimmy Carter	1980
Franklin Roosevelt	1944	Ronald Reagan	1984
Harry Truman	1948	Michael Dukakis	1988
Adlai Stevenson	1952	Bill Clinton	1992
Dwight Eisenhower	1956	Bill Clinton	1996
John Kennedy	1960	George W. Bush	2000
Lyndon Johnson	1964	George W. Bush	2004

Wisconsin (1848)(10)
30/40=75%
D-16; R-26; O-1

Lewis Cass	1848	Herbert Hoover	1928
Franklin Pierce	1852	Franklin Roosevelt	1932
John Fremont	1856	Franklin Roosevelt	1936
Abraham Lincoln	1860	Franklin Roosevelt	1940
Abraham Lincoln	1864	Thomas Dewey	1944
Ulysses Grant	1868	Harry Truman	1948
Ulysses Grant	1872	Dwight Eisenhower	1952
Rutherford Hayes	1876	Dwight Eisenhower	1956
James Garfield	1880	Richard Nixon	1960
James Blaine	1884	Lyndon Johnson	1964
Benjamin Harrison	1888	Richard Nixon	1968
Grover Cleveland	1892	Richard Nixon	1972
William McKinley	1896	Jimmy Carter	1976
William McKinley	1900	Ronald Reagan	1980
Theodore Roosevelt	1904	Ronald Reagan	1984
William Taft	1908	Michael Dukakis	1988
Woodrow Wilson	1912	Bill Clinton	1992
Charles Hughes	1916	Bill Clinton	1996
Warren Harding	1920	Al Gore	2000
Robert LaFollette[23]	1924	John Kerry	2004

Wyoming (1892)(3)
22/29=75.86%
D-8; R-21

Benjamin Harrison	1892	Woodrow Wilson	1912
William Bryan	1896	Woodrow Wilson	1916
William McKinley	1900	Warren Harding	1920
Theodore Roosevelt	1904	Calvin Coolidge	1924
William Taft	1908	Herbert Hoover	1928

Wyoming (cont.)

Franklin Roosevelt	1932	**Richard Nixon**	1972
Franklin Roosevelt	1936	Gerald Ford	1976
Franklin Roosevelt	1940	**Ronald Reagan**	1980
Thomas Dewey	1944	**Ronald Reagan**	1984
Harry Truman	1948	**George Bush**	1988
Dwight Eisenhower	1952	George Bush	1992
Dwight Eisenhower	1956	Bob Dole	1996
Richard Nixon	1960	**George W. Bush**	2000
Lyndon Johnson	1964	George W. Bush	2004
Richard Nixon	1968		

Washington D.C. (1964²⁴)(3)
(4/11=36.36%)
(D-11)

Lyndon Johnson	1964	Michael Dukakis	1988
Hubert Humphrey	1968	**Bill Clinton**	1992
George McGovern	1972	**Bill Clinton**	1996
Jimmy Carter	1976	Al Gore	2000
Jimmy Carter	1980	John Kerry	2004
Walter Mondale	1984		

NOTES

1. Alabama was a Confederate state and did not vote in the 1864 Presidential election.

2. Arkansas was a Confederate state and did not vote in the 1864 Presidential election.

3. Delaware cast a blank ballot in the House of Representatives vote to decide the election.

4. Florida was a Confederate state and did not vote in the 1864 Presidential election.

5. Georgia was a Confederate state and did not vote in the 1864 Presidential elections. She was readmitted in 1868 but her delegation was unseated in 1868 and readmitted in 1870.

6. The Indiana vote was cast Dec. 3, 1816, two weeks before the state's formal admission to the Union. Congress counted its votes (3) for Monroe despite this abnormality.

7. Louisiana was a Confederate state and did not vote in the 1864 Presidential election.

8. Maryland was awarded to Jefferson by congressional decision.

9. Massachusetts is the only state Webster carried.

10. Massachusetts is the only state McGovern carried. He also carried the District of Columbia.

11. Minnesota is Mondale's home state, and the only state he carried. In addition he carried the District of Columbia.

12. Mississippi was a Confederate state and did not vote in the 1864 or 1868 Presidential elections. Mississippi was readmitted to the Union in 1870.

13. While the Missouri constitution was adopted in 1820, actual admission was 1821. The vote was Monroe 231 with Missouri and 228 without.

14. Missouri is the only state carried by Douglas.

15. Although a member of the Union, New York did not select a slate of electors for the 1789 Electoral College.

16. North Carolina did not ratify the Constitution in time for the 1789 election. As a Confederate state, North Carolina did not vote in the 1864 Presidential election.

17. In the 1892 election, North Dakota's three electoral votes were divided amongst three candidates. Thus no candidate carried the state.

18. South Carolina was a Confederate state and did not vote in the 1864 Presidential election.

19. The election of 1800 was decided by the House of Representatives. South Carolina cast a blank ballot in the House vote.

20. Tennessee was a Confederate state and did not vote in the 1864 Presidential election.

21. Texas was a Confederate state and did not vote in the 1864 or 1868 Presidential elections.

22. Virginia was a Confederate state and did not vote in the 1864 or 1868 Presidential elections.

23. Wisconsin is the only state LaFollette carried; he ran on the Progressive Party ticket.

24. Washington D.C. first elected an electoral delegation in 1964.

---

32. Also-Rans

Some elections are easy. They went one way and nothing else need be said. Others are more interesting and are still today the subject of speculation and heated discussion. The elections of 1800, 1876, and 2000 are three of the better known controversial elections. Here are all of the second place candidates and some others who also ran.

Year	Runner-Up	Other Candidates
1789[1]	John Adams	
1792	John Adams	
1796	Thomas Jefferson	
1800	John Adams*	Aaron Burr[2]
1804	Charles Pickney	
1808	Charles Pickney	Dewitt Clinton

*Denotes defeated incumbent President

Year	Runner-Up	Other Candidates
1812	Dewitt Clinton	
1816	Rufus King	
1820	John Quincy Adams[3]	
1824	Andrew Jackson[4]	Clay; Crawford
1828	John Q. Adams*	
1832	Henry Clay	
1836	W. H. Harrison	White; Webster
1840	Martin Van Buren*	
1844	Henry Clay	
1848	Lewis Cass	
1852	Winfield Scott	
1856	John Fremont	
1860	Stephen Douglas	Breckinridge; Bell
1864	George McClellan	
1868	Horatio Seymour	
1872	Horace Greeley[5]	(Hendricks; Brown; Jenkins; Davis)[6]
1876	Samuel Tilden[7]	
1880	Winfield Hancock	
1884	James Blaine	
1888	Grover Cleveland*	
1892	Benjamin Harrison*	James Weaver[8]
1896	William Jennings Bryan	
1900	William Jennings Bryan	
1904	Alton Parker	Eugene Debs
1908	William Jennings Bryan	Eugene Debs
1912	T. Roosevelt*	William H. Taft[†9]
1916	Charles E. Hughes	
1920	James Cox	Eugene Debs
1924	John Davis	Robert La Follette
1928	Al Smith	
1932	Herbert Hoover	
1936	Alfred Landon	
1940	Wendell Willkie	
1944	Thomas Dewey	Thurmond; Wallace
1948	Thomas Dewey	
1952	Adlai Stevenson	
1956	Adlai Stevenson	
1960	Richard Nixon	Byrd
1964	Barry Goldwater	
1968	Hubert Humphrey	Wallace
1972	George McGovern	Hospers
1976	Gerald Ford*	Reagan

*Denotes defeated incumbent President
†Denotes defeated former President

Year	Runner-Up	Other Candidates
1980	Jimmy Carter*	Anderson
1984	Walter Mondale	
1988	Michael Dukakis	
1992	George H. W. Bush*	Perot
1996	Robert Dole	Perot
2000	Albert Gore	Nader; Buchanan; Browne
2004	John Kerry	

NOTES

1. The constitution was ratified in May 1788. The first presidential election was held in 1789, instead of the leap year 1788. This is the only time a presidential election was held in an odd numbered year.

2. Burr was actually the vice-presidential candidate. When he and Jefferson tied in the electoral vote, he refused to concede the election. This act sent the matter to the House of Representatives which, with the help of Hamilton, decided the election in favor of Jefferson. This also led to the passage of the 12th Amendment and the famous duel between Burr and Hamilton.

3. Monroe won all of the electors in. Urban legend states that Governor William Plumer of New Hampshire voted for John Q. Adams, then Secretary of State, to preserve Washington as the only President to unanimously win the Electoral College. And there are those who say that Plumer genuinely disliked Monroe.

4. Jackson won the popular vote, but did not have a majority of the electoral vote. When the election went to the House, Clay withdrew and threw his support to Adams.

5. Greeley was founder of the *New Yorker* and the *New York Tribune.* He encouraged development of the country by urging "Go west, young man, and grow up with the country."

6. Greeley died before the election. Votes that he won were divided amongst these four candidates.

7. Tilden won the popular vote and the electoral vote, but was one electoral vote shy of the Presidency. The electoral votes of three states, South Carolina, Louisiana, and, of course, Florida, were challenged by the Republicans. There was also one disputed vote in Oregon. The election was decided by a House appointed commission. The commission consisted of three Republican senators, and two Democratic senators, along with three Democratic representatives and two Republican representatives, two Democratic Supreme Court Justices and two Republican Supreme Court Justices. One more member was chosen by these four Justices. He was Joseph Bradley, a staunch Republican.

8. Weaver won 4 states. No other third party would win a single state again, until Teddy Roosevelt did it in 1912.

9. This is the only election in the nation's history that featured two Presidents losing. It also was the last time a third party came in second.

*Denotes defeated incumbent President

33. Age at Inauguration

Theodore Roosevelt was the youngest; Ronald Reagan the oldest. In between there are 40 Presidents whose average age at inauguration is 55 years (calculated on age shown, not actual age including months). Ten Presidents were in their sixties when they took the oath of office. Reagan was just 17 days shy of seventy. Prior to Reagan, W. H. Harrison was the oldest President. One hundred and forty years separate them. Eight presidents were in their forties when they became President.

Here they are beginning with the youngest. Where the years are the same, they are listed by actual age: i.e. Clinton was 46 years 5 months; Grant 46 years 11 months.

President	Age	President	Age
T. Roosevelt	42	Harding	55
Kennedy	43	B. Harrison	55
Clinton	46	Cleveland	55†
Grant	46	Nixon	56
Pierce	48	Wilson	56
Cleveland	48*	A. Johnson	56
Garfield	49	Washington	56
Polk	49	J. Q. Adams	57
Fillmore	50	Jefferson	57
Tyler	51	Madison	57
Coolidge	51	Monroe	58
F. Roosevelt	51	Truman	60
Taft	51	Ford	61
Arthur	52	J. Adams	61
Lincoln	52	Jackson	61
Carter	52	Eisenhower	62
McKinley	54	Taylor	64
Van Buren	54	G. H. W. Bush	64
Hayes	54	Buchanan	65
G. W. Bush	54	W. H. Harrison	68
Hoover	54	Reagan	69
L. Johnson	55		

*Age shown is for Cleveland's first term.
†Age shown is for Cleveland's second term.

34. Length of Inaugural Address

William H. Harrison, after one hundred and sixty-four years, still holds the record for the longest inaugural address. George Washington gave the shortest at the start of his second term. From the wordy to the concise, all elected Presidents give a speech after they take the oath of office. Lincoln had much to say at his first inauguration, but spoke just 700 words for his second inauguration. "Silent Cal" Coolidge proved to be less than silent when he gave his speech. He is number six on our list.

Beginning with the longest down to the shortest, here they are. The list does not include those who succeeded to office, by death or resignation.

President	Year	Words
William H. Harrison	1841	8,444
William H. Taft	1909	5,428
James K. Polk	1845	4,800
James Monroe	1821	4,461
Benjamin Harrison	1889	4,387
Calvin Coolidge	1925	4,055
William McKinley	1897	3,966
Martin Van Buren	1837	3,834
Herbert C. Hoover	1929	3,801
Abraham Lincoln	1861	3,635
James Monroe	1817	3,370
Franklin Pierce	1853	3,333
Warren G. Harding	1921	3,327
James A. Garfield	1881	2,977
John Q. Adams	1825	2,912
James Buchanan	1857	2,824
Ronald Reagan	1985	2,602
Rutherford B. Hayes	1877	2,481
Dwight D. Eisenhower	1957	2,449
Dwight D. Eisenhower	1953	2,446
Ronald Reagan	1981	2,433
John Adams	1797	2,318
George Bush	1989	2,316
Harry S Truman	1949	2,272
William McKinley	1901	2,217
William J. Clinton	1997	2,170
Thomas Jefferson	1805	2,158

President	Year	Words
Richard M. Nixon	1969	2,124
George W. Bush	2005	2,095
Grover Cleveland	1893	2,014
Franklin D. Roosevelt	1933	1,880
Franklin D. Roosevelt	1937	1,808
Woodrow Wilson	1913	1,802
Thomas Jefferson	1801	1,721
Grover Cleveland	1885	1,682
Richard M. Nixon	1973	1,654
George W. Bush	2001	1,588
Woodrow Wilson	1917	1,529
William J. Clinton	1993	1,507
Lyndon B. Johnson	1965	1,491
George Washington	1789	1,428
John F. Kennedy	1961	1,390
Franklin D. Roosevelt	1941	1,343
Ulysses S. Grant	1873	1,339
James Madison	1813	1,210
James Madison	1809	1,175
Andrew Jackson	1833	1,173
Ulysses S. Grant	1869	1,127
Andrew Jackson	1829	1,126
Zachary Taylor	1841	1,088
Jimmy Carter	1977	1,087
Theodore Roosevelt	1905	983
Abraham Lincoln	1865	700
Franklin D. Roosevelt	1945	558
George Washington	1793	135

35. Living Former Presidents at Start of Term

Both Bill Clinton and George W. Bush started their terms in office with five living past Presidents. The only other President to have that much experience available was Lincoln.

The longest period with no Presidential death was from 1799 (Washington) to 1826, 27 years. Both Jefferson and John Adams died on the same day: July 4, 1826. Adams' final words were "Jefferson lives." In fact, Jefferson had died a few hours earlier.

In recent times Eisenhower, Truman and Lyndon Johnson all died during Nixon's tenure. Johnson died in 1973. It would be 21 years before another President died. The next Presidential death would be Richard Nixon's in 1994.

From most to least.

President	Number Living	Presidents	Died During Term
Lincoln	5	Van Buren	1862
		Tyler	1862
		Fillmore	
		Pierce	
		Buchanan	
Clinton	5	Nixon	1994
		Ford	
		Carter	
		Reagan	
		G. H. W. Bush	
G. W. Bush	5	Ford	
		Carter	
		Reagan	2004
		G. H. W. Bush	
		Clinton	
John Q. Adams	4	Adams	1826
		Jefferson	1826
		Madison	
		Monroe	
Polk	4	John Q. Adams	1848
		Jackson	1845
		Van Buren	
		Tyler	
Buchanan	4	Van Buren	
		Tyler	
		Fillmore	
		Pierce	
G. H. W. Bush	4	Nixon	
		Ford	
		Carter	
		Reagan	
Monroe	3	Adams	
		Jefferson	
		Madison	
Jackson	3	Madison	1836
		Monroe	1831
		John Q. Adams	
W. H. Harrison[1]	3	John Q. Adams	

35. Living Former Presidents at Start of Term 101

President	Number Living	Presidents	Died During Term
		Jackson	
		Van Buren	
Tyler	3	John Q. Adams	
		Jackson	
		Van Buren	
Taylor[2]	3	Van Buren	
		Tyler	
		Polk	1849
Pierce	3	Van Buren	
		Tyler	
		Fillmore	
A. Johnson	3	Fillmore	
		Pierce	
		Buchanan	1868
Grant	3	Fillmore	1874
		Pierce	1869
		A. Johnson	1875
Cleveland[3]	3	Grant	1885
		Hayes	
		Arthur	1886
Kennedy[4]	3	Hoover	
		Truman	
		Eisenhower	
L. Johnson	3	Hoover	1964
		Truman	
		Eisenhower	
Nixon[5]	3	Truman	1972
		Eisenhower	1969
		L. Johnson	1973
Reagan	3	Nixon	
		Ford	
		Carter	
B. Harrison	2	Hayes[6]	1893
		Cleveland	
Madison	2	Adams	
		Jefferson	
Van Buren	2	John Q. Adams	
		Jackson	
Fillmore	2	Van Buren	
		Tyler	
Garfield[7]	2	Grant	
		Hayes	
Arthur	2	Grant	
		Hayes	

President	Number Living	Presidents	Died During Term
McKinley[8]	2	B. Harrison	1901
		Cleveland	
Wilson	2	T. Roosevelt	1919
		Taft	
Harding[9]	2	Taft	
		Wilson	
Coolidge	2	Taft	
		Wilson	1924
Hoover	2	Taft	1930
		Coolidge	1933
Eisenhower	2	Hoover	
		Truman	
Carter	2	Nixon	
		Ford	
Adams	1	Washington	1799
Jefferson	1	Adams	
Hayes	1	Grant	
Cleveland[10]	1	B. Harrison	
T. Roosevelt	1	Cleveland	1908
Taft	1	T. Roosevelt	
F. Roosevelt[11]	2	Hoover	
Truman	1	Hoover	
Ford	1	Nixon	

NOTES

1. W. H. Harrison was the first President to die in office. He was President for only 31 days.

2. Taylor died in office.

3. First term.

4. Kennedy was assassinated.

5. Nixon resigned the Presidency 9 Aug. 1974.

6. Hayes died after B. Harrison's defeat for re-election, but before Cleveland was inaugurated.

7. Garfield was assassinated in 1881.

8. McKinley died of assassination wounds Sept. 1901. Harrison died in March of the same year.

9. Harding died in office.

10. Second term.

11. FDR died in office.

36. Vice Presidents

Most Presidents had at least one. FDR had three. Thomas Jefferson was the first to have two.

Some became President through succession, some achieved greatness, and many are obscure footnotes in our history. George Clinton was the first to die in office. Clinton was also the only Vice President to serve two consecutive terms in office under different Presidents. Both of Madison's Vice Presidents died in office.

Between "Little Van" (Martin Van Buren) and George Bush, none were elected directly to the Presidency from the Vice Presidency. While many presidents have vowed to have an active Vice President, the office is still, generally, overshadowed by the First Lady. Or in the words of one Vice President, John Nance Garner, "Not worth a bucket of warm spit."

Presented here in the order in which they served.

President	Vice President
George Washington	John Adams 1789–1797
John Adams	Thomas Jefferson 1797–1801
Thomas Jefferson	Aaron Burr 1801–1805[1]
	George Clinton 1805–1809[2]
James Madison	George Clinton 1809–1812[3]
	Elbridge Gerry 1813–1814[4]
James Monroe	Daniel Tompkins 1817–1825
John Q. Adams	John C. Calhoun 1825–1829
Andrew Jackson	John C. Calhoun 1829–1832[5]
	Martin Van Buren 1833–1837
Martin Van Buren	Richard M. Johnson 1837–1841
William H. Harrison*	John Tyler 1841
John Tyler	(No Vice President) 1841–1845
James K. Polk	George Dallas[6] 1845–1849
Zachary Taylor*	Millard Fillmore 1849–1850
Millard Fillmore	(No Vice President) 1850–1853
Franklin Pierce	William King 1853[7]
James Buchanan	John C. Breckinridge 1857–1861
Abraham Lincoln*	Hannibal Hamlin 1861–1865
	Andrew Johnson 1865[8]
Andrew Johnson	(No Vice President) 1865–1869
Ulysses Grant	Schuyler Colfax 1869–1873

*Denotes the 8 Presidents who died in office

President	*Vice President*
	Henry Wilson 1873–1875[9]
Rutherford B. Hayes	William Wheeler 1877–1881
James Garfield*	Chester A. Arthur 1881
Chester A. Arthur	(No Vice President) 1881–1885
Grover Cleveland	Thomas Hendricks 1885[10]
Benjamin Harrison	Levi Morton 1889–1893
Grover Cleveland	Adlai Stevenson[11] 1893–1897
William McKinley	Garret Hobart[12] 1897–1899
	Theodore Roosevelt 1901
Theodore Roosevelt	(No Vice President 1901–1905)
	Charles Fairbanks (1905–1909)
William H. Taft	James Sherman[13] 1909–1912
Woodrow Wilson	Thomas Marshall 1913–1921
Warren G. Harding*	Calvin Coolidge 1921–1923
Calvin Coolidge	(No Vice President) 1923–1925
	Charles Dawes 1925–1929
Herbert Hoover	Charles Curtis 1929–1933
Franklin D. Roosevelt	John Nance Garner 1933–1941
	Henry A. Wallace 1941–1945
	Harry S Truman 1945
Harry S Truman	(No Vice President) 1945–1949
	Alben Barkley 1949–1953
Dwight D. Eisenhower	Richard M. Nixon 1953–1961
John F. Kennedy	Lyndon B. Johnson 1961–1963
Lyndon B. Johnson	(No Vice President) 1963–1965
	Hubert H. Humphrey 1965–1969
Richard M. Nixon	Spiro Agnew 1969–1973[14]
	Gerald Ford 1973–1974[15]
Gerald Ford	Nelson Rockefeller 1974–1977[16]
James E. Carter	Walter Mondale 1977–1981
Ronald Reagan	George H. W. Bush 1981–1989
George H. W. Bush	Dan Quayle 1989–1993
William Clinton	Al Gore 1993–2001
George W. Bush	Richard Cheney 2001

NOTES

1. Burr had actually been a candidate for Vice President. After the election he refused to accept the Vice Presidency and forced the issue into the House. The result was twofold. First was the duel in which Burr killed Hamilton, and the second was the passage of the 12th Amendment to the Constitution.

2. First Vice President under the 12th Amendment. (Provides for the direct election of the Vice President.)

*Denotes the 8 Presidents who died in office

3. First Vice President to die in office. (4-20-1812)

4. Died in office. (11-23-1814)

5. Calhoun resigned the Vice Presidency in Dec. of 1832. Other than Spiro Agnew, he is the only Vice President to resign.

6. Dallas, Texas, is named for him.

7. Died in Cuba, April 1852. King went to Cuba after being struck by tuberculosis. He took his oath of office in Cuba and died there a month later. He never returned to the States.

8. Only Vice President since the adoption of the 12th Amendment to be a member of a party different from the President's.

9. Died in office 1885. He was born Jeremiah Jones; he changed his name to Henry Wilson after reading an obscure biography.

10. Died in office.

11. Grandfather of Adlai Stevenson III, two-time candidate for President against Dwight Eisenhower, 1952 & 1956.

12. Hobart died in office in 1899.

13. Died in office of Bright's disease, 1912.

14. Agnew was forced to resign office in 1973 due to an alleged kickback scheme while he was governor of Maryland.

15. Ford is the first Vice President be appointed under the Twenty-fifth Amendment.

16. Appointed to Vice Presidency by President Gerald Ford. Ford and Rockefeller are the only two appointed Vice Presidents.

37. Cabinets

The Constitution allows the President to appoint advisors who then must be confirmed to the position by Congress. Presidential Cabinet officers are commonly referred to as the "secretaries" of various government areas of interest, such as State, Agriculture, Treasury, and Defense. The purpose of the Cabinet officers is to advise the President as well as to function as the heads of the various departments of the government.

Washington's Cabinet was composed of only four members. Today President Bush has a Cabinet of fifteen.

The government, now well over 200 years old, is still growing.

George Washington

Secretary of State

Thomas Jefferson[1]	1790–1793
Edmund Jennings Randolph	1794–1795
Timothy Pickering	1795–1797

Secretary of the Treasury

Alexander Hamilton[2]	1789–1795
Oliver Wolcott	1795–1797

Secretary of War

Henry Knox[3]	1789–1794
Timothy Pickering	1795
James McHenry	1796–1797

Attorney General

Edmund Jennings Randolph	1789–1794
William Bradford	1794–1795
Charles Lee	1795–1797

John Adams

Secretary of State

Timothy Pickering[4]	1795–1800
John Marshall	1800–1801

Secretary of the Treasury

Oliver Wolcott	1796–1800
Samuel Dexter	1801

Secretary of War

James McHenry	1795–1800
Samuel Dexter[5]	1800–1801

Attorney General

Charles Lee	1795–1801

Secretary of the Navy

Benjamin Stoddert	1798–1801

Thomas Jefferson

Secretary of State

James Madison	1801–1809

Secretary of the Treasury

Samuel Dexter[6]	1801
Albert Gallatin	1801–1809

Secretary of War

Henry Dearborn	1801–180_

Attorney General

Levi Lincoln	1801–1804
John Breckenridge	1805–1806
Caesar Rodney	1807–1809

Secretary of the Navy

Robert Smith	1801–1809

James Madison

Secretary of State

Robert Smith	1809–1811
James Monroe	1811–1817

Secretary of the Treasury

Albert Gallatin	1801–1814
George W. Campbell	1814
Alexander Dallas	1814–1816
William Crawford	1816–1817

Secretary of War

William Eustis	1809–1812
John Armstrong	1813–1814
James Monroe[7]	1814–1815
William Crawford	1815–1816

Attorney General

Caesar Rodney	1807–1811
William Pinkney	1811–1814
Richard Rush	1814–1817

Secretary of the Navy

Paul Hamilton	1809–1812
William Jones	1813–1814
Benjamin Crowninshield	1815–1817

James Monroe

Secretary of State

John Quincy Adams	1817–1825

Secretary of the Treasury

William Crawford	1816–1825

Secretary of War

John C. Calhoun	1817–1825

Attorney General

Richard Rush	1817
William Wirt	1817–1825

Secretary of the Navy

Benjamin Crowninshield	1815–1818
Smith Thompson	1819–1823
Samuel L. Southard	1823–1825

John Quincy Adams

Secretary of State

Henry Clay	1825–1829

Secretary of the Treasury
Richard Rush   1825–1829

Secretary of War
James Barbour   1825–1828
Peter Porter   1828–1829

Attorney General
William Wirt   1825–1829

Secretary of the Navy
Samuel Southard   1825–1829

Andrew Jackson

Secretary of State
Martin Van Buren[8]   1829–1831
Edward Livingston   1831–1833
Louis McLane   1833–1834
John Forsyth   1834–1837

Secretary of the Treasury
Samuel Ingham   1829–1831
Louis McLane   1831–1833
William Duane   1833
Levi Woodbury   1834–1837

Secretary of War
John Eaton[9]   1829–1831
Lewis Cass   1831–1836

Attorney General
John Berrien   1829–1831
Roger Taney   1831–1833
Benjamin Butler   1833–1837

Secretary of the Navy
John Branch   1829–1831
Levi Woodbury   1831–1834
Mahlon Dickerson   1834–1837

Postmaster General
William Barry   1829–1835
Amos Kendall   1835–1837

Martin Van Buren

Secretary of State
John Forsyth   1837–1841

Secretary of the Treasury
Levi Woodbury   1837–1841

Secretary of War
Joel Poinsett[10]   1837–1841

Attorney General
Benjamin Butler   1837–1838
Felix Grundy   1838–1839
Henry Gilpin   1840–1841

Secretary of the Navy
Mahlon Dickerson   1837–1838
James Paulding   1838–1841

Postmaster General
Amos Kendall   1837–1840
John Niles   1840–1841

Wiliam H. Harrison

Secretary of State
Daniel Webster   1841

Secretary of the Treasury
Thomas Ewing   1841

Secretary of War
John Bell   1841

Attorney General
John Crittenden   1841

Secretary of the Navy
George Badger   1841

Postmaster General
Francis Granger   1841

John Tyler

Secretary of State
Daniel Webster   1841–1843
Abel Upshur   1843–1844
John Calhoun   1844–1845

Secretary of the Treasury
Thomas Ewing   1841
Walter Forward   1841–1843
John Spencer   1843–1844
George Bibb   1844–1845

Secretary of War
John Bell   1841
John Spencer   1841–1843
William Wilkins   1844–1845

Attorney General

John Crittenden	1841
Hugh Legare	1841–1843
John Nelson	1843–1845

Secretary of the Navy

George Badger	1841
Abel Upshur	1841–1843
Thomas Gilmer[11]	1844
John Mason	1844–1845

Postmaster General

Francis Granger	1841
Charles Wickliffe	1841–1845

James K. Polk

Secretary of State

James Buchanan[12]	1845–1849.

Secretary of the Treasury

Robert Walker	1845–1849

Secretary of War

William Marcy	1845–1849

Attorney General

John Mason	1845–1846
Nathan Clifford	1846–1848
Isaac Toucey	1848–1849

Secretary of the Navy

George Bancroft[13]	1845–1846
John Mason	1846–1849

Postmaster General

Cave Johnson[14]	1845–1849

Zachary Taylor

Secretary of State

John Clayton	1849–1850

Secretary of the Treasury

William Meredith	1849–1850

Secretary of War

George Crawford	1849–1850

Attorney General

Reverdy Johnson	1849–1850

Secretary of the Navy
William Preston 1849–1850

Postmaster General
Jacob Collamer 1849–1850

Secretary of Interior[15]
Thomas Ewing 1849–1850

Millard Fillmore

Secretary of State
Daniel Webster[16] 1850–1852
Edward Everett 1852–1853

Secretary of the Treasury
Thomas Corwin 1850–1853

Secretary of War
Charles Conrad 1850–1853

Attorney General
John Crittenden 1850–1853

Secretary of the Navy
William Graham 1850–1852
John Kennedy 1852–1853

Postmaster General
Nathan Hall 1850–1852
Samuel Hubbard 1852–1853

Secretary of Interior
Thomas McKennan 1850
Alexander Stuart[17] 1850–1853

Franklin Pierce

Secretary of State
William Marcy 1853–1857

Secretary of the Treasury
James Guthrie 1853–1857

Secretary of War
Jefferson Davis[18] 1853–1857

Attorney General
Caleb Cushing 1853–1857

Secretary of the Navy
James Dobbin 1853–1857

Postmaster General

| James Campbell | 1853–1857 |

Secretary of Interior

| Robert McClelland | 1853–1857 |

James Buchanan

Secretary of State

| Lewis Cass | 1857–1860 |
| Jeremiah Black | 1860–1861 |

Secretary of the Treasury

Howell Cobb	1857–1860
Phillip Thomas	1860–1861
John Dix[19]	1861

Secretary of War

| John Floyd | 1857–1860 |
| Joseph Holt | 1861 |

Attorney General

| Jeremiah Black | 1857–1860 |
| Edwin Stanton | 1860–1861 |

Secretary of the Navy

| Isaac Toucey | 1857–1861 |

Postmaster General

Aaron Brown	1857–1859
Joseph Holt[20]	1859–1860
Horatio King	1861

Secretary of Interior

| Jacob Thompson | 1857–1861 |

Abraham Lincoln

Secretary of State

| William Seward | 1861–1865 |

Secretary of the Treasury

Salmon P. Chase[21]	1861–1864
William Fessenden	1864–1865
Hugh McCulloch	1865

Secretary of War

| Simon Cameron | 1861–1862 |
| Edwin Stanton | 1862–1865 |

Attorney General

| Edward Bates[22] | 1861–1864 |
| James Speed | 1864–1865 |

Secretary of the Navy
Gideon Welles   1861–1865

Postmaster General
Montgomery Blair   1861–1864
William Dennison   1861–1865

Secretary of the Interior
Caleb Smith   1861–1862
John Usher   1862–1865

Andrew Johnson

Secretary of State
William Seward[23]   1865–1869

Secretary of the Treasury
Hugh McCulloch   1865–1869

Secretary of War
Edwin Stanton[24]   1865–1868
John Schofield   1868–1869

Attorney General
James Speed[25]   1865–1866
Henry Stanbery   1866–1868
William Evarts   1868–1869

Secretary of the Navy
Gideon Welles   1865–1869

Postmaster General
William Dennison   1865–1866
Alexander Randall   1866–1869

Secretary of the Interior
John Usher   1865
James Harlan   1865–1866
Orville Browning   1866–1869

Ulysses Grant

Secretary of State
Elihu Washburne[26]   1869
Hamilton Fish   1869–1877

Secretary of the Treasury
George Boutwell   1869–1873
William Richardson   1873–1874
Benjamin Bristow   1874–1876
Lot Morrill   1876–1877

Secretary of War
John Rawlins[27]	1869
William T. Sherman	1869
William Belknap[28]	1869–1876
Alphonso Taft[29]	1876
James Cameron	1876–1877

Attorney General
Ebenezer Hoar	1869–1870
Amos Akerman	1870–1871
George Williams	1872–1875
Edwards Pierrepont	1875–1876
Alfonso Taft	1876–1877

Secretary of the Navy
| Adolph Borie | 1869 |
| George Robeson | 1869–1877 |

Postmaster General
John Creswell[30]	1869–1874
James Marshall	1874
Marshall Jewell	1874–1876
James Tyner	1876–1877

Secretary of the Interior
Jacob Cox	1869–1870
Columbus Delano	1870–1875
Zachariah Chandler	1875–1877

Rutherford Hayes

Secretary of State
| William Evarts | 1877–1881 |

Secretary of the Treasury
| John Sherman | 1877–1881 |

Secretary of War
| George McCrary | 1877–1879 |
| Alexander Ramsey | 1879–1881 |

Attorney General
| Charles Devens | 1877–1881 |

Secretary of the Navy
| Richard Thompson | 1877–1880 |
| Nathan Goff | 1881 |

Postmaster General
| David Key | 1877–1880 |
| Horace Maynard | 1880–1881 |

Secretary of the Interior
Carl Schurz   1877–1881

James Garfield

Secretary of State
James Blaine   1881

Secretary of the Treasury
William Windom   1881

Secretary of War
Robert Todd Lincoln[31]   1881

Attorney General
Wayne MacVeagh   1881

Secretary of the Navy
William Hunt   1881

Postmaster General
Thomas James   1881

Secretary of the Interior
Samuel Kirkwood   1881

Chester Arthur

Secretary of State
James Blaine   1881
Frederick Frelinghuysen   1881–1885

Secretary of the Treasury
William Windom   1881
Charles Folger[32]   1881–1884
Walter Gresham   1884
Hugh McCulloch[33]   1884–1885

Secretary of War
Robert Todd Lincoln   1881–1885

Attorney General
Wayne MacVeagh   1881
Benjamin Brewster   1881–1885

Secretary of the Navy
William Hunt   1881–1882
William Chandler   1882–1885

Postmaster General
Thomas James   1881
Timothy Howe[34]   1882–1883

| Walter Gresham | 1883–1884 |
| Frank Hatton | 1884–1885 |

Secretary of the Interior

| Samuel Kirkwood | 1881–1882 |
| Henry Teller | 1882–1885 |

Grover Cleveland 1st Term

Secretary of State

| Thomas Bayard | 1885–1889 |

Secretary of the Treasury

| Daniel Manning | 1885–1887 |
| Charles Fairchild | 1887–1889 |

Secretary of War

| William Endicott | 1885–1889 |

Attorney General

| Augustus Garland | 1885–1889 |

Secretary of the Navy

| William Whitney | 1885–1889 |

Postmaster General

| William Vilas | 1885–1888 |
| Donald Dickinson | 1888–1889 |

Secretary of the Interior

| Lucius Lamar | 1885–1888 |
| William Vilas | 1888–1889 |

Secretary of Agriculture

| Norman Colman[35] | 1889 |

Benjamin Harrison

Secretary of State

| James Blaine | 1889–1892 |
| John Foster | 1892–1893 |

Secretary of the Treasury

| William Windom[36] | 1889–1891 |
| Charles Foster | 1891–1893 |

Secretary of War

| Redfield Proctor | 1889–1891 |
| Stephen Elkins | 1891–1893 |

Attorney General

| William Miller | 1889–1893 |

Secretary of the Navy
Benjamin Tracy   1889–1893

Postmaster General
John Wanamaker   1889–1893

Secretary of the Interior
John Noble   1889–1893

Secretary of Agriculture
Jeremiah Rusk   1889–1893

Grover Cleveland 2nd Term

Secretary of State
Walter Gresham[37]   1893–1895
Richard Olney   1895–1897

Secretary of the Treasury
John Carlisle   1893–1897

Secretary of War
Daniel Lamont   1893–1897

Attorney General
Richard Olney   1893–1895
Judson Harmon   1895–1897

Secretary of the Navy
Hilary Herbert   1893–1897

Postmaster General
Wilson Bissell   1893–1895
William Wilson   1895–1897

Secretary of the Interior
Hoke Smith   1893–1896
David Francis   1896–1897

Secretary of Agriculture
J. Sterling Morton   1893–1897

William McKinley

Secretary of State
John Sherman   1897–1898
William Day   1898
John Hay   1898–1901

Secretary of the Treasury
Lyman Gage   1897–1901

Secretary of War
Russell Alger   1897–1899
Elihu Root   1899–1901

Attorney General

Joseph McKenna	1897–1898
John Griggs	1898–1901
Philander Knox	1901

Secretary of the Navy

John Long	1897–1901

Postmaster General

James Gary	1897–1898
Charles Emory	1898–1901

Secretary of the Interior

Cornelius Bliss	1897–1898
Ethan Hitchcock	1898–1901

Secretary of Agriculture

James Wilson	1897–1901

Theodore Roosevelt

Secretary of State

John Hay	1901–1905
Elihu Root[38]	1905–1909

Secretary of the Treasury

Lyman Gage	1901–1902
Leslie Shaw	1902–1907
George Cortelyou	1907–1909

Secretary of War

Elihu Root	1901–1904
William H. Taft[39]	1904–1908
Luke Wright	1908–1909

Attorney General

Philander Knox	1901–1904
William Moody	1904–1906
Charles Bonaparte[40]	1906–1909

Secretary of the Navy

John Long[41]	1901–1902
William Moody	1902–1904
Paul Morton	1904–1905
Charles Bonaparte	1905–1906
Victor Metcalf	1906–1908
Truman Newberry	1908–1909

Postmaster General

Charles Smith	1901–1902
Henry Payne[42]	1902–1904

Robert Wynne	1904–1905
George Cortelyou	1905–1907
George von L. Meyer	1907–1909

Secretary of the Interior
| Ethan Hitchcock | 1901–1907 |
| James Garfield[43] | 1907–1909 |

Secretary of Agriculture
| James Wilson | 1901–1909 |

Secretary of Commerce and Labor
George Cortelyou	1903–1904
Victor Meccalf	1904–1906
Oscar Straus[44]	1906–1909

William H. Taft

Secretary of State
| Philander Knox | 1909–1913 |

Secretary of the Treasury
| Franklin MacVeagh | 1909–1913 |

Secretary of War
| Jacob Dickinson | 1909–1911 |
| Henry Stimson | 1911–1913 |

Attorney General
| George Wickersham | 1909–1913 |

Secretary of the Navy
| George von L. Meyer | 1909–1913 |

Postmaster General
| Frank Hitchcock | 1909–1913 |

Secretary of the Interior
| Richard Ballinger | 1909–1911 |
| Walter Fisher | 1911–1913 |

Secretary of Agriculture
| James Wilson | 1911–1913 |

Secretary of Commerce and Labor
| Charles Nagel | 1911–1913 |

Woodrow Wilson

Secretary of State
William Jennings Bryan[45]	1913–1915
Robert Lansing	1915–1920
Bainbridge Colby	1920–1921

Secretary of the Treasury
William McAdoo	1913–1918
Carter Glass	1918–1920
David Houston	1920–1921

Secretary of War
Lindley Garrison	1913–1916
Newton Baker	1916–1921

Attorney General
James McReynolds	1913–1914
Thomas Gregory	1914–1919
Mitchell Palmer	1919–1921

Secretary of the Navy
Josephus Daniels	1913–1921

Postmaster General
Albert Burleson	1913–1921

Secretary of the Interior
Franklin Lane	1913–1920
John Payne	1920–1921

Secretary of Agriculture
David Houston	1913–1920
Edwin Meridith	1920–1921

Secretary of Commerce
William Redfield	1913–1919
Joshua Alexander	1919–1921

Secretary of Labor
William Wilson	1913–1921

Warren Harding

Secretary of State
Charles Hughes	1921–1923

Secretary of the Treasury
Andrew Mellon	1921–1923

Secretary of War
John Weeks	1921–1923

Attorney General
Harry Daugherty	1921–1923

Secretary of the Navy
Edwin Denby[46]	1921–1923

Postmaster General
Will Hays	1921–1922

| Hubert Work | 1922–1923 |
| Harry New | 1923 |

Secretary of the Interior
| Albert Fall[47] | 1921–1923 |
| Hubert Work | 1923 |

Secretary of Agriculture
| Henry Wallace | 1921–1923 |

Secretary of Commerce
| Herbert Hoover[48] | 1921–1923 |

Secretary of Labor
| James Davis | 1921–1923 |

Calvin Coolidge

Secretary of State
| Charles Hughes | 1923–1925 |
| Frank Kellogg[49] | 1925–1929 |

Secretary of the Treasury
| Andrew Mellon | 1923–1929 |

Secretary of War
| John Weeks[50] | 1923–1925 |
| Dwight Davis[51] | 1925–1929 |

Attorney General
Harry Daugherty	1923–1924
Harlan F. Stone[52]	1924–1925
John Sargent	1925–1929

Secretary of the Navy
| Edwin Denby | 1923–1924 |
| Curtis Wilbur | 1924–1929 |

Postmaster General
| Harry New | 1923–1929 |

Secretary of the Interior
| Hubert Work | 1923–1928 |
| Roy West | 1928–1929 |

Secretary of Agriculture
Henry Wallace[53]	1923–1924
Howard Gore	1924–1925
William Jardine	1925–1929

Secretary of Commerce
| Herbert Hoover | 1921–1928 |
| William Whiting | 1928–1929 |

Secretary of Labor
James Davis   1923–1929

Herbert Hoover

Secretary of State
Henry Stimson   1929–1933

Secretary of the Treasury
Andrew Mellon   1929–1932
Ogden Mills   1932–1933

Secretary of War
James Good[54]   1929
Patrick Hurley   1929–1933

Attorney General
William Mitchell   1929–1933

Secretary of the Navy
Charles Adams[55]   1929–1933

Postmaster General
Walter Brown   1929–1933

Secretary of the Interior
Ray Lyman Wilbur   1929–1933

Secretary of Agriculture
Arthur Hyde   1929–1933

Secretary of Commerce
Robert Lamont   1929–1932
Roy Chapin   1932–1933

Secretary of Labor
James Davis   1929–1930
William Doak   1930–1933

Franklin D. Roosevelt

Secretary of State
Cordell Hull[56]   1933–1944
Edward Stettinius, Jr.   1944–1945

Secretary of the Treasury
William Woodin   1933
Henry Morgenthau, Jr.   1934–1945

Secretary of War
George Dern[57]   1933–1936
Harry Woodring   1936–1940
Henry Stimson   1940–1945

Attorney General

Homer Cummings	1933–1939
Frank Murphy	1939–1940
Robert Jackson	1940–1941
Francis Biddle	1941–1945

Secretary of the Navy

Claude Swanson[58]	1933–1939
Charles Edison[59]	1940
Frank Knox[60]	1940–1944
James Forrestal	1945

Postmaster General

James Farley	1933–1940
Frank Walker	1940–1945

Secretary of the Interior

Harold Ickes[61]	1933–1945

Secretary of Agriculture

Henry Wallace[62]	1933–1940
Claude Wickard	1940–1945

Secretary of Commerce

Daniel Roper	1933–1938
Harry Hopkins	1938–1940
Jesse Jones	1940–1945
Henry Wallace	1944–1945

Secretary of Labor

Frances Perkins[63]	1933–1945

Harry S Truman

Secretary of State

Edward Stettinius, Jr.	1945
James Byrnes	1945–1947
George Marshall[64]	1947–1949
Dean Acheson	1949–1953

Secretary of the Treasury

Henry Morgenthau	1945
Frederick Vinson	1945–1946
John Snyder	1946–1953

Secretary of War

Henry Stimson	1945
Robert Patterson	1945–1947
Kenneth Royall[65]	1947

Secretary of Defense

James Forrestal[66]	1947–1949

Louis Johnson	1949–1950
George Marshall[67]	1950–1951
Robert Lovett	1951–1953

Attorney General

Francis Biddle	1945
Thomas Clark	1945–1949
J. Howard McGrath	1949–1952
James McGranery	1952–1953

Secretary of the Navy

James Forrestal[68]	1945–1947

Postmaster General

Frank Walker	1945
Robert Hannegan	1945–1947
Jesse Donaldson	1947–1953

Secretary of the Interior

Harold Ickes	1945–1946
J. A. Krug	1946–1949
Oscar Chapman	1949–1953

Secretary of Agriculture

Claude Wickard	1945
Clinton Anderson	1945–1948
Charles Brannan	1948–1953

Secretary of Commerce

Henry Wallace	1945–1946
Averell Harriman	1946–1948
Charles Sawyer	1948–195

Secretary of Labor

Frances Perkins	1945
Lewis Schwellenbach[69]	1945–1948
Maurice Tobin	1948–1953

Dwight D. Eisenhower

Secretary of State

John Foster Dulles	1953–1959
Christian Herter	1959–1961

Secretary of the Treasury

George Humphrey	1953–1957
Robert Anderson	1957–1961

Secretary of Defense

Charles Wilson	1953–1957
Neil McElroy	1957–1959
Thomas Gates	1959–1961

Attorney General
Herbert Brownell[70]   1953–1957
William Rogers   1957–1961

Postmaster General
Arthur Summerfield   1953–1961

Secretary of the Interior
Douglas McKay   1953–1956
Frederick Seaton   1956–1961

Secretary of Agriculture
Ezra Benson   1953–1961

Secretary of Commerce
Sinclair Weeks   1953–1958
Frederick Mueller   1959–1961

Secretary of Labor
Martin Durkin   1953
James Mitchell   1953–1961

*Secretary of Health, Education
  and Welfare*
Oveta Culp Hobby[71]   1953–1955
Marion Folsom   1955–1958
Arthur Flemming   1958–1961

John Kennedy

Secretary of State
Dean Rusk   1961–1963

Secretary of the Treasury
Douglas Dillon   1961–1963

Secretary of Defense
Robert McNamara   1961–1963

Attorney General
Robert Kennedy[72]   1961–1963

Postmaster General
J. Edward Day   1961–1963
John Gronouski   1963

Secretary of the Interior
Stewart Udall   1961–1963

Secretary of Agriculture
Orville Freeman   1961–1963

Secretary of Commerce
Luther Hodges   1961–1963

Secretary of Labor

| Arthur Goldberg | 1961–1962 |
| Willard Wirtz | 1962–1963 |

**Secretary of Health, Education
and Welfare**

| Abraham Ribicoff | 1961–1962 |
| Anthony Celebrezze | 1962–1963 |

Lyndon Johnson

Secretary of State

| Dean Rusk | 1963–1969 |

Secretary of the Treasury

Douglas Dillon	1963–1965
Henry Fowler	1965–1968
Joseph Barr	1968–1969

Secretary of Defense

| Robert McNamara | 1963–1968 |
| Clark Clifford | 1968–1969 |

Attorney General

Robert Kennedy	1963–1964
Nicholas deB. Katzenbach	1965–1966
Ramsey Clark[73]	1966–1969

Postmaster General

John Gronouski	1963–1965
Lawrence O'Brien[74]	1965–1968
Marvin Watson	1968–1969

Secretary of the Interior

| Stewart Udall | 1963–1969 |

Secretary of Agriculture

| Orville Freeman | 1963–1969 |

Secretary of Commerce

Luther Hodges	1963–1965
John Connor	1965–1967
Alexander Trowbridge	1967–1968
C.R. Smith	1968–1969

Secretary of Labor

| Willard Wirtz | 1963–1969 |

**Secretary of Health, Education
and Welfare**

| Anthony Celebrezze | 1963–1965 |

| John Gardner | 1965–1968 |
| Wilbur Cohen | 1968–1969 |

Secretary of Housing and Urban Development

| Robert Weaver[75] | 1966–1969 |
| Robert Wood | 1969 |

Secretary of Transportation

| Alan Boyd | 1967–1969 |
| Richard Nixon | |

Richard Nixon

Secretary of State

| William Rogers | 1969–1973 |
| Henry Kissinger[76] | 1973–1974 |

Secretary of the Treasury

David Kennedy	1969–1971
John Connally	1971–1972
George Schultz	1972–1974
William Simon	1974

Secretary of Defense

Melvin Laird	1969–1973
Elliot Richardson	1973
James Schlesinger	1973–1974

Attorney General

John Mitchell	1969–1972
Richard Kleindienst	1972–1973
Elliot Richardson	1973
William Saxbe	1974

Postmaster General

| William Blount[77] | 1969–1971 |

Secretary of the Interior

| Walter Hickel | 1969–1970 |
| Rogers Morton | 1971–1974 |

Secretary of Agriculture

| Clifford Hardin | 1969–1971 |
| Earl Butz | 1971–1974 |

Secretary of Commerce

Maurice Stans	1969–1972
Peter Peterson	1972–1973
Frederick Dent	1973–1974

Secretary of Labor

| George Shultz | 1969–1970 |

| James Hodgson | 1970–1973 |
| Peter Brennan | 1973–1974 |

Secretary of Health, Education and Welfare

Robert Finch	1969–1970
Elliott Richardson	1970–1973
Casper Weinberger	1973–1974

Secretary of Housing and Urban Development

| George Rommey | 1969–1973 |
| James Lynn | 1973–1974 |

Secretary of Transportation

| John Volpe | 1969–1973 |
| Claude Brinegar | 1973–1974 |

Gerald Ford

Secretary of State

| Henry Kissinger | 1974–1977 |

Secretary of the Treasury

| William Simon | 1974–1977 |

Secretary of Defense

| James Schlesinger | 1974 |
| Donald Rumsfeld | 1975–1977 |

Attorney General

| William Saxbe | 1974–1975 |
| Edward Levi | 1975–1977 |

Secretary of the Interior

Rogers Morton	1974–1975
Stanley Hathaway	1975
Thomas Kleppe	1975–1977

Secretary of Agriculture

| Earl Butz | 1974–1976 |
| John Knebel | 1976–1977 |

Secretary of Commerce

Frederick Dent	1974–1975
Rogers Morton	1975
Elliott Richardson	1975–1977

Secretary of Labor

Peter Brennan	1974–1975
John Dunlop	1975–1976
W. J. Usery, Jr.	1976–1977

Secretary of Health, Education and Welfare

Caspar Weinberger	1974–1975
David Matthews	1975–1977

Secretary of Housing and Urban Development

James Lynn	1974–1975
Carla Hills	1975–1977

Secretary of Transportation

Claude Brinegar	1974–1975
William Coleman	1975–1977

Jimmy Carter

Secretary of State

Cyrus Vance	1977–1980
Edmund Muskie[78]	1980–1981

Secretary of the Treasury

Michael Blumenthal	1977–1979
William Miller	1979–1981

Secretary of Defense

Harold Brown	1977–1981

Attorney General

Griffin Bell	1977–1979
Benjamin Civiletti	1979–1981

Secretary of the Interior

Cecil Andrus	1977–1981

Secretary of Agriculture

Robert Bergland	1977–1981

Secretary of Commerce

Juanita Kreps	1977–1979
Phillip Klutznick	1980–1981

Secretary of Labor

Ray Marshall	1979–1981

Secretary of Health, Education and Welfare[79]

Joseph Califano, Jr.	1977–1979
Patricia Roberts Harris	1979–1981

Secretary of Housing and Urban Development

Patricia Roberts Harris	1977–1979
Moon Landrieu	1979–1981

Secretary of Transportation

Brock Adams	1977–1979
Neil Goldschmidt	1979–1981

Secretary of Energy

James Schlesinger	1977–1979
Charles Duncan, Jr.	1979–1981

Secretary of Education

Shirley Hufstedler	1979–1981

Ronald Reagan

Secretary of State

Alexander Haig	1981–1982
George Schultz	1982–1989

Secretary of the Treasury

Donald Regan	1981–1985
James Baker	1985–1988
Nicholas Brady	1988–1989

Secretary of Defense

Caspar Weinberger	1981–1987
Frank Carlucci	1987–1989

Attorney General

William French Smith	1981–1985
Edwin Meese	1985–1988
Richard Thornburgh	1988–1989

Secretary of the Interior

James Watt	1981–1983
William Clark	1983–1985
Donald Hodel	1985–1989

Secretary of Agriculture

John Block	1981–1986
Richard Lyng	1986–1989

Secretary of Commerce

Malcolm Baldridge	1981–1987
William Verity, Jr.	1987–1989

Secretary of Labor

Raymond Donovan[80]	1981–1985
William Brock	1985–1987
Ann Dore McLaughlin	1987–1989

Secretary of Health and Human Services

Richard Schweiker	1981–1983

| Margaret Heckler | 1983–1985 |
| Otis Bowen | 1985–1989 |

Secretary of Housing and Urban Development

| Samuel Pierce | 1981–1989 |

Secretary of Transportation

Andrew Lewis	1981–1983
Elizabeth Dole	1983–1987
James Burnley	1987–1989

Secretary of Energy

James Edwards	1981–1982
Donald Hodel	1982–1985
John Herrington	1985–1989

Secretary of Education

Terrel Bell	1981–1985
William Bennett	1985–1988
Lauro Cavazos	1988–1989

George Bush

Secretary of State

| James Baker | 1989–1992 |
| Lawrence Eagleburger | 1992–1993 |

Secretary of the Treasury

| Nicholas Brady | 1989–1993 |

Secretary of Defense

| Richard Cheney[81] | 1989–1993 |

Attorney General

| Richard Thornburgh | 1989–1991 |
| William Barr | 1991–1993 |

Secretary of the Interior

| Manuel Lujan | 1989–1993 |

Secretary of Agriculture

| Clayton Yeutter | 1989–1991 |
| Edward Madigan | 1991–1993 |

Secretary of Commerce

| Robert Mosbacher | 1989–1992 |
| Barbara Franklin | 1992–1993 |

Secretary of Labor

| Elizabeth Dole[82] | 1989–1990 |
| Lynn Martin | 1990–1993 |

Secretary of Health and Human Services
Louis Sullivan ... 1989–1993

Secretary of Housing and Urban Development
Jack Kemp ... 1989–1993

Secretary of Transportation
Samuel Skinner ... 1989–1991
Andrew Card ... 1992–1993

Secretary of Energy
James Watkins ... 1989–1993

Secretary of Education
Lauro Cavazos ... 1989–1990
Lamar Alexander ... 1991–1993

Secretary of Veterans Affairs
Edward Derwinski[83] ... 1989–1992

William Clinton

Secretary of State
Warren Christopher ... 1993–1997
Madeleine Korbel Albright[84] ... 1997–2001

Secretary of the Treasury
Lloyd Bentsen ... 1993–1994
Robert Rubin ... 1995–1999
Lawrence Summers ... 1999–2001

Secretary of Defense
Les Aspin, Jr. ... 1993–1994
William Perry ... 1994–1997
William Cohen ... 1997–2001

Attorney General
Janet Reno ... 1993–2001

Secretary of the Interior
Bruce Babbitt ... 1993–2001

Secretary of Agriculture
Mike Espy ... 1993–1994
Dan Glickman ... 1995–2001

Secretary of Commerce
Ronald Brown[85] ... 1993–1996
Mickey Kantor ... 1996–1997
William Daley[86] ... 1997–2001

Secretary of Labor
Robert Reich   1993–1997
Alexis Herman   1997–2001

*Secretary of Health and Human
  Services*
Donna Shalala[87]   1993–2001

*Secretary of Housing and Urban
  Development*
Henry Cisneros[88]   1993–1997
Andrew Cuomo[89]   1997–2001

Secretary of Transportation
Federico Pena   1993–1997
Rodney Slater   1997–2001

Secretary of Energy
Hazel O'Leary   1993–1997
Federico Pena   1997–1998
Bill Richardson   1998–2001

Secretary of Education
Richard Riley   1993–2001

Secretary of Veterans Affairs
Jesse Brown   1993–1997
Togo West, Jr.   1997–2001

George W. Bush

Secretary of State
Colin Powell   2001–2005
Condoleezza Rice   2005

Secretary of the Treasury
Paul O'Neill   2001–2003
John Snow   2003

Secretary of Defense
Donald Rumsfeld   2001–

Attorney General
John Ashcroft   2001–2005
Alberto Gonzales   2005–

Secretary of the Interior
Gale Norton   2001–

Secretary of Agriculture
Ann Veneman   2001–2005
Mike Johanns   2005–

Secretary of Commerce
Donald Evans	2001–2005
Carlos Gutierrez	2005–

Secretary of Labor
Elaine Chao	2001–

Secretary of Health and Human Services
Tommy Thompson	2001–2005
Michael O. Leavitt	2005–

Secretary of Housing and Urban Development
Mel Martinez	2001–2003
Alphonso Jackson	2004–

Secretary of Transportation
Norman Mineta	2001–

Secretary of Energy
Spencer Abraham	2001–2005
Samuel Bodman	2005–

Secretary of Education
Roderick Paige	2001–2005
Margaret Spellings	2005–

Secretary of Veterans Affairs
Anthony Principi	2001–2005
Jim Nicholson	2005–

Secretary of Homeland Security
Tom Ridge	2003–2005
Michael Chertoff	2005–

NOTES

1. Third President of the United States. See also the two dollar bill.
2. See illustration on the ten dollar bill.
3. Fort Knox, home of our nation's gold supply, is named for Henry Knox. He was General George Washington's Chief of Artillery in the Revolutionary War.
4. Pickering was a holdover from Washington's administration. Adams learned that Pickering was in cahoots with Hamilton working against his administration. Adams requested his resignation. Pickering refused. Adams fired him. This makes Pickering the only Secretary of State to be directly fired.
5. Dexter left the Secretary of War post to briefly serve as Secretary of the Treasury.

6. Dexter stayed on until Jefferson could find an appointee of his own.

7. Monroe was both Secretary of State and Secretary of War concurrently for Madison. He was also the fifth President of the United States.

8. Because of Van Buren's support of Jackson during the Peggy Eaton affair, Jackson hand picked Van Buren as his successor.

9. The infamous Peggy Eaton affair involved Peggy O'Neale Timberlake. Her husband, a civilian Navy employee, had died at sea. Peggy then married John, with whom she purportedly had been having an affair. But, this being 1828, she had failed to observe a proper mourning period. She was thus snubbed by the Cabinet wives. Jackson, who had suffered in a similar fashion with his wife, ordered his Cabinet members to have their wives be civil to Mrs. Eaton. The wives refused. Only Martin Van Buren, a widower, socialized with her.

10. He introduced the poinsettia to the United States.

11. Gilmer was killed in an explosion aboard the USS *Princeton*. President Tyler was also aboard, but was not injured. He only served for 9 days.

12. The fifteenth President of the United States.

13. Founder of the U.S. Naval Academy at Annapolis.

14. He introduced the use of postage stamps.

15. This post was established to deal with patents, public land, Indian affairs, and pensions.

16. Webster was the first Secretary of State to be appointed to the post by two Presidents. He died in office 1852.

17. He organized this department.

18. The future president of the Confederate States of America. He was responsible for modernizing the Army and making it a more efficient fighting machine, a machine which would be used against the Confederacy.

19. He served in the Civil War as a Major General. Fort Dix in New Jersey is named for him.

20. He was responsible for the Pony Express.

21. See illustration on $10,000 bill.

22. He was the first Cabinet member from west of the Mississippi River.

23. During the Johnson Administration Seward negotiated the purchase of Alaska from Russia.

24. When Johnson fired Stanton the Tenure of Office Act was invoked and the first impeachment of a President went to trial in the Senate. Stanton barricaded himself his office until Johnson was acquitted.

25. He resigned his post to defend the President in the impeachment trial.

26. Washburne served as Secretary of State for 9 days and resigned to become minister to France.

27. Died in office.

28. Faced with impeachment for taking bribes, Belknap resigned.

29. William Taft's father. He resigned to become Attorney General.

30. He introduced the penny postcard.

31. Son of President Lincoln.

32. Died in office.

33. Served as Secretary of the Treasury for Presidents Lincoln & Johnson.

34. Died in office.

35. This Cabinet post was created late in Cleveland's first term. Colman served for the last two months of the term: February & March.

36. Died in office.

37. Died in office.

38. Won the Nobel Peace Prize in 1912 for his works in Latin America and resolving the fishing rights dispute with Great Britain.

39. Our next President.

40. A grandnephew of Napoleon.

41. He was TR's boss when Roosevelt was an assistant secretary of the Navy.

42. Died in office.

43. Son of the 20th President.

44. He is the first Jewish Cabinet member.

45. The oft-defeated Presidential candidate.

46. Denby released federal oil reserves to the Interior Department. He did this with no sense of wrongdoing; however this was the basis of the Teapot Dome Scandal.

47. Fall was the main villain of the Teapot Dome Scandal. He persuaded Harding to transfer the federal oil reserves to his department. He then allowed Mammoth Oil Company to tap the reserves. In exchange Fall received $308,000 and some cattle. He also accepted a bribe from Pan-American Petroleum. He was convicted and served ten months in New Mexico State Prison.

48. Our 31st President.

49. He was awarded the 1929 Nobel Peace Prize for negotiating the Kellogg-Briand Pact. This called for its signatories to renounce war as a means of settling their differences.

50. He clashed with Billy Mitchell over the future of aviation in defense.

51. Davis was an avid tennis player. He donated the Davis Cup as an international tennis trophy in 1900.

52. Stone organized the FBI, and appointed 29-year-old J. Edgar Hoover as its director.

53. Died in office.

54. Died in office.

55. Great grandson of President John Q. Adams

56. Hull served longer than any Secretary of State.

57. Died in office.

58. Died in office.

59. Son of Thomas Edison.

60. Died in office.

61. Along with Perkins the only secretaries to serve the entire twelve years.

62. Wallace introduced such things as the School Milk Program; Domestic Allotment Plan (paid farmers to reduce output); and the Food Stamp Program.

63. Perkins was the first woman Cabinet officer. She died in 1965.

64. Winner of the 1953 Nobel Peace Prize for designing the European Recovery Program, aka the Marshall Plan, which helped war-damaged European Nations recover from WWII.

65. The last Secretary of War. In 1947 this department became the Defense Department.

66. Committed suicide.

67. He was granted a congressional exemption from the law barring military men from the post of Defense Secretary.

68. This position also went to the Department of Defense in 1947, through Forrestal's efforts. This makes the Truman and Nixon administrations the only ones to reduce the size of the Cabinet.

69. Died in office.

70. Brownell filed the *Brown vs. Board of Education of Topeka* case. This became a landmark civil rights decision.

71. The first person to hold this office and the second woman Cabinet officer.

72. The President's younger brother.

73. Son of Supreme Court Justice Thomas Clark.

74. O'Brien, in an effort to eliminate door to door delivery, ordered that all new housing developments have curbside boxes.

75. First African-American Cabinet officer.

76. Along with Le Duc Tho of North Viet Nam, co-winner of the 1973 Nobel Peace Prize.

77. Blount worked himself out of the Cabinet. He converted the U.S. Post Office into the U.S. Postal Service, a semi-independent organization that no longer had a seat in the Cabinet.

78. Democratic Vice-Presidential nominee, 1968.

79. In 1979 this department was changed to the Department of Health and Human Services. The department was added to the Cabinet at that time.

80. Donovan was the first Cabinet member to be indicted while in office. The charges of fraud and larceny were brought in conjunction with a New Jersey subway project on which his construction firm was working.

81. Cheney served George H. W. Bush's son as Vice President.

82. First woman to serve in two different Cabinet positions under two different administrations.

83. Derwinski resigned under pressure from veteran groups. The remainder of his term was served by his deputy, Anthony Principi, who was acting secretary for a few months.

84. First female Secretary of State.

85. Brown was killed in an airline crash while on a trade mission to Bosnia.

86. Chicago Mayor Richard Daley's son.

87. She served in this post longer than any other Secretary of Health and Human Services.

88. Cisneros was convicted, while in office, of misdemeanor charges about payments to his mistress. He received a Presidential pardon from President Clinton.

89. Son of then New York Governor Mario Cuomo.

38. Supreme Court Appointees

William Howard Taft was happier on the United States Supreme Court than he ever was as the country's Chief Executive.

It is the duty of the President to fill, by appointment approved by the Senate, any vacancies in the Supreme Court. Senate confirmation, in the past, was fairly automatic. Of late, however, it has been harder to find an appointee who would please both sides of the aisle of a more divided Senate.

The court consists of eight Associate Justices and a Chief Justice. Appointment to the court is for life or until a Justice chooses to retire.

These are the Justices appointed by our country's Presidents. Years served are in parentheses.

President	Supreme Court Appointees
Washington (10)	John Jay[1] (1789–1795)
	John Rutledge (1789–1791)
	William Cushing (1789–1810)
	James Wilson (1789–1798)
	John Blair (1789–1796)
	James Iredell[2] (1790–1799)
	Thomas Johnson (1791–1793)
	William Paterson (1793–1806)
	Samuel Chase[3] (1796–1811)
	Oliver Ellsworth (1796–1800)
Adams (J) (3)	Bushrod Washington[4] (1798–1829)
	Alfred Moore (1799–1804)
	John Marshall[5] (1801–1835)
Jefferson (3)	William Johnson (1804–1834)
	Brockholst Livingston (1806–1823)
	Thomas Todd (1807–1826)
Madison (2)	Joseph Story (1811–1845)
	Gabriel Duval (1812–1835)
Monroe (1)	Smith Thompson (1823–1843)
Adams J. Q (1)	Robert Trimble (1826–1828)
Jackson (6)	John McLean (1829–1861)
	Henry Baldwin (1830–1844)
	James Wayne (1835–1867)
	Phillip Barbour (1836–1841)
	Roger Taney (1836–1864)
	John Catron (1837–1865)
Van Buren (2)	John McKinley (1837–1860)
	Peter Daniel (1841–1860)
Harrison, W. H. (0)	
Tyler (1)	Samuel Nelson (1845–1872)
Polk (2)	Levi Woodbury (1845–1851)
	Robert Grier (1845–1870)
Taylor (0)	
Fillmore (1)	Benjamin Curtis (1851–1867)
Pierce (1)	John Campbell[6] (1853–1861)
Buchanan (1)	Nathan Clifford (1858–1881)
Lincoln (5)	Noah Swayne (1862–1881)
	Samuel Miller (1862–1890)
	David Davis (1862–1877)
	Stephen Field (1863–1897)
	Salmon Chase[7] (1864–1873)
Johnson, A. (0)	

President	*Supreme Court Appointees*
Grant (4)	William Strong (1870–1890)
	Joseph Bradley (1870–1892)
	Ward Hunt (1873–1882)
	Morrison Waite (1874–1888)
Hayes (2)	John Harlan (1877–1911)
	William Woods[8] (1881–1887)
Garfield (1)	Stanley Matthews (1881–1889)
Arthur (2)	Horace Gray (1882–1902)
	Samuel Blatchford (1882–1893)
Cleveland (1st Term) (2)	Lucius Lamar (1888–1893)
	Melville Fuller (1888–1910)
Harrison, B. (4)	David Brewer (1889–1910)
	Henry Brown (1891–1906)
	George Shiras (1892–1903)
	Howell Jackson (1893–1895)
Cleveland (2nd Term) (2)	Edward White[9] (1891–1921)
	Rufus Peckham (1896–1909)
McKinley (1)	Joseph McKenna (1898–1925)
Roosevelt, T. (3)	Oliver Wendell Holmes (1902–1932)
	William Day (1903–1922)
	William Moody (1906–1910)
Taft (6)	Horace Lurton (1910–1914)
	Charles Hughes[10] (1910–1916)
	Edward White[11] (1910–1921)
	Willis Van Devanter (1911–1937)
	Joseph Lamar (1911–1916)
	Mahlon Pitney (1912–1922)
Wilson (3)	James McReynolds (1914–1941)
	Louis Brandeis[12] (1916–1939)
	John Clarke (1916–1922)
Harding (4)	William Howard Taft[13] (1921–1930)
	George Sutherland (1922–1938)
	Pierce Butler (1922–1939)
	Edward Stanford (1923–1930)
Coolidge (1)	Harlan Stone[14] (1925–1946)
Hoover (3)	Charles Evans Hughes[15] (1930–1941)
	Owen Roberts (1930–1945)
	Benjamin Cardozo (1932–1938)
Roosevelt, F. (9)	Hugo Black[16] (1937–1971)
	Stanley Reed (1938–1957)
	Felix Frankfurter (1939–1962)
	William O. Douglas (1939–1975)
	Frank Murphy (1940–1949)
	Harlan Fiske Stone[17] (1925–1941)
	James Byrnes (1941–1942)

President	*Supreme Court Appointees*
	Robert Jackson (1941–1954)
	Wiley Rutledge (1943–1949)
Truman (4)	Harold Burton (1945–1958)
	Frederick Vinson (1946–1953)
	Thomas Clark (1949–1967)
	Sherman Minton (1949–1956)
Eisenhower (5)	Earl Warren[18] (1954–1969)
	John Marshall Harlan[19] (1955–1971)
	William Brennan (1956–1990)
	Charles Whittaker (1957–1962)
	Potter Stewart (1959–1981)
Kennedy (2)	Byron "Whizzer" White[20] (1962–1993)
	Arthur Goldberg (1962–1965)
Johnson, L. (2)	Abe Fortas (1965–1969)
	Thurgood Marshall (1967–1991)
Nixon (4)	Warren Burger (1969–1986)
	Harry Blackmun (1970–1994)
	Lewis Powell, Jr. (1972–1987)
	William Rehnquist (1972–2005)
Ford (1)	John Stevens (1975–present)
Carter (0)	
Reagan (4)	Sandra Day O'Connor[21] (1981–present)
	William Rehnquist[22] (1972–2005)
	Antonin Scalia (1986–present)
	Anthony Kennedy (1988–present)
Bush, G.H.W. (2)	David Souter (1990–present)
	Clarence Thomas (1991–present)
Clinton (2)	Ruth Ginsberg (1993–present)
	Stephen G. Breyer (1994–present)
Bush, G. W. (2)	John Roberts, Jr. (2005–present)
	Samuel Alito, Jr. (2006–present)

Notes

1. Jay is to the Supreme Court as Washington is to the country. Jay set precedents followed by subsequent Chiefs Justice. His decisions are studied and debated today.

2. James Iredell is the youngest Supreme Court Justice at the age of 38.

3. Samuel Chase is the only Supreme Court Justice to face impeachment. He was acquitted by the Senate with a margin of 4 votes.

4. Nephew of President Washington.

5. Arguably the greatest Chief Justice the nation has known.

6. Although opposed to secession, he resigned from the court to become Assistant Secretary of War with the Confederacy. He was sentenced to four months in prison at the end of the war.

7. Chase presided over the impeachment trial of Andrew Johnson.

8. Woods was from Georgia. He was the first post–Civil War southerner appointed to the Court.

9. White was the first Associate Justice elevated to Chief Justice by Presidential appointment (Taft). He was also the first southern (Louisiana) Chief Justice since the Civil War.

10. Hughes resigned in 1916 to run for President against Wilson.

11. Appointed by Cleveland, Taft elevated White to Chief Justice.

12. He was the first Jewish appointment to the court.

13. Taft is the only U.S. President to be appointed to the U.S. Supreme Court. He served as Chief Justice. Taft's court struck down the Tenure of Office Act which was used to bring impeachment proceedings against A. Johnson.

14. Stone served as Chief Justice, 1941–1946.

15. Hoover returned Hughes to the court after an unsuccessful try for the Presidency against Wilson.

16. Black had been a member of the Ku Klux Klan. After being confirmed, he became a staunch civil rights activist on the court.

17. Roosevelt elevated Stone from Associate Justice to Chief Justice.

18. Chaired the Warren Commission which investigated the assassination of Kennedy. The commission included future President Ford.

19. Grandson of John Harlan, who served on the court 1877–1911.

20. White got his nickname as a football player for the University of Colorado. He was also a Rhodes Scholar.

21. After 192 years a woman is appointed to the court.

22. In 1986 Reagan elevated Justice Rehnquist to Chief Justice.

---

39. House Composition

Logic would seem to dictate that a President needs his party to be the majority party in Congress to facilitate the passage of his favored legislation. This is not always the case. Presidents Hoover and Carter both had majority memberships but still had problems getting legislation passed. President Reagan's party was in the minority yet he was able to get his favorite bills through the House.

President	Congress	Years	President's Party		Opposition Party	
Washington	1st	1789–1791	Federalist	38	Anti-Federalist	26
Washington	2nd	1791–1793	Federalist	37	Dem-Rep[1]	33
Washington	3rd	1793–1795	Federalist	48	Dem-Rep	57
Washington	4th	1795–1797	Federalist	54	Dem-Rep	52

President	Congress	Years	President's Party		Opposition Party	
Adams	5th	1797–1799	Federalist	58	Dem-Rep	48
Adams	6th	1799–1801	Federalist	64	Dem-Rep	42
Jefferson	7th	1801–1803	Dem-Rep	69	Federalist	36
Jefferson	8th	1803–1805	Dem-Rep	102	Federalist	39
Jefferson	9th	1805–1807	Dem-Rep	116	Federalist	25
Jefferson	10th	1807–1809	Dem-Rep	118	Federalist	24
Madison	11th	1809–1811	Dem-Rep	94	Federalist	48
Madison	12th	1811–1813	Dem-Rep	108	Federalist	36
Madison	13th	1813–1815	Dem-Rep	112	Federalist	68
Madison	14th	1815–1817	Dem-Rep	117	Federalist	65
Monroe	15th	1817–1819	Dem-Rep	141	Federalist	42
Monroe	16th	1819–1821	Dem-Rep	156	Federalist	27
Monroe	17th	1821–1823	Dem-Rep	158	Federalist	25
Monroe	18th	1823–1825	Dem-Rep	187	Federalist	26
J. Q. Adams	19th	1825–1827	Proadmin[2]	105	Antiadmin	97
J. Q. Adams	20th	1827–1829	Proadmin	94	Antiadmin	119
Jackson	21st	1829–1831	Democrat	139	Nat. Rep.[3]	74
Jackson	22nd	1831–1833	Democrat	141	Nat. Rep.	58
					Other	14
Jackson	23rd	1833–1835	Democrat	147	Anti-Mason	53
					Other	60
Jackson	24th	1835–1837	Democrat	145	Whig	98
Van Buren	25th	1837–1839	Democrat	108	Whig	107
					Other	24
Van Buren	26th	1839–1841	Democrat	124	Whig	118
W. H. Harrison	27th[4]	1841–1843	Whig	133	Democrat	102
					Other	6
Tyler	28th	1843–1845	Whig	79	Democrat	142
					Other	1
Polk	29th	1845–1847	Democrat	143	Whig	77
					Other	6
Polk	30th	1847–1849	Democrat	108	Whig	115
					Other	4
Taylor[5]	31st	1849–1851	Whig	109	Democrat	112
					Other	6
Fillmore	32nd	1851–1853	Whig	88	Democrat	140
					Other	5
Pierce	33rd	1853–1855	Democrat	159	Whig	71
					Other	4
Pierce	34th	1855–1857	Democrat	83	Republican	108
					Other	43
Buchanan	35th	1857–1859	Democrat	131	Republican	92
					Other	14
Buchanan	36th	1859–1861	Democrat	101	Republican	113

President	Congress	Years	President's Party		Opposition Party	
					Other	23
Lincoln	37th	1861–1863	Republican	106	Democrat	42
			Other	28	Vacant	2
Lincoln	38th	1863–1865	Republican	103	Democrat	86
Lincoln	39th[6]	1865–1867	Nat. Union[7]	143	Democrat	48
A. Johnson	40th	1867–1869	Nat. Union	143	Democrat	49
					Vacant	2
Grant	41st	1869–1871	Republican	170	Democrat	73
Grant	42nd	1871–1873	Republican	139	Democrat	104
					Other	5
Grant	43rd	1873–1875	Republican	194	Democrat	92
			Other	14	Vacant	2
Grant	44th	1875–1877	Republican	107	Democrat	181
			Other	14	Vacant	2
Hayes	45th	1877–1879	Republican	137	Democrat	156
Hayes	46th	1879–1881	Republican	150	Democrat	125
			Other	14	Vacant	1
Garfield	47th[8]	1881–1883	Republican	152	Democrat	103
					Other	11
Arthur	48th	1883–1885	Republican	119	Democrat	206
					Other	6
Cleveland	49th	1885–1887	Democrat	182	Republican	140
			Other	2	Vacant	1
Cleveland	50th	1887–1889	Democrat	170	Republican	151
					Other	4
B. Harrison	51st	1889–1891	Republican	173	Democrat	158
					Other	1
B. Harrison	52nd	1891–1893	Republican	88	Democrat	231
					Other	14
Cleveland	53rd	1893–1895	Democrat	220	Republican	126
					Other	10
Cleveland	54th	1895–1897	Democrat	104	Republican	246
					Other	7
McKinley	55th	1897–1899	Republican	206	Democrat	134
					Other	16
McKinley	56th	1899–1901	Republican	185	Democrat	163
					Other	9
McKinley	57th[9]	1901–1903	Republican	198	Democrat	153
			Other	5	Vacant	1
T. Roosevelt	58th	1903–1905	Republican	207	Democrat	178
					Vacant	1
T. Roosevelt	59th	1905–1907	Republican	250	Democrat	136
T. Roosevelt	60th	1907–1909	Republican	222	Democrat	164
Taft	61st	1909–1911	Republican	219	Democrat	172

39. House Composition

President	Congress	Years	President's Party		Opposition Party	
Taft	62nd	1911–1913	Republican	162	Democrat	228
					Other	1
Wilson	63rd	1913–1915	Democrat	291	Republican	127
					Other	17
Wilson	64th	1915–1917	Democrat	231	Republican	193
			Other	8	Vacant	3
Wilson	65th	1917–1919	Democrat	210	Republican	216
					Other	9
Wilson	66th	1919–1921	Democrat	191	Republican	237
					Other	7
Harding	67th	1921–1923	Republican	300	Democrat	132
			Other	1	Vacant	2
Harding	68th[10]	1923–1925	Republican	225	Democrat	207
					Other	3
Coolidge	69th	1925–1927	Republican	247	Democrat	183
					Other	5
Coolidge	70th	1927–1929	Republican	237	Democrat	195
					Other	3
Hoover	71st	1929–1931	Republican	267	Democrat	163
					Other	1
Hoover	72nd	1931–1933	Republican	216	Democrat	218
					Other	1
F. Roosevelt	73rd	1933–1935	Democrat	313	Republican	103
					Other	5
F. Roosevelt	74th	1935–1937	Democrat	322	Republican	103
					Other	10
F. Roosevelt	75th	1937–1939	Democrat	337[11]	Republican	89 [12]
					Other	13
F. Roosevelt	76th	1939–1941	Democrat	262	Republican	169
					Other	4
F. Roosevelt	77th	1941–1943	Democrat	267	Republican	162
					Other	6
F. Roosevelt	78th	1943–1945	Democrat	222	Republican	209
					Other	4
F. Roosevelt	79th[13]	1945–1947	Democrat	243	Republican	190
					Other	2
Truman	80th	1947–1949	Democrat	188	Republican	245
					Other	1
Truman	81st	1949–1951	Democrat	263	Republican	171
					Other	2
Truman	82nd	1951–1953	Democrat	234	Republican	199
					Other	1
Eisenhower	83rd	1953–1955	Republican	221[14]	Democrat	213
					Other	1

President	Congress	Years	President's Party		Opposition Party	
Eisenhower	84th	1955–1957	Republican	203	Democrat	232
Eisenhower	85th	1957–1959	Republican	201[15]	Democrat	234
Eisenhower	86th	1959–1961	Republican	153	Democrat	283
Kennedy	87th	1961–1963	Democrat	262	Republican	175
Kennedy	88th[16]	1963–1965	Democrat	258	Republican	176
					Vacant	1
L. Johnson	89th	1965–1967	Democrat	295	Republican	140
L. Johnson	90th	1967–1969	Democrat	248	Republican	187
Nixon	91st	1969–1971	Republican	192	Democrat	243
Nixon	92nd	1971–1973	Republican	180	Democrat	255
Nixon	93rd[17]	1973–1975	Republican	192	Democrat	242
					Other	1
Ford	94th	1975–1977	Republican	144	Democrat	291
Carter	95th	1977–1979	Democrat	292	Republican	143
Carter	96th	1979–1981	Democrat	277	Republican	158
Reagan	97th	1981–1983	Republican	192	Democrat	242
Reagan	98th	1983–1985	Republican	166	Democrat	269
Reagan	99th	1985–1987	Republican	182	Democrat	253
Reagan	100th	1987–1989	Republican	177	Democrat	258
Bush	101st	1989–1991	Republican	175	Democrat	260
Bush	102nd	1991–1993	Republican	167	Democrats	267
					Other	1
Clinton	103rd	1993–1995	Democrat	258	Republican	176
					Other	1
Clinton	104th	1995–1997	Democrat	204	Republican	230[18]
					Other	1
Clinton	105th	1997–1999	Democrat	207	Republican	226
					Other	2
Clinton	106th	1999–2001	Democrat	211	Republican	223
					Other	1
G. W. Bush	107th	2001–2003	Republican	221	Democrat	212
					Other	2
G. W. Bush	108th	2003–2005	Republican	229	Democrat	205
				Other	1	Vacant	1
G. W. Bush	109th	2005–2007	Republican	232	Democrat	201
					Other	2

NOTES

1. Democratic-Republican party.

2. At this point in our nation's history there were no formal parties. For that reason we will use Proadmin(istration) for the President, and Antiadmin(istration) against the President.

3. National Republican party.

4. Harrison died a month and a half after inauguration and the term was finished by Tyler.

5. Taylor died in office. His Vice President, Millard Fillmore, finished the session.

6. Lincoln was assassinated at the beginning of his second term. Andrew Johnson succeeded him.

7. This is another name for the Republican Party. It was adopted to appease the Democrats who supported the war effort. It is also the last Presidential election won by a party labeled other than Democrat or Republican.

8. Garfield was assassinated in 1881. Chester Arthur succeeded him.

9. McKinley was assassinated six months after his inauguration to a second term. His Vice President, Teddy Roosevelt, finished the term.

10. This term was finished by Coolidge due to Harding's death in 1923.

11. This represents the highest number of members either party ever had.

12. This is the last time either of the major parties was below triple digits in the House. The Congress was in session from 1937–1939.

13. Roosevelt died in early 1945. Truman finished FDR's fourth term.

14. This is the last Republican majority in the House of Representatives until 1995.

15. This is the last Congress in which the Republicans had 200 members until 1995.

16. Kennedy was assassinated November 22, 1963. Lyndon Johnson finished the term.

17. Nixon resigned in August of 1974. Ford succeeded him.

18. This is the first Republican majority, and the first time the Republicans had over 200 House members in 40 years.

---

40. Senate Composition

The Senate is the upper house of Congress. It was created to give each state equal representation in the government. Each state sends two senators to Congress. Senators serve a six year term.

Initially senators were appointed by their state legislatures. This changed with the passage of the Seventeenth Amendment enacted in 1913. This amendment provided for the direct election of senators by the voters.

Here are the Senate compositions throughout the years.

President	Congress	Years	President's Party		Opposition Party	
Washington	1st	1789–1791	Federalist	17	Anti-Federalist	9
Washington	2nd	1791–1793	Federalist	16	Dem-Rep[1]	13
Washington	3rd	1793–1795	Federalist	17	Dem-Rep	13
Washington	4th	1795–1797	Federalist	19	Dem-Rep	13

President	Congress	Years	President's Party		Opposition Party	
Adams	5th	1797–1799	Federalist	20	Dem-Rep	12
Adams	6th	1799–1801	Federalist	19	Dem-Rep	13
Jefferson	7th	1801–1803	Dem-Rep	18	Federalist	14
Jefferson	8th	1803–1805	Dem-Rep	25	Federalist	9
Jefferson	9th	1805–1807	Dem-Rep	27	Federalist	7
Jefferson	10th	1807–1809	Dem-Rep	28	Federalist	6
Madison	11th	1809–1811	Dem-Rep	28	Federalist	6
Madison	12th	1811–1813	Dem-Rep	30	Federalist	6
Madison	13th	1813–1815	Dem-Rep	27	Federalist	9
Madison	14th	1815–1817	Dem-Rep	25	Federalist	11
Monroe	15th	1817–1819	Dem-Rep	34	Federalist	10
Monroe	16th	1819–1821	Dem-Rep	35	Federalist	7
Monroe	17th	1821–1823	Dem-Rep	44	Federalist	4
Monroe	18th	1823–1825	Dem-Rep	44	Federalist	4
J. Q. Adams	19th	1825–1827	Proadmin[2]	26	Antiadmin	20
J. Q. Adams	20th	1827–1829	Proadmin	20	Antiadmin	28
Jackson	21st	1829–1831	Democrat	26	Nat. Rep.[3]	22
Jackson	22nd	1831–1833	Democrat	25	Nat. Rep.	21
					Other	2
Jackson	23rd	1833–1835	Democrat	20	Nat. Rep.	20
					Other	8
Jackson	24th	1835–1837	Democrat	27	Whig	25
Van Buren	25th	1837–1839	Democrat	30	Whig	18
					Other	4
Van Buren	26th	1839–1841	Democrat	28	Whig	22
W. H. Harrison	27th[4]	1841–1843	Whig	28	Democrat	22
					Other	2
Tyler	28th	1843–1845	Whig	28	Democrat	25
					Other	1
Polk	29th	1845–1847	Democrat	31	Whig	25
Polk	30th	1847–1849	Democrat	36	Whig	21
					Other	1
Taylor	31st[5]	1849–1851	Whig	25	Democrat	35
					Other	2
Fillmore	32nd	1851–1853	Whig	24	Democrat	35
					Other	3
Pierce	33rd	1853–1855	Democrat	38	Whig	22
					Other	2
Pierce	34th	1855–1857	Democrat	42	Republican	15
					Other	5
Buchanan	35th	1857–1859	Democrat	39	Republican	20
					Other	5
Buchanan	36th	1859–1861	Democrat	38	Republican	26
					Other	2

President	Congress	Years	President's Party		Opposition Party	
Lincoln	37th	1861–1863	Republican	31	Democrat	11
			Other	7	Vacant	1
Lincoln	38th	1863–1865	Republican	36	Democrat	9
					Other	5
Lincoln	39th[6]	1865–1867	Nat. Union[7]	42	Democrat	10
Johnson	40th	1867–1869	Nat. Union	42	Democrat	11
Grant	41st	1869–1871	Republican	61	Democrat	11
					Vacant	2
Grant	42nd	1871–1873	Republican	57	Democrat	17
Grant	43rd	1873–1875	Republican	54	Democrat	19
					Vacant	1
Grant	44th	1875–1877	Republican	46	Democrat	29
					Vacant	1
Hayes	45th	1877–1879	Republican	39	Democrat	36
					Other	1
Hayes	46th	1879–1881	Republican	33	Democrat	43
Garfield	47th[8]	1881–1883	Republican	37	Democrat	37
					Other	2
Arthur	48th	1883–1885	Republican	40	Democrat	36
Cleveland	49th	1885–1887	Democrat	34	Republican	41
					Vacant	1
Cleveland	50th	1887–1889	Democrat	37	Republican	39
B. Harrison	51st	1889–1891	Republican	47	Democrat	37
B. Harrison	52nd	1891–1893	Republican	47	Democrat	39
					Other	2
Cleveland	53rd	1893–1895	Democrat	44	Republican	38
			Other	3	Vacant	3
Cleveland	54th	1895–1897	Democrat	39	Republican	44
					Other	5
McKinley	55th	1897–1899	Republican	46	Democrat	34
					Other	10
McKinley	56th	1899–1901	Republican	53	Democrat	26
					Other	11
McKinley	57th[9]	1901–1903	Republican	56	Democrat	29
			Other	3	Vacant	2
T. Roosevelt	58th	1903–1905	Republican	58	Democrat	32
T. Roosevelt	59th	1905–1907	Republican	58	Democrat	32
T. Roosevelt	60th	1907–1909	Republican	61	Democrat	29
					Vacant	2
Taft	61st	1909–1911	Republican	59	Democrat	32
					Vacant	1
Taft	62nd	1911–1913	Republican	49	Democrat	42
					Vacant	1
Wilson	63rd	1913–1915	Democrat	51	Republican	44

President	Congress	Years	President's Party		Opposition Party	
					Other	1
Wilson	64th	1915–1917	Democrat	56	Republican	39
					Other	1
Wilson	65th	1917–1919	Democrat	53	Republican	42
					Other	1
Wilson	66th	1919–1921	Democrat	47	Republican	48
					Other	1
Harding	67th	1921–1923	Republican	59	Democrat	37
Harding	68th[10]	1923–1925	Republican	51	Democrat	43
					Other	2
Coolidge	69th	1925–1927	Republican	54	Democrat	40
			Other	1	Vacant	1
Coolidge	70th	1927–1929	Republican	48	Democrat	47
					Other	1
Hoover	71st	1929–1931	Republican	56	Democrat	39
					Other	1
Hoover	72nd	1931–1933	Republican	48	Democrat	47
					Other	1
F. Roosevelt	73rd	1933–1935	Democrat	59	Republican	36
					Other	1
F. Roosevelt	74th	1935–1937	Democrat	69	Republican	25
					Other	2
F. Roosevelt	75th	1937–1939	Democrat	75	Republican	17
					Other	4
F. Roosevelt	76th	1939–1941	Democrat	69	Republican	23
					Other	4
F. Roosevelt	77th	1941–1943	Democrat	66	Republican	28
					Other	1
F. Roosevelt	78th	1941–1945	Democrat	57	Republican	38
					Other	1
F. Roosevelt	79th[11]	1945–1947	Democrat	57	Republican	38
					Other	1
Truman	80th	1947–1949	Democrat	45	Republican	51
Truman	81st	1949–1951	Democrat	54	Republican	42
Eisenhower	82nd	1951–1953	Republican	47	Democrat	48
					Other	1
Eisenhower	83rd	1953–1955	Republican	48	Democrat	46
					Other	2
Eisenhower	84th	1955–1957	Republican	47	Democrat	48
					Other	1
Eisenhower	85th	1957–1959	Republican	47	Democrat	49
Eisenhower	86th	1959–1961	Republican	34	Democrat	64
Kennedy	87th	1961–1963	Democrat	64	Democrat	36
Kennedy	88th[12]	1963–1965	Democrat	67	Republican	33

President	Congress	Years	President's Party		Opposition Party	
L. Johnson	89th	1965–1967	Democrat	68	Republican	32
L. Johnson	90th	1967–1969	Democrat	64	Republican	36
Nixon	91st	1969–1971	Republican	42	Democrat	58
Nixon	92nd	1971–1973	Republican	44	Democrat	54
					Other	2
Nixon	93rd[13]	1973–1975	Republican	42	Democrat	56
					Other	2
Ford	94th	1975–1977	Republican	37	Democrat	61
					Other	2
Carter	95th	1977–1979	Democrat	61	Republican	38
					Other	1
Carter	96th	1979–1981	Democrat	58	Republican	41
					Other	1
Reagan	97th	1981–1983	Republican	53	Democrat	46
					Other	1
Reagan	98th	1983–1985	Republican	54	Democrat	46
Reagan	99th	1985–1987	Republican	53	Democrat	47
Reagan	100th	1987–1989	Republican	45	Democrat	55
Bush	101st	1989–1991	Republican	45	Democrat	55
Bush	102nd	1991–1993	Republican	44	Democrat	56
Clinton	103rd	1993–1995	Democrat	57	Republican	43
Clinton	104th	1995–1997	Democrat	48	Republican	52
Clinton	105th	1997–1999	Democrat	45	Republican	55
Clinton	106th	1999–2001	Democrat	45	Republican	55
G. W. Bush	107th	2001–2003	Republican	50	Democrat	50
G. W. Bush	108th	2003–2005	Republican	51	Democrat	48
					Other	1
G. W. Bush	109th	2005–2007	Republican	55	Democrat	44
					Other	1

NOTES

1. Democratic-Republican Party.

2. At this point in our nation's history there were no formal parties. For that reason we will use Proadmin(istration) for the President, and Antiadmin(istration) against the President.

3. National Republican Party.

4. Harrison died a month and a half after inauguration and the term was finished by Tyler.

5. Taylor died in office. His Vice President, Millard Fillmore, finished the session.

6. Lincoln was assassinated at the beginning of his second term. Andrew Johnson succeeded him.

7. This is another name for the Republican Party. It was adopted to appease the

Democrats who supported the war effort. It is also the last Presidential election won by a party named other than Democrat or Republican.

   8. Garfield was assassinated in 1881. Chester Arthur succeeded him.
   9. McKinley was assassinated six months after his inauguration to a second term. His Vice President, Teddy Roosevelt, finished the term.
   10. This term was finished by Coolidge due to Harding's death in 1923.
   11. Roosevelt died in early 1945. Truman finished FDR's fourth term.
   12. Kennedy was assassinated in November 1963. Lyndon Johnson finished the term.
   13. Nixon resigned in August 1974. Ford succeeded him.

41. Presidential Accomplishments and Significant Issues

   William Henry Harrison was President for a scant 30 days and was bed-ridden for that period. He had no opportunity to propose legislation nor guide the country in any meaningful way.

   Franklin Delano Roosevelt led the country for more than 12 years and had an impact on the nation that is still felt today over 60 years later.

   Here is a summary of what the Presidents accomplished during their tenures.

George Washington 1789–1797
   Set precedents for: relying on department heads for advice; choosing own Cabinet; 2 term limit.
   Jay's treaty with Great Britain.
   Pinckney's treaty with Spain.
   Important laws: Oaths of allegiance; First tariffs; Departments of State, War and the Treasury; Offices of Postmaster General, Attorney General; organized the Federal Court System (1789).
   Federal Census; Patent and copyright laws; Removal of federal capitol from Philadelphia to Washington[1] (1790).
   Established the Bank of the United States (1791).
   Presidential Succession[2]; Established the U.S. Mint in Philadelphia (1792).
   Naturalization law (1796).

John Adams 1797–1801
   XYZ Affair[3] (1797).

Alien and Sedition Acts (1798).
Logan Act[4]; Fries Rebellion[5] (1799).

Thomas Jefferson 1801–1809
Louisiana Purchase (1803).
Lewis & Clark Expedition (1804–1806).
Abolition of Slave Trade[6]; Executive Privilege[7] (1807).
Embargo Act (1807–1809).

James Madison 1809–1817
Non-intercourse Act[8] (1809–1810).
Macon's Bill no. 2[9] (1810).
Second Bank of the United States (1816).

James Monroe 1817–1825
Rush-Bagot Agreement[10]; Convention of 1818[11] (1818).
Adams-Otis Treaty (1819).
Missouri Compromise (1820).
Monroe Doctrine (1823).

John Q. Adams 1825–1829
The Panama Congress (1826).

Andrew Jackson 1829–1837
Internal improvements[12] (1830).
Spoils System; Tariff and Nullification[13]; The Bank of the United States.
  (These all took place over several years during Jackson's Administration).

Martin Van Buren 1837–1841
Panic of 1837.
Texas statehood[14] (1837).

William H. Harrison 1841
None

John Tyler 1841–1845
Right of Succession[15]; The Bank of the United States; Mass Cabinet resignations; Preemption Act (1841).
Webster-Ashburton Treaty (1842).
Princeton Explosion[16] (1844).
Texas Annexation (1845).

James Polk 1845–1849
Oregon Treaty; Walker Tariff; Independent Treasury Act (1846).

Zachary Taylor 1849–1850
Clayton Bulwer Treaty; Galphin Claim[17] (1850).

Millard Fillmore 1850–1853
The Compromise of 1850.
Commodore Perry's Mission to Japan (1850–1854).

Franklin Pierce 1853–1857
Gadsden Purchase (1853).
Kansas-Nebraska Act; Ostend Manifesto[18] (1854).

James Buchanan 1857–1861
Panic of 1857.
Succession (1861).

Abraham Lincoln 1861–1865
Martial law.
Homestead Act; Morrill Act[19] (1862).
Reconstruction (1865).

Andrew Johnson 1865–1869
Reconstruction.
Alaska Purchase (1867).
Impeachment (1868).

Ulysses Grant 1869–1877
Reconstruction.
Treaty of Washington (1871).
Panic of 1873.
Resumption of Specie Act (1875).

Rutherford Hayes 1877–1881
Reconstruction Ends; Civil Service Reform[20] (1877).
Bland-Allison Act[21] (1878).
Resumption of Specie Act (1879).

James Garfield 1881
None[22]

Chester Arthur 1881–1885
Chinese Exclusion Act; River and Harbors Act (1882).
Pendleton Act[23]; Mongrel Tariff (1883).

Grover Cleveland 1885–1889
Presidential Succession Act[24] (1886).
Interstate Commerce Act; Dawes Severalty Act[25]; Hatch Act (1887).

Benjamin Harrison 1889–1893
Dependent and Disability Pensions Act; Sherman Anti-Trust Act; Sherman Silver Purchase Act; McKinley Tariff Act (1890).

Grover Cleveland 1893–1897
Hawaii[26]; Panic of 1893; Repeal of the Sherman Silver Purchase Act (1893). Wilson-Gorman Act; Pullman Strike (1894).

William McKinley 1897–1901
Dingley Tariff Act (1897).
Annexation of Hawaii (1898).
Gold Standard Act (1900).

Theodore Roosevelt 1901–1909
Panama Canal Treaty; Antitrust policy[27] (1901).
Anthracite coal strike; Reclamation Act[28] (1902).
Pelican Island, Florida National Wildlife Refuge (1903).
Russo-Japanese War[29]; Big Stick Policy (1904–1905).
Meat Inspection Act; Pure Food and Drug Act; Devils Tower in Wyoming[30] (1906).

William Taft 1909–1913
Payne-Aldrich Tariff Act (1909).
Mann-Elkins Act (1910).
Webb-Kenyon Interstate Liquor Shipments Act[31](1913).

Woodrow Wilson 1913–1921
Underwood Tariff; Federal Reserve Act (1913).
Federal Trade Commission; Clayton Anti-Trust Act (1914).
Child labor laws; Adamson Act[32] (1916).

Warren Harding 1921–1923
Refusal to enter the League of Nations; Formal conclusion of WWI[33]; Establishment of the Budget Bureau; Pardon of Eugene Debs; Civil rights; Emergency Tariff Act (1921).
Fordeny-McCumber Tariff Act (1922).

Calvin Coolidge 1923–1929
Immigration Act; Tax reduction; Veterans Bonus[34] (1924).
Tax reduction; Commercial aviation[35] (1926).
Kellogg-Briand Act (1928).

Herbert Hoover 1929–1933
Agricultural Marketing Act; Stock Market Crash (1929).
Hawley-Smoot Tariff; London Naval Treaty (1930).
Norris-LaGuardia Act[36]; Bonus March (1932).

Franklin Roosevelt 1933–1945

Bank Holiday; Civilian Conservation Corps; Agricultural Adjustment Act; Tennessee Valley Authority; Federal Emergency Relief Administration; National Industrial Recovery Act[37]; Recognition of the Soviet Union (1933).

Securities and Exchange Commission; National Housing Act (1934).

Works Progress Administration; Rural Electrification Administration; Wagner Act[38]; Social Security Act (1935).

Court packing plan (1937).

Hatch Act (1939).

Harry Truman 1945–1953

Nuremberg Trials (1945–1946).

United Nations (1945).

Presidential Succession Act; Taft Hartley Act (1947).

Israel; End of segregation in military (1948).

Seizure of steel mills; H-bomb (1952).

Cold War; Marshall Plan.

Dwight Eisenhower 1953–1961

End of McCarthy Hearings (1954).

Interstate Highway System (1956).

Little Rock school integration (1957).

St. Lawrence Seaway opening (1959).

John Kennedy 1961–1963

Bay of Pigs Invasion; Alliance for Progress; Peace Corps; Berlin Wall; Space Program (1961).

Steel price rollback; Civil rights; Cuban Missile Crisis (1962).

Atmospheric Test Ban Treaty (1963).

Lyndon Johnson 1963–1969

War on Poverty; Civil rights (1964).

Medicare and Medicaid; Water Quality Act; Dominican Republic (1965).

Clean Water Restoration Act; The Fair Packaging and Labeling Act; The National Traffic Safety Act (1966).

Wholesome Meat Act (1967).

Pueblo incident (1968).

Richard Nixon 1969–1974

Environmental Quality Policy Act; Moon Landing (1969).

Seabed Treaty[39]; Environmental Protection Agency; Water Improvement Act; National Air Quality Standards; Resource Recovery Act (1970).

China admitted to U.N.; Chemical Weapons Treaty; Wage & price controls (1971).

Water Pollution Act; Consumer Product Safety Act; Watergate; SALT Agreement; Revenue Sharing (1972).

Resignation (1974).

Gerald Ford 1974–1977

Nixon Pardon; Clemency for draft evaders & deserters; WIN buttons; Campaign Reform Law (1974).

Mayguez Incident; Helsinki Agreement; Fair Credit Billing Act; Real Estate Settlement Procedure Act; Equal Credit Opportunity Act; Magnuson-Moss Warranty Act; Financial bail-out of New York City; Voting Rights Extension (1975).

Jimmy Carter 1975–1981

Pardon of draft evaders; Deregulation of cargo airlines; Ban on dumping of raw sewage into the ocean; Strip Mining Reclamation Act; Bill making Food Stamps free; Panama Canal Treaty (1977).

Deregulation of commercial airlines; Deregulation of natural gas prices; Humphrey-Hawkins Full Employment Act; Camp David Accords (1978).

Deregulation of trucking industry; Three Mile Island; Diplomatic relations with China; Afghanistan; Iran Crisis (1979).

Alaska Land Act (1980).

Ronald Reagan 1981–1889

Assassination attempt (1981).

Reaganomics (1982).

Social Security; Grenada (1983).

Iran Contra Scandal (1985).

U.S.-Canadian trade pact (1988).

George H. W. Bush 1989–1993

Savings and Loan Crisis; Third World debt[40]; Alaska Oil Spill (1989).

Capture of Manuel Noriega; Americans with Disabilities Act; Clean Air Act (1990).

Somalian aid (1992).

Bill Clinton 1993–2001

New York World Trade Center bomb; Branch Davidian incident, Waco, TX; Aid to Russia (1993).

General Agreement on Tariffs and Trade (GATT) treaty (1994).

Oklahoma City Bombing; Anti-Terrorism Act; Effective Death Penalty Act; Budget crisis (1995).

Kennedy-Kassenbaum Act; Immigration reform (1996).
President's Initiative on Race (1997).
Monica Lewinski (1998).
Impeachment proceedings; Budget surplus[41] (1999).
China given Permanent Normal Trade Relations (2000).

George W. Bush 2001–Present
9–11 (2001).
Afghanistan invasion (2001).
Iraq invasion (2003).
Supreme Court appointments (2005).

NOTES

1. The actual move took place during the Presidency of John Adams in 1800.
2. This law provided for the succession to the office after the Vice President. Next in line would have been the President Pro Tempore of the Senate and then the Speaker of the House. This was pretty much outdated with the passage of the 25th Amendment.
3. Adams sent a three-man mission to France to negotiate a settlement to privateering by the French against U.S. shipping. The French foreign minister refused to receive the mission, and instead sent three men to demand a payment of $250,000 in order to receive them.
4. Logan had tried to mediate a settlement with France. This law forbids private citizens from entering into diplomatic relations with other countries. It is still in effect.
5. This little-known incident established the federal government's authority to levy and collect taxes on private property.
6. This act made it illegal to import slaves. Smuggling of slaves continued until the Civil War.
7. Summoned to appear before Congress for the Burr trial, Jefferson refused and released only such information as he saw fit. By these acts he established the precedent of Executive Privilege.
8. This was a follow up to the failed embargo. It forbade dealings with France and Great Britain.
9. Repealed the Non-intercourse Act
10. Demilitarized the Great Lakes.
11. Gave U.S. fishermen the rights to certain Canadian waters and set the border between the U.S. and Canada from Minnesota to the Rockies.
12. Jackson vetoed the Maysville Road bill which would have used federal funds for the construction of a highway in Kentucky.
13. Jackson wanted a strong tariff, but the Southern States would have suffered from it. They threatened "Nullification" (secession) if it passed. Jackson drew a line and stuck to it.
14. After winning its freedom from Mexico, Texas applied for admission to the Union. Van Buren opposed statehood.
15. Tyler believed himself to be President, not a care-taker as many believed him to be. Because Tyler was the first to face this issue he set a precedent to be followed by eight other Vice Presidents.

16. 28 Feb. 1844 Tyler and other dignitaries were inspecting the USS *Princeton*, when a deck gun misfired. President Tyler was below decks and uninjured; however, the Secretary of State and the Secretary of Navy were among those killed. Also killed was a diplomat named David Gardiner, father of the President's future wife.

17. This was an alleged conflict of interest case. The Galphin family of Georgia had filed and settled a claim against the U.S. government. They now wanted interest. Their lawyer had been George Crawford, Taylor's War Secretary who now stood to gain half of the interest to be paid.

18. This was an attempt to purchase Cuba from Spain.

19. Granted each state lands which were to be sold and the proceeds used to finance agricultural and mechanical arts colleges.

20. By executive order, Hayes barred government employees from participating in elections.

21. Hayes vetoed this "soft money" bill. His veto was overridden.

22. Garfield was assassinated less than four months after inauguration.

23. Created the modern civil service system.

24. Superseded the Presidential Succession Act of 1792.

25. Granted citizenship to Indians willing to renounce their tribal allegiance.

26. Cleveland condemned the complicity of Americans in the overthrow of Queen Liliuokalani.

27. Roosevelt delivered his first annual message to Congress Dec. 1901. In that speech he outlined his antitrust policy.

28. This was the beginning of Roosevelt's attempt to preserve the American West.

29. Roosevelt was awarded the Nobel Peace Prize in 1906 for his part in mediating peace in this conflict. He was the first American to win this award.

30. This is the nation's first national monument.

31. Barred shipment of liquor to dry states. Passed over Taft's veto.

32. Passed in order to prevent a railroad strike in the advent of U.S. entry into WWI, this act gave the railway workers an eight hour day.

33. The Republican Congress rejected the Treaty of Versailles. Thus it fell to Harding to conclude the U.S. role in the war.

34. Coolidge vetoed this bill. Congress overrode his veto.

35. Placed civil aviation under federal authority. Established the first commercial air routes.

36. Banned strikes that threatened public safety.

37. This program included the Public Works Administration and the National Recovery Administration (NRA). The NRA was declared unconstitutional by the Supreme Court in 1935.

38. The Wagner Act corrected the parts of the NRA which the Supreme Court found objectionable.

39. Banned nuclear testing in international waters.

40. Reversing Reagan's policy, Bush forgave as much as 20 percent, or around $60,000,000,000, in debt owed by 39 Third World countries.

41. It had been over 30 years since the United States had a surplus.

42. Vetoes

In 212 years there have been 2,550 vetoes by 43 Presidents. That averages 12 a year, or 59 per President. Of those only 106 have been overridden. Andrew Johnson had 15 out of 29 vetoes, or 52 percent, overturned.

A veto is a rejection of congressional legislation. On a straight veto the President sends Congress an explanation of the reason the bill is being rejected. The President can also use a "pocket veto." A pocket veto allows the President to simply hold the bill until time runs out for signing it. This permits the President to reject the legislation without providing a reason.

By the number of vetoes.

President	Vetoes	Pocket Vetoes	Total	Overridden
F. Roosevelt	372	263	635	9
Cleveland[1]	304	110	414	2
Truman	180	70	250	12
Eisenhower	73	108	181	2
Cleveland[2]	42	128	170	5
Grant	45	48	93	4
T. Roosevelt	42	40	82	1
Reagan	39	39	78	9
Ford	48	18	66	12
Coolidge	20	30	50	4
B. Harrison	19	25	44	1
Wilson	33	11	44	6
G. H. W. Bush	29	15	44	1
Nixon	28	17	45	7
McKinley	6	36	42	0
Taft	30	9	39	1
Hoover	21	16	37	3
Clinton	36	1	37	2
Carter	13	18	31	2
L. Johnson	16	14	30	0
A. Johnson	21	8	29	15
Kennedy	12	9	21	0
Hayes	12	1	13	1
Jackson	5	7	12	0
Arthur	4	8	12	1
Tyler	6	4	10	1
Pierce	9	0	9	5
Madison	5	2	7	0

President	Vetoes	Pocket Vetoes	Total	Overridden
Buchanan	4	3	7	0
Lincoln	2	5	7	0
Harding	5	1	6	0
Polk	2	1	3	0
Washington	2	0	2	0
Monroe	1	0	1	0
Van Buren	0	1	1	0
J. Adams	0	0	0	0
Jefferson	0	0	0	0
J. Q. Adams	0	0	0	0
W. H. Harrison	0	0	0	0
Taylor	0	0	0	0
Fillmore	0	0	0	0
Garfield	0	0	0	0
G. W. Bush[3]	0	0	0	0

NOTES

1. First term.
2. Second term.
3. As of the end of November, 2005.

43. States Admitted During Administration

When Washington came to office there were eleven states in the United States. These were, in order of ratification: Delaware (12-7-1787); Pennsylvania (12-12-1787); New Jersey (12-27-1787); Georgia[1] (1-2-1788); Connecticut (1-9-1788); Massachusetts (2-6-1788); Maryland (4-28-1788); South Carolina[2] (5-23-1788); New Hampshire (6-21-1788); Virginia[3] (6-25-1788); and New York (7-26-1788). North Carolina[4] (11-21-1789) and Rhode Island (5-29-1790) both joined after the United States federal government was in place and Washington had taken his oath of office. The most years between states being admitted is 46. The most consecutive presidents between admissions is nine, our current status.

President	State(s)	Admitted
Washington (3)	Vermont	March 4, 1791
	Kentucky	June 1, 1792
	Tennessee[5]	June 1, 1796
Adams	None	
Jefferson (1)	Ohio	June 17, 1803
Madison (2)	Louisiana[6]	April 30, 1812
	Indiana	Dec. 11, 1816
Monroe (5)	Mississippi[7]	Dec. 10, 1817
	Illinois	Dec. 3, 1818
	Alabama[8]	Dec. 14, 1819
	Maine	March 15, 1820
	Missouri[9]	Aug. 10, 1821
Adams, J. Q.	None	
Jackson (2)	Arkansas[10]	June 15, 1836
	Michigan	Jan. 26, 1837
Van Buren	None	
W. H. Harrison	None	
Tyler (1)	Florida[11]	March 3, 1845
Polk (3)	Texas[12]	Dec. 29, 1845
	Iowa	Dec. 28, 1846
	Wisconsin	May 29, 1848
Taylor	None	
Fillmore (1)	California	Sept. 9, 1850
Pierce	None	
Buchanan (3)	Minnesota	May 11, 1858
	Oregon	Feb. 14, 1859
	Kansas	Jan. 29, 1861
Lincoln (2)	W. Virginia[13]	June 20, 1863
	Nevada	Oct. 31, 1864
Johnson A. (1)	Nebraska	March 1, 1867
Grant (1)	Colorado	Aug. 1, 1876
Hayes	None	
Garfield	None	
Arthur	None	
Cleveland[14]	None	
B. Harrison (6)	North Dakota	Nov. 2, 1889
	South Dakota	Nov. 2, 1889
	Montana	Nov. 8, 1889
	Washington	Nov. 11, 1889
	Idaho	July 3, 1890
	Wyoming	Nov. 11, 1890
Cleveland[15]	Utah	Jan. 4, 1896
McKinley	None	
Roosevelt T. (1)	Oklahoma	Nov. 16, 1907
Taft (2)	New Mexico	Jan. 6, 1912

President	State(s)	Admitted
	Arizona	Feb. 14, 1912
Wilson	None	
Harding	None	
Coolidge	None	
Hoover	None	
Roosevelt, F.	None	
Truman	None	
Eisenhower (2)	Alaska	Jan. 3, 1959
	Hawaii	Aug. 21, 1959

No states have been admitted since 1959. Being considered for statehood, at present, are Guam, Puerto Rico, and Washington, D.C.

NOTES

1. Georgia was readmitted to the Union, under President A. Johnson, July 21, 1868. The congressional delegation was unseated March 5, 1869, and Georgia was then readmitted under President Grant July 15, 1870.

2. South Carolina was readmitted to the Union, under President A. Johnson, July 9, 1868.

3. Virginia was readmitted to the Union, under President Grant, April 17, 1870.

4. North Carolina was readmitted, under President A. Johnson, July 4, 1868.

5. Tennessee was readmitted to the Union, under President A. Johnson, July 24, 1866.

6. Louisiana was readmitted to the Union, under President A. Johnson, January 26, 1868.

7. Mississippi was readmitted to the Union, under President Grant, February 23, 1870.

8. Alabama was readmitted to the Union, under President A. Johnson, July 25, 1868.

9. This was the Missouri Compromise. Maine was carved out of New Hampshire as a free state, while Missouri was the admitted as a slave state.

10. Arkansas was readmitted to the Union, under President A. Johnson, June 22, 1868.

11. Florida was readmitted to the Union, under President A. Johnson, June 25, 1868.

12. Texas was readmitted to the Union, under President Grant, March 30, 1870.

13. West Virginia was carved from a section of northern Virginia. The citizens of this northern area remained loyal to the Union during the Civil War.

14. First term.

15. Second term.

44. Constitutional Amendments

The Founding Fathers showed ample humility in providing a manner in which to amend the Constitution. Of the 27 times this process has been utilized, ten were almost before the ink had dried on the Constitution. We call these ten amendments the Bill of Rights. They were necessary in order to have all 13 states agree to the Constitution, and were ratified in 1791.

Only eleven presidents have signed amendments. Here they are in the order of the amendments passed.

Amendment	President	Purpose
1st Amendment	Washington	Guarantees freedom of worship, speech, the press, and assembly.
2nd Amendment		The right to bear arms openly.
3rd Amendment		Freedom from quartering soldiers without the owner's consent.
4th Amendment		Protection from unreasonable search and seizure.
5th Amendment		Guarantees freedom from double jeopardy. Freedom from self incrimination. Guarantees "due process of law."
6th Amendment		Right to trial by a jury of one's peers.
7th Amendment		Right to trial by jury.
8th Amendment		Freedom from excessive bail, fines and "cruel and unusual punishment."
9th Amendment		"The enumeration in the Constitution of certain rights shall not be construed to deny or disparage others retained by the people."
10th Amendment		Reserves, to the states, those rights not given to the federal government by the Constitution.
11th Amendment		Restricts the ability of a citizen of one state to sue another state (1795).
12th Amendment	Jefferson	Changes the election of the Vice President from runner-up in the popular vote to separate electors in the Electoral College (1804).
13th Amendment	A. Johnson	Abolition of slavery (1865).
14th Amendment		Protects privileges and immunities of all citizens without regard to race; provides for due process; equal protection of citizens; apportionment of representatives; & Civil War Disqualification and Debt (1868).

Amendment	President	Purpose
15th Amendment	Grant	Equal rights for all citizens (1870).
16th Amendment	Wilson	Allows income tax (1913).
17th Amendment		Provides for direct election of U.S. Senators (1913).
18th Amendment		Enacted Prohibition (1919).
19th Amendment		Gives right to vote to women (1920).
20th Amendment	Hoover	Moves inaugurations for President from March 4 to January 20 (1933).
21st Amendment	F. Roosevelt	Repeals Prohibition (1933).
22nd Amendment	Truman	Limits future Presidents to two terms in office (1951).
23rd Amendment	Kennedy	Gives residents of Washington, D.C., Presidential electors (1961).
24th Amendment	L. Johnson	Prohibits poll tax (1964).
25th Amendment		Allows the President, with approval of Congress, to fill a vacancy in the Vice Presidency by appointment (1967).
26th Amendment	Nixon	Changes the federal voting age to 18 (1971).
27th Amendment	G.H.W. Bush	Prohibits Congress from giving itself a pay raise in the current session (1992).

45. Wars

The Bible tells us "There shall be wars, and rumors of wars." In its history the United States has been involved in armed conflict on a regular basis. No generation has been spared some sort of fighting.

Only sixteen of our Presidents have avoided the use of troops in major conflict.

Following is a list of conflicts in Presidential order served.

President	War
Washington	Ohio Indian Wars (1791–1795)
	Whiskey Rebellion[1] (1794)
John Adams	None
Jefferson	Tripolitan War[2] (1801–1805)
Madison	War of 1812[3] (1812–1814)
	Creek War (1813–1814)
Monroe	Indian Wars of 1817–1821
	First Seminole War (1817–1818)

President	*War*
John Q. Adams	None
Jackson	Black Hawk War (1832)
	Second Seminole War (1835–1842)
Van Buren	None
W. H. Harrison	None
Tyler	None
Polk	Mexican War (1846–1848)
Taylor	None
Fillmore	None
Pierce	Third Seminole War (1855–1858)
Buchanan	Civil War[4] (1861–1865)
Lincoln	Civil War (1861–1865)
Andrew Johnson	None[5]
Grant	Indian Wars[6]
Hayes	Apache Wars (1876–1886)
Garfield	Apache Wars (1876–1886)
Arthur	Apache Wars (1876–1886)
Cleveland (first term)	Apache Wars (1876–1886)
Benjamin Harrison	None
Cleveland (second term)	None
McKinley	Spanish-American War (1898)
Theodore Roosevelt	None[7]
Taft	None
Wilson	World War I[8]
Harding	None
Coolidge	None
Hoover	None
Franklin Roosevelt	WWII (1941–1945)[9]
Harry Truman	WWII (1941–1945)
	Korean War (1950–1953)
Eisenhower	Korean War (1950–1953)
Kennedy	Viet Nam War (1962–1975)
Lyndon Johnson	Viet Nam War (1962–1975)
Nixon	Viet Nam War (1962–1975)
Ford	None
Carter	None
Reagan	Grenada; Lebanon[10]
George H. W. Bush	Persian Gulf War (1990)
Clinton	None
George Bush	Afghanistan (2001 to present)
	Iraq (2003 to present)

NOTES

1. This was not an actual war. The federal government placed an excise tax on liquor. Farmers in Pennsylvania, who made their own whiskey, refused to pay the tax.

Washington ordered a force of 15,000 troops into the field and there he personally inspected them and the issue was settled.

2. It was this war that gave the U.S. Marine Corps Hymn the line "to the shores of Tripoli." Today Tripoli is known as Libya.

3. This was also called "Mr. Madison's War."

4. The Civil War actually began on the end of Buchanan's Presidency. The South fired on *The Star of the West*, an unarmed merchant ship sent to reinforce Fort Sumter in January, 1861. This act, and the subsequent attack on the fort itself, set the nation at war.

5. Johnson did preside over the last few battles of the Civil War. Lee had surrendered before Lincoln was assassinated, but due to slow communications and the stubbornness of some commanders there were some residual battles.

6. These included the Battle of Little Bighorn.

7. On the subject of war, Roosevelt was awarded the Nobel Peace Prize for 1906 for his role in negotiating a settlement to the Russo-Japanese War.

8. In 1919 Wilson was given the Noble Peace Prize for his work to establish the League of Nations.

9. 1941 is the year the United States entered WWII. It had been in progress for several years at that time.

10. While not actual wars, these were brief military conflicts in which U.S. soldiers died.

---

46. Presidential Pardons

In September 1974, upon taking office, President Ford granted perhaps the most notable pardon in U.S. history. He issued his predecessor, Richard Nixon, a full pardon for all crimes which he had committed, or may have committed against the United States. This brought the Watergate Era to a close. President Clinton drew heavy criticism for his use of the pardon during the closing days of his administration, yet he used it sparingly. He ranks as 21 out of 41 presidents in the use of this instrument.

President	Pardons	President	Pardons
F. Roosevelt	3,687	Cleveland[1]	1,107
Wilson	2,480	T. Roosevelt	981
Truman	2,044	Nixon	926
Coolidge	1,545	McKinley	918
Hoover	1,385	Hayes	893
Grant	1,332	Harding	800
L. Johnson	1,187	Taft	758
Eisenhower	1,157	A. Johnson	654

President	Pardons	President	Pardons
B. Harrison	613	J. Q. Adams	183
Kennedy	575	Fillmore	170
Carter	566	Van Buren	168
Clinton	456	Buchanan	150
Monroe	419	Pierce	142
Ford	409	Jefferson	119
Reagan	406	G. Bush	77
Jackson	386	Taylor	38
Lincoln	343	G. W. Bush	31[2]
Arthur	337	J. Adams	21
Polk	268	Washington	16
Tyler	209	W. H. Harrison	0
Madison	196	Garfield	0

NOTE

1. Both terms combined.
2. This figure is for January of 2005. Based on his record as governor of Texas, President Bush is not likely to be free with Presidential pardons.

47. White House Pets

In addition to the Presidents and their families, the White House has been home to a variety of animals. Common pets such as birds, fish, cats, and dogs would seem likely, but in addition there have been lions, tigers, and bears. All have been a part of the White House. No President would ever admit to hating pets. Teddy Roosevelt, although a noted hunter, certainly could not be called an animal hater. He kept a zoo at the White House. Not all the animals in this chapter actually lived at 1600 Pennsylvania Avenue. Checkers would have been over 17 years old when the Nixons moved to the White House.

Alphabetically by animal, including names where known:

Alligators

John Quincy Adams

Antelopes

Calvin Coolidge

Badgers

Theodore Roosevelt — "Josiah"

Bears

Thomas Jefferson[1]
Theodore Roosevelt (5)
Calvin Coolidge

Birds

George Washington — "Polly" Parrot
Thomas Jefferson — Mockingbird
James Madison — "Macaw" Parrot
Andrew Jackson — "Pol" Parrot
John Tyler— "Johnny Ty" Canary
James Buchanan — Eagle
Abraham Lincoln — "Jack" Turkey
Ulysses Grant — Parrot; Roosters
Rutherford Hayes— Canaries
Grover Cleveland—Canaries & Mockingbirds
William McKinley — Parrot
Theodore Roosevelt — Chickens; Owl; & "Eli" Macaw
Woodrow Wilson — Chickens
Warren Harding — Canaries
Calvin Coolidge — "Nip" "Tuck" & "Snowflake" Canaries; "Old Bill" Thrush; "Enoch" Goose; Mockingbird
John Kennedy — "Bluebell" & "Marybelle" Parakeets
Lyndon Johnson — Lovebirds

Bobcats

Calvin Coolidge — Smokey

Cats

Abraham Lincoln
Rutherford Hayes— "Siam" Siamese
William McKinley — Angora with kittens
Theodore Roosevelt— "Tom Quartz" & "Slippers"
Woodrow Wilson

Calvin Coolidge — "Rounder," "Tiger," & "Blacky"
Harry Truman
John Kennedy — "Tom Kitten"
Gerald Ford— "Chan" Siamese
Jimmy Carter — "Misty Malarky Ying Yang" Siamese
Bill Clinton — "Socks"
George W. Bush — "Willie," "Ernie"[2]

Cows

William H. Harrison
Rutherford Hayes
William Taft — "Pauline Wayne"

Dogs

George Washington — 36 hounds
James Madison — Spaniel
John Tyler — "Le Beau" Greyhound
James Buchanan — "Lara" Newfoundland
Abraham Lincoln
Ulysses Grant — "Faithful" Newfoundland, & an Irish Setter
Rutherford Hayes— "Grim" Greyhound; "Duke" English Mastiff; & "Dot" terrier; "Hector" Newfoundland; plus other dogs
James Garfield — "Veto"
Grover Cleveland — Poodle
Benjamin Harrison — "Dash"
Theodore Roosevelt — "Sailor Boy" Chesapeake Bay Retriever; "Manchu" Pekingese; "Skip"; "Jack" & "Pete" Bull Terriers; & a Coyote
Warren Harding— "Laddie Boy" Airedale; "Old Boy" Bulldog
Calvin Coolidge — "Peter Pan" terrier; "Paul Pry" Airedale; "Calamity Jane" sheepdog; "Boston Beans" Bulldog; "King Cole" shepherd; "Palo Alto" birder; "Rob Roy," "Prudence Prim," "Ruby Rough," & "Bessie" Collies; "Blackberry" & "Tiny Tim" Chows
Herbert Hoover—"Glen" Collie; "Yukon" Malamute; "Patrick" Irish

Wolfhound; "Eaglehurst Gillette" setter; "Weejie" Elkhound; "Big Ben" & "Sonnie" Fox Terriers; "King Tut" & "Pat" shepherds

Franklin Roosevelt—"Fala" & "Meggie" Scottish Terriers; "Major" German Shepherd; "Tiny" Old English Sheepdog; "President" Great Dane; "Blaze" Bull Mastiff; & "Winks" Llewellyn Setter.

Harry Truman—"Mike" Irish Setter; "Feller"

Dwight Eisenhower—"Heidi" Weimaraner

John Kennedy—"Charlie" Welsh Terrier; "Pushinka"[3]; "Shannon"; "Wolf" and "Clipper"; Pushinka and Charlie's pups, "Blackie," "Butterfly," "Streaker" & "White Tips"

Lyndon Johnson—"Him," "Her" & "Freckles"[4] Beagles; "Blanco," Collie; "Edgar" & "Yuki" mutts

Richard Nixon—"Checkers" Cocker Spaniel; "Pasha" Terrier; "Vicky" Poodle; "King Timahoe" Irish Setter

Gerald Ford—"Liberty" Golden Retriever

Jimmy Carter—"Grits"

Ronald Reagan—"Rex" King Charles Spaniel; "Lucky" Bouvier des Flandres

George Bush—"Millie" & "Ranger" Springer Spaniels

Bill Clinton—"Buddy" Chocolate Labrador Retriever

George W. Bush—"Spot"[5] Springer Spaniel; "Barney" Scottish Terrier

Donkey

Calvin Coolidge—"Ebeneezer"

Elephants

James Buchanan

Fish

James Garfield
Richard Nixon

Goats

William Harrison
Abraham Lincoln
Rutherford Hayes
Benjamin Harrison—"Whiskers"
Harry Truman

Guinea Pigs

Theodore Roosevelt
John Kennedy—"Debbie" & "Billie"

Hippos

Calvin Coolidge[6]

Horses & Ponies

George Washington
John Adams
Andrew Jackson—"Truxton," "Sam Patches," "Emily," "Lady Nashville," "Bolivia" horses; ponies
John Tyler—"The General" horse
James Polk—horse
Zachary Taylor—"Old Whitey"[7]
Abraham Lincoln—ponies
Ulysses Grant—"Jeff Davis,"[8] "Julia," "Jennie," "Mary," "Butcher Boy," "Cincinnatus," "Egypt," and "St. Louis" horses; "Reb" and "Billy Button" ponies
Rutherford Hayes—horses
James Garfield—"Kit" horse
Theodore Roosevelt—12 horses and "Algonquin" pony
John Kennedy—"Sardar" horse; "Macaroni," "Tex," & "Leprechaun" ponies
Ronald Reagan—horses

Hyenas

Theodore Roosevelt

Lion

Theodore Roosevelt
Calvin Coolidge

Lizards

Theodore Roosevelt

Mice

Andrew Johnson—white mice

Opossum

Benjamin Harrison
Herbert Hoover

Pigs

Abraham Lincoln
Theodore Roosevelt
Dwight Eisenhower

Rabbits

Abraham Lincoln—white rabbit
Theodore Roosevelt
John Kennedy—"Zsa Zsa"

Raccoons

Theodore Roosevelt
Calvin Coolidge—"Rebecca" & "Horace"

Rats

Theodore Roosevelt—"Jonathan" piebald rat & two kangaroo rats

Sheep

James Madison
Woodrow Wilson

Silkworms

John Q. Adams

Snakes

Theodore Roosevelt—"Emily Spinach" garter snake; other snakes

Squirrels

Theodore Roosevelt—flying squirrel

Tigers

Martin Van Buren—tiger cubs

Wallaby

Calvin Coolidge

Zebra

Theodore Roosevelt

NOTES

1. Jefferson had two bear cubs. They were a gift from Lewis & Clark.
2. Ernie was a polydactyl with more than five toes per foot. He was deemed unfit for White House duty and shipped off to a family in California.
3. Pushinka was a gift from Nikita Khrushchev, Premier of the USSR, and was from a litter by Strelka, a veteran of space travel.
4. Freckles was sired by Him.
5. Spot was Millie's pup, born in the White House during G. H. W. Bush's tenure.
6. It was a pygmy hippo.
7. Old Whitey was General Taylor's horse in the Mexican War.
8. This is fact. Grant named a horse after the president of the Confederacy.

48. Time Spent in Office

Of the 11 Presidents (including Washington) who served two full terms, 3 were Republicans, and 5 were Democrats. Washington, Jefferson, Madison, and Monroe all served parties which no longer exist. Three others (all Republicans) were elected to a second term but did not complete it. Two were assassinated (Lincoln and McKinley) and one resigned. No President between Jackson and Grant (ten Presidents) was in office eight years. Of those ten only Lincoln was reelected. By years in office/order served.

President	*Time in Office*
Roosevelt, F.	12 years, 1 month, 8 days[1]
Jefferson	8 years
Madison	8 years
Monroe	8 years
Jackson	8 years
Grant	8 years
Cleveland	8 years[2]
Wilson	8 years
Eisenhower	8 years
Reagan	8 years
Clinton	8 years
Washington	7 years, 10 months, 27 days[3]
Truman	7 years, 9 months, 8 days
Roosevelt, T.	7 years, 6 months, 20 days
Nixon	5 years, 6 months, 20 days
Coolidge	5 years, 5 months, 2 days
Johnson, L.	5 years, 1 month, 28 days
McKinley	4 years, 5 months, 10 days
Lincoln	4 years, 1 month, 11 days
Adams	4 years
Adams, J.Q.	4 years
Van Buren	4 years
Polk	4 years
Pierce	4 years
Buchanan	4 years
Hayes	4 years
Harrison, B.	4 years
Taft	4 years
Hoover	4 years
Carter	4 years

President	*Time in Office*
Bush	4 years
Tyler	3 years, 10 months, 29 days
Johnson, A.	3 years, 10 months, 19 days
Arthur	3 years, 6 months, 15 days
Kennedy	2 years, 10 months, 2 days
Fillmore	2 years, 7 months, 25 days
Ford	2 years, 5 months, 10 days
Harding	2 years, 4 months, 28 days
Taylor	1 year, 4 months, 5 days
Garfield	5 months, 15 days
Harrison, W.H.	1 month, 1 day

NOTES

1. During Roosevelt's first term the date of inauguration was changed from March 4 to January 20.

2. Cleveland served two nonconsecutive 4 year terms. (1885–1889 & 1893–1897 and is counted as both the 22nd and 24th president.)

3. Washington was sworn in for his first term on 30 April, 1789. Thus his first term was only 3 years, 10 months, 26 days.

49. Age Upon Leaving Office

Reagan was the oldest in and out. Cleveland's age is upon completion of his second term. Should George W. Bush serve two full terms he will be 63 upon leaving office.

President	*Age*	*President*	*Age*
Reagan	77.9	Jefferson	65.8
Eisenhower	70.2	Taylor+	65.6
Jackson	69.9	J. Adams	65.3
Buchanan	69.8	Washington	65
Truman	68.7	Wilson	64.1
George Bush	68.6	Ford	63.5
W. H. Harrison+	68.1	F. Roosevelt	63.2+
Monroe	66.1	J. Q Adams	61.6
Madison	65.9	Nixon*	61.5

President	Age		President	Age
L. Johnson	60.4		Taft	55.4
A. Johnson	60.1		Arthur	55.4
Cleveland**	59.9		Tyler	54.9
B. Harrison	59.5		Grant	54.8
McKinley+	58.6		Clinton	54.4
Hoover	58.5		Polk	53.3
Hayes	58.4		Fillmore	53.1
Van Buren	58.2		Pierce	52.2
Harding+	57.7		Cleveland***	51.9
Coolidge	56.6		T. Roosevelt	50.3
Carter	56.3		Garfield+	49.8
Lincoln+	56.1		Kennedy+	46.4

+Died in office
*Resigned
**Second Term
***First Term

50. How the Presidents Relaxed

The Presidency is a very demanding position. Pictures of Presidents leaving office show men who have aged more than the years in office would seem to justify.

Presidents need activities to allow them to unwind and escape the burdens of office.

Here is how each President found his relaxation.

President	Enjoyed
Washington	Billiards; Fox hunting; Reading; Walking
Adams, J.	Walking; Smoking; Reading; Whist[1]; Tending private library; Fishing
Jefferson	Architecture; Botany; Animal husbandry; Meteorology; Mechanical engineering; Reading; Wine; Horseback riding; Music[2]; Book collecting[3]
Madison	Walking; Nature; Horseback riding; Chess; Reading
Monroe	Horseback riding; Hunting
Adams, J.Q.	Billiards; Reading; Diarist; Nature; Botany; Walking; Horseback riding; Swimming[4]; Theater; Wine

President	Enjoyed
Jackson	Race horse breeding; Gamecocks[5]; Practical jokes; Reading; Pipe collecting
Van Buren	Theater; Fishing; Wine; Gambling[6]; Opera
Harrison, W. H.	Walking; Horseback riding; Reading the Bible
Tyler	Violin; Hunting; Fox hunting; Pets
Polk	Politics[7]
Taylor	Chewing tobacco[8]; Friends
Fillmore	Reading[9]; Civic affairs
Pierce	Fishing
Buchanan	Reading; Cards; Social activities
Lincoln	Reading; Theater; Chess; Jokes; Poetry
Johnson, A.	Checkers; Gardening; Circus & minstrel shows
Grant	Cigars; Art[10]; Fast horses[11]
Hayes	Hunting; Fishing; Chess; Walking; Gardening; Reading
Garfield	Hunting; Fishing; Chess; Cards (Euchre[12] & Whist); Billiards; Reading; Moderate drinking
Arthur	Social activities; Fishing; Hunting
Cleveland	Fishing; Hunting[13]; Walking; Carriage rides; Cards (Euchre, Cribbage, Pinochle & Poker); Beer; German food
Harrison, B.	Walking; Carriage rides; Duck hunting; Billiards; Cigars
McKinley	Walking; Carriage rides; Opera; Theater; Cards (Euchre, Cribbage, & Whist); Cigars; Alcohol
Roosevelt, T.	Wrestling; Boxing; Jiu Jitsu; Horseback riding; Tennis; Hiking; Swimming[14]; Hunting; Polo; Rowing; Animals; Reading; Animal studies
Taft	Golf[15]; Baseball[16]; Theater
Wilson	Golf[17]; Horseback riding; Theater; Billiards; Reading
Harding	Golf; Baseball; Boxing; Burlesque[18]; Poker; Liquor; Auto Trips; Yachting; Fishing
Coolidge	Walking; Horseback riding; Fishing; Skeet shooting; Practical jokes; Animals; Circus; Yachting; Cigars[19]
Hoover	Medicine ball; Fishing; Reading; Liquor
Roosevelt, F.	Swimming; Birdwatching; Stamp collecting; Sailing; Fishing; Movies; Poker; Liquor; Cigarettes
Truman	Walking; Poker; Piano; Concerts; Art; Liquor
Eisenhower	Golf; Painting; Fly-fishing; Hunting; Poker; Bridge; Canasta; Cooking; Reading; TV; Movies; Liquor; Cigarettes[20]
Kennedy	Sailing; Swimming; Golf; Touch football; Movies; Theater; Reading; Cigars
Johnson, L.	Dominoes; Poker; Golf; Swimming; Liquor; Cigarettes[21]
Nixon	Golf; Bowling; Swimming; Poker[22]; Reading; Movies; Pipe smoker
Ford	Golf; Swimming; Tennis; Skiing; Football[23]; Pipe smoker; Exercise
Carter	Jogging; Hiking; Cross country skiing; Bicycling; Tennis;

President	*Enjoyed*
	Bowling; Fishing; Speed reading; Classical music; Movies; Liquor; Cigars
Reagan	Gym; Horseback riding; Ranch work; Reading; Wine
Bush, G. H. W.	Jogging; Tennis; Golf; Racquetball; Hunting; Horseshoes; Fishing; Speedboat; Baseball; Reading; TV; Movies; Music; Liquor; Socializing
Clinton	Swimming; Golf; Basketball; Cards; Trivial Pursuit; Crosswords; Collecting porcelain; Jogging; Beer; Reading; Movies; Saxophone; Cigars
Bush, G. W.	Baseball[24]; Golf; Playing with family dog; Fishing; Hunting; Country music; Computer solitaire; Internet

NOTES

1. Whist is a card game, roughly equivalent to modern day Bridge. It was popular in the 18th and 19th centuries.

2. Jefferson played the fiddle.

3. Jefferson sold his book collection, 6,500 volumes, to the United States after the British burned the Capitol in 1815. He received $23,950 for the collection which formed the new Library of Congress.

4. J.Q. Adams enjoyed skinny dipping in the Potomac.

5. Gamecock fighting was a popular sport in Jackson's time. Today it is illegal.

6. Van Buren liked to bet on the outcome of elections.

7. Polk was absorbed by politics. He had no other interests outside of his family and the political realm.

8. Taylor was said to have been a marksman at hitting the spittoon.

9. Fillmore was a bibliophile. He established the first permanent White House Library.

10. Grant painted and drew horses.

11. While President, Grant was given a ticket for riding too fast in Washington, D.C. He paid the $20.00 fine.

12. Euchre is a card game still played today. It is popular mainly in the British Commonwealth.

13. Cleveland called his rifle "Death and Destruction."

14. Teddy also enjoyed skinny dipping in the Potomac.

15. Golf in America may date back to early colonial times. The USGA was founded in 1894. Taft was the first President to be an active golfer. Out of the next 16 Presidents 9 were golfers.

16. The tradition of the President throwing out the opening day pitch began with Taft.

17. Wilson once said that golf was "an intellectual attempt to put an elusive ball into an obscure hole with implements ill-adapted to the purpose." Wilson reportedly shot about 115.

18. Burlesque, in Harding's time, was a form of theater, not necessarily sexual in nature.

19. Coolidge liked the Fonesca Corona Fines de Lux costing 21 cents apiece.

20. Ike quit smoking in 1949.

21. Lyndon was a three-pack-a-day smoker. He quit in 1955 after a heart attack.

22. It is reported that Nixon was a master poker player, and won thousands of dollars during his time in the service. He used this money to finance his first campaign for Congress.

23. Ford played center for his high school football team and for the Michigan Wolverines.

24. At one point Bush owned part of the Texas Rangers.

51. Places of Retirement

Some Presidents retired to private life. John Quincy Adams and Andrew Johnson returned to Congress. Taft became Chief Justice of the United States Supreme Court.

Here are the others and where they retired. (Presidents W. H. Harding, Zachary Taylor, Abraham Lincoln, James Garfield, William McKinley, Warren Harding, Franklin D. Roosevelt, and John Kennedy will not appear in this chapter.)

President	*Retired to*
George Washington[1]	Mt. Vernon Plantation, VA
John Adams	Quincy, MA
Thomas Jefferson	Monticello Plantation, VA
James Madison	Montpelier Plantation, VA
James Monroe	Oak Hill Estate, VA
John Q. Adams[2]	Quincy, MA
Andrew Jackson	Hermitage Plantation, near Nashville, TN
Martin Van Buren	Kinderhook, NY
John Tyler	Sherwood Forest, near Richmond VA
James Polk[3]	Nashville, TN
Millard Fillmore	Buffalo, NY
Franklin Pierce	Concord, NH
James Buchanan	Lancaster, PA
Andrew Johnson[4]	Greenville, TN
Ulysses Grant	New York City[5]
Rutherford Hayes	Spiegel Grove in Fremont, OH
Chester Arthur	New York City
Grover Cleveland[6]	Buzzard Bay, MA
Benjamin Harrison	Indianapolis, IN
Grover Cleveland[7]	Princeton, NJ
Theodore Roosevelt	Sagamore Hill Estate, Oyster Bay, NY

President	*Retired to*
William Taft[8]	Washington, D.C.
Woodrow Wilson	Washington, D.C.
Calvin Coolidge	Northampton, MA
Herbert Hoover	Palo Alto, CA[9]
Harry Truman	Independence, MO
Dwight Eisenhower	Gettysburg, PA
Lyndon Johnson	LBJ Ranch; Johnson City, TX
Richard Nixon	San Clemente, CA[10]
Gerald Ford	Rancho Mirage, CA
Jimmy Carter	Plains, GA
Ronald Reagan	Bel Air, CA[11]
George H. W. Bush	Houston, TX
William Clinton	New York City

NOTES

1. John Adams appointed Washington Lt. General and Commander in Chief of American forces. Although he never took to the field, he is the only former President to hold this post.

2. After one year of retirement, Adams was elected to the House of Representatives. He served there for 17 years. Adams collapsed on the floor of the House and died in the Speaker's Room.

3. Polk spent only a few weeks there before death claimed him.

4. In 1875 Johnson returned to the U.S. Senate. He is the only President to serve in the Senate after being President. He died in office.

5. Originally Grant retired to Galena, IL. He moved to New York City in 1881.

6. After his first term Cleveland also practiced law in New York City.

7. Second term.

8. After his Presidency he was a law professor at Yale. Taft retired from the Supreme Court, and died less than a month later in Washington, D. C.

9. Hoover also spent much of his time at a suite of rooms he had at the Waldorf-Astoria Hotel in New York City.

10. Nixon later moved to New York City.

11. Reagan also had a ranch in the Simi Valley north of Los Angeles.

---

52. Years Lived
After the Presidency

The Presidency is a demanding taskmaster. The average number of years the President lives after leaving office is a scant 12.9. This figure takes into account only the thirty-three presidents who left the White House. One of them, Polk, lived only eight months after serving his country. The average will certainly change upward. Two former chief executives have already passed the twenty-year mark. Ford, Carter and G. H. W. Bush have all passed the twelve-year mark.

Strangely enough the President who probably loved the job the most, and drew strength from it, Teddy Roosevelt, lived just nine years after being the youngest president to leave the office. His successor, Big Bill Taft, who had no taste for the office, lived just twelve days less than seventeen years out of office.

President	Years Lived Out of Office	President	Years Lived Out of Office
Herbert Hoover	31.6	Theodore Roosevelt	9.8
John Adams	25.3	Ulysses S. Grant	8.4
Martin Van Buren	21.4	Andrew Jackson	8.3
Millard Fillmore	21	Dwight Eisenhower	8.2
Richard M. Nixon	20.3	Benjamin Harrison	8
Harry S Truman	19.9	James Buchanan	7.2
James Madison	19.3	Andrew Johnson	6.4
John Q. Adams	19	James Monroe	6.3
Thomas Jefferson	17.3	Lyndon B. Johnson	4
William H. Taft	17	Calvin Coolidge	3.8
John Tyler	16.9	Woodrow Wilson	2.9
Ronald Reagan	15.5	George Washington	2.8
Franklin Pierce	12.6	Chester Arthur	1.7
Rutherford B. Hayes	11.9	James K. Polk	.7
Grover Cleveland	11.3		

53. Last Words

Final words are important. Our Presidents, much as they did in office, leave us with dying words which range from the profound to the mundane, the wordy to the simple. Grant's final word may surprise some. Lincoln and Kennedy, for obvious reasons, are not included in this section. Others for whom no last words are known: Monroe, Van Buren, Polk, Pierce, Buchanan, A. Johnson, Arthur, B. Harrison, Taft, Coolidge, Hoover, Truman, L. Johnson, Nixon, and Reagan.

President	Final Words
Washington	"'Tis Well."
Adams	"Jefferson still survives."[1]
Jefferson	"Is it the fourth? I resign my spirit to God, my daughter to my Country."
Madison	"Nothing more than a change of mind, my dear."[2]
Monroe	Unknown
J. Q. Adams	"This is the end of earth; I am content."[3]
Jackson	"I hope and trust to meet you in heaven, both white and black, both white and black.... [in response to wails heard outside] Oh do not cry. Be good children and we shall meet in heaven."
Van Buren	"There is but one reliance."
W. H. Harrison	"I wish you to understand the true principles of the government. I wish them carried out. I ask nothing more."
Tyler	"Perhaps it is best."
Polk	Unknown
Taylor	"I regret nothing, but I am sorry that I am about to leave my friends."
Fillmore	"The nourishment is palatable."
Pierce	Unknown
Buchanan	"O Lord, God Almighty, as Thou wilt."
Lincoln	Unknown
A. Johnson	Unknown
Grant	"Water."
Hayes	"I know that I am going where Lucy is."
Garfield	"Swaim, can't you stop this? Swaim!"[4]
Arthur	Unknown
Cleveland	"I have tried so hard to do right."
B. Harrison	"Are the doctors here? Doctor ... please my lungs."
McKinley	"Good bye, good bye to all. It's God's way. His will, not ours, be done."
T. Roosevelt	"Please put out the light."[5]
Taft	Unknown
Wilson	"I am ready."
Harding	"That's good. Go on. Read some more."[6]
Coolidge	Unknown
Hoover	Unknown
F. Roosevelt	"I have a terrible headache."
Truman	Unknown
Eisenhower	"I want to go. God take me."
Kennedy	Unknown
L. Johnson	Unknown
Nixon	Unknown
Reagan	Unknown

NOTES

1. In fact Jefferson had died a few hours earlier.
2. To one of his nieces who inquired "What is the matter, Uncle James?"
3. There is some dispute as to whether Adams said content or composed.
4. Dr. Swaim was Garfield's attending physician.
5. To his valet, James Amos.
6. To his wife who was reading an article from the *Saturday Evening Post*.

54. Date of Death

Three Presidents have died on the Fourth of July. Each of them played a significant role in the formation of our nation.

Here are the dates of death in calendar order.

Month	Date	Year	President
January	5	1933	Coolidge
	6	1919	T. Roosevelt
	17	1893	Hayes
	18	1862	Tyler
	22	1973	L. Johnson
February	3	1924	Wilson
	23	1848	J. Q. Adams
March	8	1874	Fillmore
	8	1930	Taft
	13	1901	B. Harrison
	28	1969	Eisenhower
April	4	1841	W. H. Harrison
	12	1945	F. D. Roosevelt
	15[1]	1865	Lincoln
	22	1994	Nixon
June	1	1868	Buchanan
	5	2004	Reagan
	8	1845	Jackson
	15	1849	Polk
	24	1908	Cleveland
	28	1836	Madison
July	4	1826	Jefferson[2]
			J. Adams
		1831	Monroe
	9	1850	Taylor

Month	Date	Year	President
	23	1885	Grant
	24	1862	Van Buren
	31	1875	A. Johnson
August	2	1923	Harding
September	14[3]	1901	McKinley
	19[4]	1881	Garfield
October	8	1869	Pierce
	20	1964	Hoover
November	18	1886	Arthur
	22	1963	Kennedy
December	14	1799	Washington
	26	1972	Truman

NOTES

1. Lincoln was shot on Good Friday and died the next morning.
2. Jefferson died at approximately 12:50 P.M., Adams at around 6:00 P.M. Adams' last words were "Jefferson lives." He didn't.
3. McKinley was shot September 6, 1901.
4. Garfield was shot July 12, 1881.

---

55. Age at Death

Van Buren died short of his eightieth birthday. Had he made it to eighty, he would have been in very select company. Only eleven presidents, including Ford, Carter, and G.H.W. Bush, have lived past eighty.

Polk chose to serve one term and died shortly after leaving the White House. He was a young 53.

Adams (the senior), Jefferson, and Monroe all died on the fourth of July.

From oldest to youngest:

President	Age	President	Age
Reagan	93.3	Truman	88.6
Adams, J.[1]	90.7	Madison	85.3
Hoover	90.2	Jefferson[2]	83.2

President	Age	President	Age
Nixon	81.3	Johnson, A.	66.6
Adams, J. Q.	80.6	Taylor[5]	65
Van Buren	79.6	Pierce	64.9
Eisenhower	78.5	Johnson, L.	64.4
Jackson	78.2	Grant	63.2
Buchanan	77.1	Roosevelt, F.[6]	63.2
Fillmore	74.2	Coolidge	60.5
Monroe[3]	73.2	Roosevelt T.	60.2
Taft	72.5	McKinley[7]	58.6
Tyler	71.8	Harding[8]	57.7
Cleveland	71.3	Arthur	57.1
Hayes	70.3	Lincoln[9]	56.1
Harrison, W. H.[4]	68.1	Polk	53.6
Washington	67.8	Garfield[10]	49.8
Harrison, B.	67.6	Kennedy[11]	46.4
Wilson	67.1		

NOTES

1. Died July 4, 1826.
2. Died July 4, 1826 just hours before Adams.
3. Died July 4, 1831.
4. Died 32 days after his inauguration.
5. Died of cholera morbus.
6. Died of cerebral hemorrhage.
7. Died of wounds from an assassin.
8. Died Aug. 2, 1923, of a stroke.
9. Assassinated Good Friday April 14, 1863. Died the following morning.
10. Died Sept. 19, 1881, as the result of an assassin's attack July 2, 1881.
11. Assassinated Nov. 22, 1963.

---

56. Cause of Death

A lack of modern medicine makes the causes of the deaths of some of the Presidents speculative. Some of the listed causes of death, such as "tuberculosis" and "cholera," were perhaps just educated guesses on the part of the attending physician.

Some of the early Presidential deaths would be preventable today. Both Garfield and McKinley would, in all likelihood, have survived their gunshot wounds. W. H. Harrison probably would have survived his pneumonia.

In order served.

President	Cause of Death
George Washington	Peritonsillar Abscess[1]
John Adams	Heart Failure, Pneumonia
Thomas Jefferson	Old Age; Multiple Diseases
James Madison	Heart Failure
James Monroe	Heart Failure
John Quincy Adams	Massive Stroke[2]
Andrew Jackson	Old Age; Multiple Diseases
Martin Van Buren	Heart Failure; Pneumonia
W. H. Harrison	Pneumonia
John Tyler	Biliousness; Bronchitis
James K. Polk	Cholera
Zachary Taylor	Food Poisoning
Millard Fillmore	Stroke
Franklin Pierce	Cirrhosis; Dropsy
James Buchanan	Pneumonia; Pericarditis
Abraham Lincoln	Gunshot Wound to the Head
Andrew Johnson	Stroke
Ulysses Grant	Throat Cancer[3]
Rutherford Hayes	Heart Attack
James Garfield	Bronchopneumonia[4]
Chester Arthur	Chronic Renal Failure; Stroke
Grover Cleveland	Multiple Diseases
Benjamin Harrison	Pneumonia
William McKinley	Gangrene[5]
Theodore Roosevelt	Heart Attack
William Taft	Cardiovascular Disease
Woodrow Wilson	Multiple Diseases
Warren Harding	Heart Attack
Calvin Coolidge	Heart Attack
Herbert Hoover	Internal Bleeding
Franklin Roosevelt	Cerebral Hemorrhage[6]
Harry Truman	Old Age
Dwight Eisenhower	Congestive Heart Failure
John Kennedy	Gunshot Wound to the Head
Lyndon Johnson	Heart Attack
Richard Nixon	Stroke
Ronald Reagan	Pneumonia

NOTES

1. This is an infection of the tonsil area. Today it is easily treated.
2. J. Q. Adams suffered his final stroke on the floor of the House of Representa-

tives after casting a "No!" vote on a proposal to decorate several U.S. generals for their participation in the Mexican War.

3. Grant was a heavy cigar smoker.

4. Garfield was shot 2 July 1881. The wound was not fatal, but poor medical treatment caused blood poisoning. The President's wound was probed with unsterilized instruments and bare fingers. The result was blood poisoning and then bronchopneumonia.

5. McKinley was the victim of an assassin's bullet. The medical treatment was inadequate to deal with what would be a minor wound today. Poor sterilization caused President McKinley's wound to develop gangrene.

6. Roosevelt suffered from high blood pressure. Most likely this was a contributing factor.

---

57. Place of Death

Garfield was shot in Washington, D.C. He survived for more than two months, finally dying in New Jersey. He and Grover Cleveland are the only two Presidents to die in New Jersey. Eight have died in New York, more than in any other state. Next in line is Washington, D.C. Four Presidents were assassinated, Lincoln and Garfield in Washington, D.C., McKinley in New York, and Kennedy in Texas.

State	City	President
California	San Francisco	Harding
	Simi Valley	Reagan
Georgia	Warm Springs	F. Roosevelt
Indiana	Indianapolis	B. Harrison
Massachusetts	Northampton	Coolidge
	Quincy	J. Adams
Missouri	Kansas City	Truman
New Hampshire	Concord	Pierce
New Jersey	Elberon	Garfield
	Princeton	Cleveland
New York	Buffalo	Fillmore
		McKinley
	Kinderhook	Van Buren
	Mt. McGregor	Grant
New York	New York City	Arthur
		Hoover
		Monroe
		Nixon
	Oyster Bay	T. Roosevelt
Ohio	Fremont	Hayes
Pennsylvania	Lancaster	Buchanan

State	*City*	*President*
Tennessee	The Hermitage	Jackson
	Nashville	Polk
	Carter's Station	A. Johnson
Texas	Dallas	Kennedy
	Johnson City	L. Johnson
Virginia	Charlottesville	Jefferson
	Montpelier	Madison
	Mount Vernon	Washington
	Richmond	Tyler
Washington, D.C.		J. Q. Adams
		Eisenhower
		W. H. Harrison
		Lincoln
		Taft
		Taylor
		Wilson

---

58. Burial Places

Only one President, Woodrow Wilson, rests in our nation's capital. Two, William Howard Taft and John Fitzgerald Kennedy, are in Arlington National Cemetery. The remaining 37 are buried in 17 states.

President	*Burial Place*	*State*
George Washington	Mt. Vernon	Virginia
John Adams	Quincy	Massachusetts
Thomas Jefferson	Monticello	Virginia
James Madison	Montpelier	Virginia
James Monroe	Hollywood Cemetery[1]	Virginia
John Quincy Adams	Quincy	Massachusetts
Andrew Jackson	The Hermitage	Tennessee
Martin Van Buren	Kinderhook	New York
William H. Harrison	North Bend[2]	Ohio
John Tyler	Hollywood Cemetery	Virginia
James Polk	Nashville[3]	Tennessee
Zachary Taylor	Louisville[4]	Kentucky
Millard Fillmore	Forest Lawn Cemetery	New York
Franklin Pierce	Concord	New Hampshire
James Buchanan	Woodward Cemetery	Pennsylvania
Abraham Lincoln	Springfield	Illinois

President	Burial Place	State
Andrew Johnson	Greenville	Tennessee
Ulysses Grant	Grant's Tomb, NYC	New York
Rutherford Hayes	Spiegel Grove[5]	Ohio
James Garfield	Lakeview Cemetery	Ohio
Chester Arthur	Albany	New York
Grover Cleveland	Princeton	New Jersey
Benjamin Harrison	Indianapolis	Indiana
William McKinley	Canton	Ohio
Theodore Roosevelt	Oyster Bay	New York
William H. Taft	Arlington National Cemetery[6]	Virginia
Woodrow Wilson	Washington Cathedral	Washington, D.C.
Warren G. Harding	Marion	Ohio
Calvin Coolidge	Plymouth	Vermont
Herbert Hoover	West Branch	Iowa
Franklin Roosevelt	Hyde Park	New York
Harry Truman	Independence	Missouri
Dwight Eisenhower	Abilene	Kansas
John F. Kennedy	Arlington National Cemetery	Virginia
Lyndon Johnson	Johnson City	Texas
Richard Nixon	Yorba Linda	California
Ronald Reagan	Simi Valley	California

Notes

1. In 1858 President Monroe's remains were exhumed from Marble Cemetery, N.Y., and re-interred at Hollywood Cemetery, in Richmond, Va.

2. Originally buried in Washington, D.C., in April 1841, his remains were removed in June to Ohio.

3. Originally interred at Polk Place, Tennessee, in 1849. In 1893 his remains were moved to the state capitol in Nashville.

4. Buried in the Congressional Cemetery in July 1850, re-interred in Louisville, Ky.

5. Hayes died in 1893, and was originally buried in Fremont, Ohio. In 1915 his remains, and those of his beloved Lucy, were moved to the family plot at Spiegel Grove.

6. Taft's funeral was the first Presidential funeral to be broadcast on the radio.

---

59. Presidents Who Held No Other Elected Office

Zachary Taylor
Ulysses S. Grant

William Howard Taft
Herbert Hoover

Dwight D. Eisenhower

60. Post-Presidential Offices

J. Q. Adams— U.S. House of Representatives (Elected)
Andrew Johnson — U.S. Senate (Elected)
W. H. Taft — U.S. Chief Justice (Appointed by Harding, 1921)

61. Vice Presidents Succeeding Presidents Who Died in Office

Vice President	President	Vice President	President
Tyler	W.H. Harrison	T. Roosevelt	McKinley
Fillmore	Taylor	Coolidge	Harding
A. Johnson	Lincoln	Truman	F. Roosevelt
Arthur	Garfield	L. Johnson	Kennedy

Tyler, Fillmore, A. Johnson, and Arthur were denied their parties' nominations for terms of their own. Tyler, Johnson and Arthur had angered party officials and Fillmore was deemed unelectable.

The next four, Teddy Roosevelt, Coolidge, Truman, and L. Johnson were all nominated and elected to their own terms.

The only other President to succeed to office, Ford upon the resignation of Nixon, was nominated but defeated in the general election.

62. Bearded Presidents

Lincoln	B. Harrison	Garfield
Grant	Hayes	

63. Presidential Firsts, Lasts, and Onlies

President	First
Washington	Elected
	Veto
	2nd term
	Pardon
	Federal nominee rejected by the Senate
	Nominee for Chief Justice rejected by the Senate
J. Adams	Vice President became President
	Elected on party ticket
	Had a Vice President from a different party
	Lived in the White House
	Defeated for re-election
Jefferson	Elected by the House
	Had been Secretary of State
	Took oath of office in Washington, D.C.
	Elected under the Thirteenth Amendment
	Served eight full years
Madison	Served as U.S. Congressman
	Used pocket veto
Monroe	Former U.S. Senator
	Inaugurated on Monday, a day late (March 4 fell on a Sunday)
J. Q. Adams	Son of a President
	Married abroad
Jackson	Born in a log cabin
	Nominated at national party convention
	Walked from Capitol to the White House after inauguration
	Target of attempted assassination
	Had a Cabinet nominee rejected by Senate
Van Buren	Born after independence
W. H. Harrison	Died in office
Tyler	Born in the United States
	Succeeded to the Presidency
	Had no Vice President
	Widowed in office
	Married in office
	Veto overridden
	Threatened with impeachment

President	First
Polk	Former Speaker of the House
	Had a gaslight in the White House
	Photographed as President
Pierce	Affirmed, not swore, the oath of office
Lincoln	Born outside the original 13 states (Kentucky)
	Owned a patent (for a type of buoy)
	Suspended the writ of habeas corpus
	Assassinated
	Portrait on paper money ($10 bill, 1862)
	Portrait on coin (1909 penny)
A. Johnson	Impeached
Grant	Fined for speeding as President (on a horse; fined $20)
Cleveland	Child born in the White House
B. Harrison	Grandson of a President
	Electric lights in the White House
	Watched a professional baseball game[1]
T. Roosevelt	Traveled abroad while President
	Awarded Nobel Peace Prize
Taft	Threw opening pitch at the first game of the baseball season
Harding	Voice broadcast on radio
Coolidge	Broadcast from the White House
F. Roosevelt	Woman Cabinet member
	Traveled abroad during war
	Appeared on TV
Truman	First White House telecast[2]
Eisenhower	Held pilot's license
Kennedy	Debated on TV
L. Johnson	Black Cabinet member
Carter	Incumbent debated on TV
Reagan	Appointed a woman to Supreme Court
G. W. Bush	Held a Masters Degree

President	Last
W. H. Harrison	Born a British Subject
Lincoln	Vice President from a different party (A. Johnson)
L. Johnson	Served without a Vice President
Clinton	Woman Secretary of State

President	Only
Washington	Elected unanimously
J. Q. Adams	Served in Congress after being President

President	Only
Jackson	Killed a man in a duel
Buchanan	Bachelor
A. Johnson	Elected Senator after being President
Cleveland	Elected to non-consecutive terms
	Married in the White House
T. Roosevelt	Congressional Medal of Honor Winner
	Nobel Peace Prize Winner
Coolidge	Born on the fourth of July
F. Roosevelt	Served more than two terms
Truman	Used nuclear weapons
Kennedy	Roman Catholic President
Ford	Appointed Vice President
Clinton	Defendant in civil court case while President
	Gave evidence to a Grand Jury
	Wife candidate for U.S. Senate

NOTES

1. Cincinnati beat Washington 7–4 in eleven innings.
2. Informing the public of his food conservation program.

---

64. Presidential Salaries

$25,000

Washington
John Adams
Jefferson
Madison
Monroe
J. Q. Adams
Jackson
Van Buren
W. H. Harrison
Tyler
Polk
Taylor
Fillmore
Pierce
Buchanan
Lincoln
A. Johnson
Grant

$50,000

Grant (2nd term)
Hayes
Garfield
Arthur
Cleveland
B. Harrison
Cleveland
McKinley
T. Roosevelt

$75,000

Taft
Wilson
Harding
Coolidge
Hoover
F. Roosevelt
Truman

$100,000

Truman
Eisenhower
Kennedy
L. Johnson

$200,000

Nixon
Ford
Carter
Reagan
G. H. W. Bush
Clinton

$400,000

G. W. Bush

65. Calendar
of Presidential Events

Many things have happened to every resident of the White House. These are simply the highlights of events and occurrences which happened when each was President.

Many events which had a direct effect on each President are not included. Instead, only those events which directly involved the President are included.

Date	Year	Occurrence
1 Jan	1796	Washington nominates Oliver Ellsworth as Chief Justice.
2 Jan	1795	Washington appoints T. Pickering Secretary of War.
	1930	Hoover meets with congressional leaders on public works.
3 Jan	1938	In his annual State of the Union address to Congress F. Roosevelt addresses defense and economic recovery.
	1961	Eisenhower breaks diplomatic ties with Cuba.
	1983	Reagan declares Times Beach, MO, a federal disaster area due to threat posed by dioxin.
	1993	G. H. W. Bush and Boris Yeltsin sign SALT II.
4 Jan	1934	F. Roosevelt requests $10,500,000,000 from Congress to advance his recovery programs.
	1935	In his State of the Union Address F. Roosevelt announces the 2nd stage of his New Deal.
	1939	In State of the Union message F. Roosevelt emphasizes foreign rather than domestic policies.
	1965	L. Johnson increases War on Poverty.
	1974	Nixon refuses to surrender tapes and documents subpoenaed by Senate Watergate Committee.
5 Jan	1838	Van Buren posts military on Canadian Border.[1]
	1933	Calvin Coolidge dies.
	1957	Eisenhower speaks to UN and proposes aid to Middle East.[2]
	1972	Nixon gives NASA approval for Space Shuttle.
6 Jan	1919	Theodore Roosevelt dies.
	1941	F. Roosevelt in State of Union message requests congressional support for Lend/Lease.
	1942	In State of Union message F. Roosevelt calls for increased production of war materials.
	1955	In his State of the Union Address, Eisenhower appeals to both parties to work to make the U.S. a world power.

Date	Year	Occurrence
	1967	L. Johnson requests 6 percent increase in income taxes to fund his Great Society.
7 Jan	1916	Wilson receives promise from Germany that it will abide by Strict international rules of maritime warfare.
	1953	Truman warns of dangers of atomic war in last State of the Union Address.
	1954	Eisenhower proposes cuts in military spending in his first State of the Union Address.
	1960	Eisenhower delivers State of the Union Address.
	1992	G. H. W. Bush departs for trip to Japan.
8 Jan	1802	Jefferson requests Congress repeal Judiciary Act of 1801.
	1918	Wilson issues "Fourteen Points" for Peace.
	1947	Truman names George C. Marshall as Secretary of State.
	1964	During his State of the Union Address, L. Johnson declares War on Poverty.
	1975	Ford appoints committee to investigate the CIA.
9 Jan	1958	Eisenhower delivers State of Union Address and advocates continuation of foreign aid and missile program.
10 Jan	1957	Eisenhower call for Congress to pass his Middle East proposal in State of the Union Address.
11 Jan	1862	Lincoln names Stanton Secretary of War.
	1962	Kennedy delivers State of the Union Address.
	1973	Nixon ends wage and price controls.
12 Jan	1803	Jefferson appoints Monroe as Minister to France.
	1966	In State of the Union Message L. Johnson pledges to continue the Great Society and aid to South Vietnam.
	1977	Ford delivers final State of the Union Address.
	1991	G. H. W. Bush receives congressional authority to use force to expel Iraq from Kuwait.
13 Jan	1868	A. Johnson's suspension of Stanton is rejected by the Senate.
	1972	Nixon withdraws 70,000 troops from Vietnam
14 Jan	1942	By proclamation F. Roosevelt requires all aliens in U.S. to register with the government.
	1943	F. Roosevelt meets Churchill in Casablanca for 10 days.
	1969	L. Johnson delivers last State of the Union Address.
15 Jan	1975	In first State of the Union Address Ford asks Congress for tax cut.
16 Jan	1953	Truman sets aside offshore oil reserves as federal property.
	1991	G. H. W. Bush orders air strike in Iraq.
17 Jan	1893	Rutherford Hayes dies.
18 Jan	1862	John Tyler dies.
19 Jan	1955	Eisenhower holds first televised press conference.
	1976	In State of the Union Message Ford asks Congress to practice fiscal responsibility.
	2001	Clinton admits to lying under oath about Monica Lewinsky.

Date	Year	Occurrence
20 Jan	1815	President Madison vetoes bill authorizing the Bank of U.S.
	1899	McKinley establishes Philippine Commission.
	1937	F. Roosevelt inaugurated for 2nd Term.
	1941	F. Roosevelt inaugurated for 3rd Term.
	1942	Japanese Removal Act is approved by F. Roosevelt.
	1945	F. Roosevelt inaugurated for 4th Term.
	1946	By Executive Order President Truman establishes the CIA.
	1949	Truman inaugurated.
	1953	Eisenhower inaugurated as the 34th President.
	1957	Eisenhower inaugurated for 2nd Term.
	1958	Eisenhower warns Congress of economic perils of wage and price increases.
	1961	John F. Kennedy inaugurated as the 35th President.
	1965	Lyndon B. Johnson inaugurated.
	1969	Richard M. Nixon inaugurated as the 37th President.
	1973	Nixon gives State of the Union Address and announces plan to reduce the size of the federal government. Nixon inaugurated for 2nd Term.
	1977	James Earl Carter inaugurated as 39th President.
	1981	Ronald Reagan inaugurated as 40th President.
	1985	Reagan inaugurated for 2nd Term.
	1989	George Herbert Walker Bush inaugurated as 41st President.
	1993	William Jefferson Clinton inaugurated as 42nd President.
	1997	Clinton inaugurated for 2nd term.
	2001	George Walker Bush inaugurated as 43rd President.
21 Jan	1957	Eisenhower follows up inauguration with televised ceremony on east portico of White House.
	1961	Kennedy appoints brother Robert as Attorney General.[3]
	1977	Carter grants unconditional pardon to Vietnam War Draft evaders.
22 Jan	1917	Wilson first mentions the League of Nations.
	1970	In State of the Union Message Nixon calls for equality of opportunity and government responsiveness to needs.
	1971	Nixon proposes "revenue sharing" in State of the Union Address.
	1973	Lyndon Johnson dies.
23 Jan	1845	Congress establishes a national election day.[4]
24 Jan	1980	Carter announces willingness to sell weapons to China.
25 Jan	1863	Lincoln fires Gen. Burnside as head of the Army of the Potomac and replaces him with Gen. Hooker.
	1961	Kennedy holds the nation's first live televised Presidential press conference.
	1972	Nixon announces 8 point peace plan proposal for Paris talks with North Vietnam.
	1984	Reagan states "America is back and standing tall" in his State of the Union Message.

Date	Year	Occurrence
	1988	Reagan delivers State of the Union Address.
26 Jan	1982	In State of the Union Address Reagan states intention to transfer federal programs to the states.
27 Jan	1862	Lincoln issues General War Order No. 1 calling for a general Union offensive. McClellan ignores the order.
28 Jan	1915	Wilson vetoes a bill requiring immigrants pass a literacy test.
	1938	F. Roosevelt recommends increased armed forces funding.
	2003	G. W. Bush, in State of the Union Address, declares Iraq has weapons of mass destruction.
29 Jan	1877	Congress establishes a committee to decide the 1876 election.[5]
30 Jan	1835	Richard Lawrence shoots at President Jackson.[6]
	1974	Nixon uses State of the Union Address to outline plans to resolve energy crisis.
31 Jan	1934	F. Roosevelt signs Farm Mortgage Refinancing Act.
	1966	L. Johnson resumes bombing raids of North Vietnam.
1 Feb	1953	Eisenhower formally joins the Presbyterian Church.
	1968	Nixon announces intentions to run for President.
2 Feb	1827	The United States Supreme Court gives the President power over the states' militias.
	1858	Buchanan asks Congress to admit Kansas to the Union.
	1872	Presidential election is changed to the first Tuesday following the first Monday of November.
	1934	F. Roosevelt signs an executive order establishing the Export-Import Bank of Washington.
	1948	Truman submits Civil Rights Package[7] to Congress.
	1953	Eisenhower delivers State of the Union Message in which he declares the 7th Fleet can no longer shield Taiwan.
	1954	Eisenhower reports first hydrogen bomb test.[8]
3 Feb	1865	Lincoln meets with Confederate Vice President Stephens.[9]
	1887	Electoral Count Act.[10]
	1924	Woodrow Wilson dies.
4 Feb	1945	F. Roosevelt, W. Churchill, & J. Stalin begin Yalta Meeting.
5 Feb	1937	F. Roosevelt announces court-packing scheme to his Cabinet.
	1993	Clinton signs Family and Medical Leave Act.
6 Feb	1933	20th Amendment adopted.[11]
	1985	In State of the Union Address, Reagan calls "for a 2nd American Revolution of hope and opportunity."
8 Feb	1966	L. Johnson concludes 3 day meeting in Hawaii with South Vietnam Premier Nguyen Cao Ky.
	1996	Clinton signs the Telecommunications Act.
7 Feb	1965	L. Johnson orders bombing of North Vietnam.
9 Feb	1825	The House of Representatives elects J. Q. Adams as the 6th President.
10 Feb	1915	Wilson warns Germany it will be held accountable for loss of lives or property.

Date	Year	Occurrence
11 Feb	1801	The 1800 Presidential election is tied between Jefferson and Burr.
	1856	Pierce warns factions in Kansas to stop fighting.
12 Feb	1999	President Clinton is acquitted of impeachment charges.
13 Feb	1861	Lincoln wins Electoral Vote.
	1964	L. Johnson asks Congress to fund John F. Kennedy Cultural Arts Center.
15 Feb	1824	J. Q. Adams nominated for President.
	1933	FDR shot at in Miami, Florida by Giuseppa Zangara.[12]
	1938	F. Roosevelt signs Agricultural Adjustment Act.
	1991	G. H. W. Bush rejects Iraq offer to pull out of Kuwait.
17 Feb	1801	The House elects Jefferson as third President.
	1815	President Madison declares end of War of 1812.
	1956	Eisenhower vetoes bill to remove price controls from natural gas.
	1976	Ford reveals plan to reform the CIA.
18 Feb	1851	Fillmore backs Fugitive Slave Law.
21 Feb	1862	Lincoln appoints Andrew Johnson military governor of the Union-controlled portions of Tennessee.
	1868	A. Johnson fires Secretary of War Stanton.
	1946	Truman establishes the Office of Economic Stabilization.
	1972	Nixon begins trip to China.
22 Feb	1868	U.S. House of Representatives votes impeachment resolution against President Johnson.
	1881	Hayes bans alcohol on military bases.
23 Feb	1848	John Quincy Adams dies.
	1966	In a message to Congress, L. Johnson calls for conservation and environmental protection.
	1991	G. H. W. Bush orders full offensive against Iraq.
24 Feb	1977	Carter announces foreign aid will be reduced to countries guilty of human rights violations.
25 Feb	1790	Washington signs bill to create the Bank of the United States.
	1804	Jefferson nominated for 2nd Term.
	1918	Wilson gives go ahead for Muscle Shoals Dam.
	1926	Coolidge signs Revenue Act.[13]
26 Feb	1931	Hoover vetoes Bonus Loan Bill.[14]
	1979	Carter asks Congress for authority to ration gas.
27 Feb	1991	G. H. W. Bush halts military action in Iraq.
28 Feb	1862	President John Tyler dies.
29 Feb	1956	Eisenhower announces he will run for 2nd Term.
1 Mar	1961	By Executive Order, Kennedy creates the Peace Corps.
	1966	L. Johnson calls for full education in message to Congress.
2 Mar	1867	Congress passes the Tenure of Office Act.[15]
	1877	The committee appointed to decide the 1876 election names Hayes as President.

Date	*Year*	*Occurrence*
	1897	Cleveland vetoes Immigration bill.
3 Mar	1801	Adams appoints "Midnight" Judges.
	1817	Madison vetoes "Bonus Bill."[16]
	1837	Jackson recognizes Republic of Texas.
	1871	Grant forms Civil Service Commission.
	1881	James Garfield inaugurated as 20th President.
	1931	Hoover vetoes the Muscle Shoals Bill.[17] Signs bill making "The Star Spangled Banner" the national anthem of the United States.
	1966	L. Johnson signs Cold War GI Bill of Rights.
4 Mar	1793	Washington sworn in for 2nd term.
	1801	Thomas Jefferson inaugurated as 3rd President.
	1805	Jefferson inaugurated to 2nd term.
	1809	James Madison inaugurated as 4th President.
	1813	Madison inaugurated for 2nd term.
	1817	James Monroe inaugurated as 5th President.
	1821	Monroe inaugurated for 2nd term.
	1825	John Q. Adams inaugurated as 6th President.
	1829	Andrew Jackson inaugurated as 7th President.
	1833	Jackson inaugurated for 2nd term.
	1837	Martin Van Buren inaugurated as 8th President.
	1841	W. H. Harrison inaugurated as the 9th President.
	1845	James Polk inaugurated as the 11th President.
	1849	Polk signs bill organizing the Minnesota Territory.
	1853	Franklin Pierce inaugurated as the 14th President.
	1857	James Buchanan inaugurated as the 15th President.
	1861	Abraham Lincoln inaugurated as the 16th President.
	1865	Lincoln inaugurated for 2nd term.
	1869	Ulysses Grant inaugurated 18th President.
	1873	Grant inaugurated for 2nd term.
	1881	James Garfield inaugurated as 20th President.
	1885	Grover Cleveland inaugurated as 22nd President.
	1889	Benjamin Harrison inaugurated as 23rd President.
	1893	Grover Cleveland inaugurated as 24th President.
	1897	William McKinley inaugurated as 25th President.
	1901	McKinley inaugurated for 2nd term.
	1909	William Howard Taft inaugurated as 27th President.
	1913	Thomas Woodrow Wilson inaugurated as 28th President.
	1921	Warren Harding inaugurated as 29th President.
	1924	Calvin Coolidge inaugurated.
	1929	Herbert Hoover inaugurated as 31st President.
	1933	Franklin D. Roosevelt inaugurated as 32nd President.
5 Mar	1849	Zachary Taylor inaugurated as the 12th President.
	1877	Rutherford B. Hayes is inaugurated as the 19th President.
	1917	Wilson inaugurated for 2nd term.

Date	Year	Occurrence
	1913	Wilson addresses Congress regarding the tariff.
	1933	F. Roosevelt proclaims 4 day bank holiday.
7 Mar	1797	John Adams inaugurated as 2nd President.
	1956	Eisenhower refuses request from Israel for arms sale.
8 Mar	1801	Jefferson delivers 1st annual message to Congress.
	1822	Monroe requests Congress recognize South American Republics.
	1874	Millard Fillmore dies.
	1930	William Howard Taft dies.
10 Mar	1955	Eisenhower indicates that in case of war, U.S. will use nuclear weapons.
11 Mar	1813	Madison accepts Czar Alexander's offer to mediate dispute with Great Britain.
	1879	Hayes vetoes bill limiting Chinese immigration.
	1941	F. Roosevelt signs Lend/Lease Bill.
12 Mar	1933	FDR's first "Fireside Chat."
13 Mar	1868	Impeachment trial of Johnson begins.
	1901	Benjamin Harrison dies.
14 Mar	1907	By Presidential order T. Roosevelt excludes Japanese laborers from entering the country.
	1929	Hoover calls a special session of Congress to deal with the economy.
	1969	Nixon announces plans for ABM System.
16 Mar	1816	Monroe nominated for Presidency.
	1868	The Senate acquits A. Johnson by one vote.
17 Mar	1932	Hoover nominated for 2nd term.
18 Mar	1959	Eisenhower signs bill to make Hawaii 49th State.
19 Mar	1798	Adams advises Congress of failed negotiations with France.
	1809	Madison reinstates trade with Great Britain.
	2000	Independent counsel Robert Ray clears Clinton administration of criminal charges of wrongdoing.
20 Mar	1807	Jefferson sends order to Pickering and Monroe. He orders them to reopen negotiations with Great Britain.
	1933	F. Roosevelt signs Economy Act.
21 Mar	1907	T. Roosevelt sends Marines to Honduras.[18]
	1947	By Executive Order Truman institutes Loyalty Program.
23 Mar	1848	J. Q. Adams dies in the House of Representatives.
24 Mar	1947	The 22nd Amendment to the Constitution is proposed by Congress.[19]
25 Mar	2003	G. W. Bush asks Congress for funds for war with Iraq.
26 Mar	1961	Kennedy meets with British Prime Minister Harold Macmillian in Key West to discuss Laos.
27 Mar	2001	G. W. Bush refuses to sign Kyoto Protocol on environment.
	2002	G. W. Bush signs campaign reform bill.
28 Mar	1834	United States Senate censures President Jackson for removal of funds from the Bank of the United States.

Date	Year	Occurrence
	1969	Dwight D. Eisenhower dies.
29 Mar	1961	The 23rd Amendment is adopted.[20]
	1969	Dwight Eisenhower dies.
30 Mar	1791	Washington selects site of future capitol of U.S.
	1867	A. Johnson sends troops to Alaska, purchased from Russia for 2 cents an acre.
	1915	Wilson protests blockade of German ports.
	1952	Truman announces he will not run for President.
31 Mar	1814	President Madison requests Congress end embargo.
	1840	President Van Buren orders 10-hour workday.[21]
	1959	Eisenhower enacts a 3 month extension of unemployment.
	1968	L. Johnson ends bombing above the 21st parallel in Vietnam. L. Johnson announces he will not run for President.
	1980	Carter signs bill deregulating the banking industry.
	1981	John Hinckley, Jr., shoots Reagan, wounding him.
1 Apr	1954	Eisenhower establishes the United States Air Force Academy near Colorado Springs, Colorado.
	1957	Emergency Housing Act signed into law by Eisenhower.
	1998	Paula Jones' case against President Clinton dismissed.
2 Apr	1811	Madison names Monroe as Secretary of State.
	1866	A. Johnson declares the Civil War over in 10 states. Texas is not included.
	1917	Wilson requests Congress for declaration of war against Germany.
	1965	L. Johnson agrees to military and economic aid to South Vietnam.
	1980	Carter signs Crude Oil Windfall Profits Act.
3 Apr	1798	Adams reveals "XYZ" Affair.
	1939	F. Roosevelt signs the Administrative Reorganization Act.[22]
	1974	Nixon agrees to pay $432,787 in back taxes.
4 Apr	1841	William H. Harrison dies. John Tyler is sworn in as the 10th President.
	2002	G. W. Bush urges Israel to withdraw forces from Palestinian held parts of West Bank.
5 Apr	1865	Lincoln tours Richmond, VA.
	1979	Carter orders gradual end to price controls on oil.
6 Apr	1789	Washington elected President.
7 Apr	1954	Eisenhower first endorses use of foreign aid for the French in Indochina (Vietnam).
	1978	Carter announces decision to delay the neutron bomb.
8 Apr	1943	F. Roosevelt freezes wages and prices to stem inflation.
9 Apr	1914	Wilson refuses to recognize Victoriano Huerta as President of Mexico.
10 Apr	1877	Hayes orders federal troops out of South Carolina.[23]
11 Apr	1865	In what would be his final speech Lincoln asks for leniency toward the South.

Date	Year	Occurrence
	1898	McKinley delivers "War Message" to Congress.
	1941	By Executive Order, F. Roosevelt creates the Office of Price Administration.
	1951	Truman removes MacArthur as commander in Korea.
	1953	Eisenhower nominates Oveta Culp Hobby as Secretary of HEW.
12 Apr	1945	President Franklin D. Roosevelt dies of a stroke in Warm Springs, GA. Harry Truman sworn in as President.
13 Apr	1830	Jackson & John C. Calhoun exchange toasts.[24]
	1943	F. Roosevelt dedicates the Jefferson Memorial.
	1972	Nixon and Canadian Prime Minister Trudeau agree on plan to free Great Lakes of pollution.
14 Apr	1789	Washington informed of election.
	1795	Washington signs Jay's treaty with Great Britain.
	1865	John W. Booth assassinates Lincoln.
	1939	F. Roosevelt requests 10 peace guarantee from Hitler and Mussolini.
	1986	Reagan orders air attack on Libya.
15 Apr	1821	Monroe appoints Andrew Jackson as governor of Florida.
	1834	Jackson protests censure by Senate.
	1861	Lincoln declares a state of insurrection.
	1865	Abraham Lincoln dies of gunshot wound to the head. Andrew Johnson is sworn in as President.
16 Apr	1789	Washington begins journey to New York City.
	1898	McKinley receives permission from Congress to use U.S. troops in Cuba.
18 Apr	1853	Vice President William King dies.
19 Apr	1861	Lincoln orders a blockade of Southern ports.
	1914	Wilson requests permission from Congress the authority to respond with arms to Huerta.[25]
	1933	F. Roosevelt proclaims end of Gold Standard.
20 Apr	1812	Vice President George Clinton dies.
	1970	Nixon promises to withdraw 150,000 troops from Vietnam by end of year.
	1983	Reagan signs compromise bill for Social Security.
22 Apr	1874	Grant vetoes the Legal Tender Bill.
	1994	Richard M. Nixon dies.
23 Apr	1789	Washington arrives in New York City.
	1898	McKinley calls for volunteers to fight in Cuba.
	1990	G. H. W. Bush signs Hate Crimes Bill.
24 Apr	1981	Reagan lifts grain embargo to USSR.
	1996	Clinton signs Antiterrorism Bill.
25 Apr	1898	McKinley responds to Spain's declaration of war by declaring war with Spain.
	2003	G. W. Bush signs law banning import of "blood" diamonds.
26 Apr	1984	Reagan visits China.

65. Calender of Presidential Events

Date	Year	Occurrence
27 Apr	1793	Washington declares U.S. neutral in British/French War.
	1846	Polk signs Congressional Resolution on Oregon.
28 Apr	1952	Truman announces the formal cessation of war with Japan.
	1965	L. Johnson sends Marines to Dominican Republic.
29 Apr	1974	Nixon issues 1,200 page edited transcript of tapes requested by Senate committee.
30 Apr	1915	Wilson creates Naval Petroleum Reserve at Teapot Dome in Wyoming.
	1970	Nixon orders troops into Cambodia.
1 May	1844	Tyler is snubbed for election as the Whigs nominate Clay.
	1893	Cleveland opens the World Columbian Exposition in Chicago.[26]
	1982	Reagan attends opening ceremonies for World's Fair in Knoxville, TN.
5 May	1740	Van Buren nominated for reelection.
	1961	Kennedy signs the Fair Labor Standards Act.[27]
	1985	Reagan lays wreath at Bergen-Belsen concentration camp in West Germany.
6 May	1800	J. Adams requests resignation of James McHenry.[28]
	1960	Eisenhower signs Civil Rights Act of 1960.
7 May	1789	George Washington inaugurated as first President of the United States.
	1914	Wilson signs bill declaring the second Sunday in May as Mother's Day.
9 May	1977	Carter requests increase in Social Security tax.
10 May	1915	Nine days after the sinking of the Lusitania, Wilson speaks against involvement in the war.
	1948	Truman orders the Army to seize the railroads.
11 May	1935	By Executive Order F. Roosevelt establishes the Rural Electrification Administration.
	1950	Truman dedicates the Grand Coulee Dam.
	1957	Eisenhower meets with Vietnamese President Ngo Dinh Diem in Washington, D.C.
	1960	Eisenhower publicly admits the U.S. has been flying reconnaissance missions over the USSR.
12 May	1800	J. Adams fires Timothy Pickering as Secretary of State.
13 May	1800	J. Adams appoints John Marshall to replace Pickering.
	1846	Congress gives Polk a requested declaration of war with Mexico.
	1889	B. Harrison appoints T. Roosevelt to the Civil Service Commission.
14 May	1975	Ford orders ground, air and sea operation to recover the U.S. cargo vessel *Mayaguez*.
15 May	1797	J. Adams calls 1st special session of Congress.
	1942	F. Roosevelt approves the Women's Auxiliary Army Corps Act.
	1990	G. H. W. Bush starts 3 day budget summit with leaders of Congress.

Date	Year	Occurrence
16 May	1940	F. Roosevelt asks Congress to increase defense spending.
17 May	1962	Kennedy states that U.S. troops in Laos are a "diplomatic solution."
18 May	1812	Madison nominated for 2nd term.
19 May	1853	Pierce orders James Gadsen to negotiate with Mexico.
20 May	1835	Van Buren nominated for President.
	1862	Lincoln signs Homestead Act.[29]
	1868	Grant nominated for President.
22 May	1832	Jackson wins nomination for 2nd term.
	1909	Taft authorizes 700,000 acres of land in Washington, Montana, and Idaho opened to settlers.
	1947	Truman signs bill to aide Greece and Turkey.
	1953	Eisenhower signs the Submerged Lands Act.
	1972	Nixon leaves for USSR visit.[30]
25 May	1836	J. Q. Adams, in Congress, speaks against annexation of Texas.
	1898	McKinley requests 75,000 military volunteers.
	1940	F. Roosevelt creates the Office of Emergency Management.[31]
26 May	1922	Harding signs bill creating Federal Narcotics Control Board.
27 May	1830	Jackson vetoes the Maysville Road Bill.
	1860	Lincoln nominated for President.
	1941	F. Roosevelt declares a state of unlimited emergency.
	1943	F. Roosevelt creates Office of War Mobilization.
	1997	Supreme Court refuses to delay Paula Jones case of sexual harassment against President Clinton.
	2003	G. W. Bush signs law funding AIDS research and prevention in 14 Caribbean and African nations.
28 May	1798	J. Adams receives authorization to seize French ships.
	1830	Jackson signs Indian Removal Act.[32]
	1845	Polk orders Zachary Taylor into Texas.
	1868	A. Johnson's impeachment trial formally ends.
	1956	Eisenhower signs bill to create Soil Bank.[33]
	1984	Reagan leads tribute to unidentified servicemen killed in Vietnam.
	2003	G. W. Bush signs tax cut.
29 May	1865	A. Johnson begins his Reconstruction policy.[34]
	1975	Ford vetoes jobs bill.
30 May	1990	G. H. W. Bush begins 3 day meeting with Soviet Premier Mikhail Gorbachev in Washington, D.C.
31 May	1797	J. Adams signs treaty of commerce with France.
	1961	Kennedy flies to Paris to meet with French President Charles de Gaulle.
1 Jun	1812	Madison asks Congress for declaration of war against Great Britain.
	1868	James Buchanan dies.
	1952	Truman meets with General Eisenhower.

Date	Year	Occurrence
4 Jun	1863	Lincoln revokes Burnside's order suppressing the *Chicago Times*.
	1924	Coolidge nominated.
	1961	Kennedy meets with USSR Premier Nikita Khrushchev.
5 Jun	1852	Pierce nominated for President.
	1888	Cleveland nominated for 2nd term.
	2004	Ronald Reagan dies.
6 Jun	1846	Polk submits treaty with Great Britain to Congress.[35]
	1865	A. Johnson offers amnesty to prisoners of war who will swear an oath of allegiance.
	1872	Grant nominated for 2nd term.
	1934	F. Roosevelt sign Securities & Exchange Act.
7 Jun	1864	Lincoln is nominated for President by the Union Party.[36]
	1979	Carter approves MX Missile project.
8 Jun	1845	Andrew Jackson dies.
	1848	Zachary Taylor nominated for President.
	1880	Garfield nominated for President.
	1905	T. Roosevelt attempts to negotiate treaty between Russia and Japan.
	1969	Nixon meets with South Vietnam Premier Nguyen Van Thieu.
9 Jun	1915	Wilson demands Germany apologize for sinking the *Lusitania*.
	1941	F. Roosevelt orders troops to take over the North American Aviation Company.
	1956	Eisenhower is hospitalized after an attack of ileitis.
10 Jun	1892	B. Harrison nominated for 2nd term.
	1940	F. Roosevelt changes U.S. policy from neutral to "non-belligerency."
	1971	Nixon ends 15 year trade embargo to Mainland China.
12 Jun	1895	Cleveland asks citizens to refrain from giving aid and comfort to Cuban rebels.
	1920	Harding nominated for President.
	1963	Kennedy signs Executive Order creating President's Advisory Council on the Arts.
	1974	Nixon begins week long peace tour of Middle East.
13 Jun	1865	A. Johnson names provisional governors for Alabama, Georgia, Mississippi, Florida, South Carolina, and Texas.
	1973	Nixon freezes prices on retail goods.
	1989	G. H. W. Bush vetoes minimum wage bill.
14 Jun	1941	F. Roosevelt freezes the assets of Germany and Italy.
15 Jun	1849	James Polk dies.
	1928	Hoover nominated for President.
16 Jun	1876	Hayes nominated for President.
	1896	McKinley nominated for President.
	1900	McKinley receives nomination for 2nd term.
	1908	Taft wins Presidential nomination.

Date	*Year*	*Occurrence*
	1916	Wilson nominated for 2nd term.
	1930	Hoover signs the Hawley-Smoot Tariff Act.
16 Jun	1941	F. Roosevelt orders closing of all German consulates.
17 Jun	1986	Reagan announces retirement of Chief Justice Burger.
	1991	The body of Zachary Taylor is exhumed to be tested for poisoning.[37]
18 Jun	1912	Taft nominated for 2nd term.
	1970	Nixon signs bill lowering voting age to 18.
	1979	Carter signs Salt II agreement.
	1983	Reagan re-appoints Paul Volker to head the Federal Reserve Board.
19 Jun	1812	Madison declares war against Great Britain.
	1942	F. Roosevelt meets with British Prime Minister W. Churchill.
20 Jun	1923	Harding begins tour of the West and Alaska.
	1931	Hoover proposes a one year moratorium on inter-governmental debts.
	1940	F. Roosevelt appoints Henry Stimson Secretary of War and Frank Knox as Secretary of the Navy.
21 Jun	1904	T. Roosevelt nominated for President.
	1938	F. Roosevelt signs Emergency Relief Appropriations Act.
	1946	Truman names F. M. Vinson as Supreme Court Chief Justice.
22 Jun	1860	Buchanan vetoes Homestead Bill.
	1944	F. Roosevelt signs Serviceman's Readjustment Act.
23 Jun	1892	Cleveland nominated for the Presidency.
24 Jun	1908	Grover Cleveland dies.
	1948	Truman signs the Selective Service Act.
25 Jun	1888	Benjamin Harrison nominated for President.
	1938	F. Roosevelt signs Fair Labor Standards Act.
	1950	Truman authorizes U.S. Troops to aid Korea south of the 38th parallel.
26 Jun	1812	Madison orders envoy to Great Britain to negotiate an armistice.
	1936	F. Roosevelt nominated for a 2nd term.
	1963	Kennedy visits Berlin.
	1968	L. Johnson accepts Earl Warren's resignation as Chief Justice, and appoints Justice Abe Fortas to replace him.
	1990	G. H. W. Bush announces plans for tax hike.
27 Jun	1809	Madison appoints J. Q. Adams minister to Russia.
	1974	Nixon begins 5 day visit to USSR.
	1980	Carter signs bill requiring draft registration.
28 Jun	1836	James Madison dies.
	1941	By Executive Order F. Roosevelt establishes the Office of Scientific Research and Development.
29 Jun	1962	Kennedy pays state visit to Mexico.
30 Jun	1921	Harding appoints William Howard Taft as Chief Justice of the United States Supreme Court.

Date	Year	Occurrence
30 Jun	1950	Truman sends additional troops to South Korea.
	1959	Eisenhower signs bill extending debt ceiling.
	1961	Kennedy signs Fair Housing Act of 1961.
	1975	Ford signs bill extending unemployment compensation.
1 Jul	1932	FDR nominated for President.
2 Jul	1798	Adams names Washington as Commander in Chief of U.S. Army.[38]
	1807	Jefferson orders British warships out of U.S. waters.[39]
	1861	Lincoln suspends habeas corpus in exceptional cases.
	1862	Lincoln signs the Morrill Act.[40]
	1881	Garfield shot by Charles Guiteau.
	1912	Wilson nominated.
	1921	Harding signs bill to formally end World War.
	1964	L. Johnson signs Civil Rights Act of 1964.
3 Jul	1894	Cleveland declares interference with mail delivery unconstitutional.
4 Jul	1826	Presidents John Adams and Thomas Jefferson die just hours apart.
	1831	James Monroe dies.
	1840	Van Buren signs Independent Treasury Act into law.
	1864	Lincoln pocket vetoes Wade-Davis Reconstruction Bill.
	1903	T. Roosevelt sends first transatlantic message to the Philippines.
	1946	Truman proclaims the Philippines a republic.
5 Jul	1935	F. Roosevelt signs the National Labor Relations Act.
6 Jul	1945	Truman establishes the Medal of Freedom.
7 Jul	1952	Eisenhower receives Presidential nomination.
	1958	Eisenhower signs bill making Alaska the 49th state.[41]
8 Jul	1972	Nixon announces trade deal with Soviet Union.
	1975	Ford announces he is a candidate for 1976.
9 Jul	1850	Zachary Taylor dies of cholera.[42] Millard Fillmore sworn in as President.
	2003	U.S. Court of Appeals upholds President's authority to designate enemy combatants.
10 Jul	1832	Jackson vetoes bill to re-charter the Bank of the United States.
	1940	F. Roosevelt again asks Congress to increase defense spending.
	1971	Nixon announces acceptance of invitation to China by Premier Chou En-lai.
11 Jul	1836	Jackson orders only gold and silver may be used to buy government lands.
11 Jul	1878	Hayes removes Chester Arthur as Collector of Customs at the Port of New York.
	1884	Cleveland receives nomination for President.
	1960	John Kennedy nominated for President.
12 Jul	1954	Eisenhower proposes modernization of U.S. highways.
	1957	Eisenhower signs Housing Act.

Date	Year	Occurrence
14 Jul	1939	F. Roosevelt requests Congress repeal arms ban.
15 Jul	1946	Truman signs bill extending wartime price controls for one year.
	1948	Truman nominated for Presidency.
	1949	Truman signs Housing Act to aid with public housing.
	1976	Carter receives Presidential nomination.
16 Jul	1980	Reagan nominated for President.
	1992	Clinton nominated for President.
17 Jul	1945	Truman attends Potsdam Conference.
18 Jul	1940	F. Roosevelt nominated for 3rd term.
	1955	Eisenhower attends Geneva Summit.
19 Jul	1993	Clinton acts to end homosexual ban in military.
20 Jul	1950	Truman requests Congress to pass rearmament bill.
	1992	G. H. W. Bush re-nominated for President.
21 Jul	1932	Hoover signs relief & reconstruction act.
	1944	F. Roosevelt nominated for 4th term.
22 Jul	1998	Clinton signs bill to revamp the IRS.
23 Jul	1885	Ulysses Grant dies.
24 Jul	1862	Martin Van Buren dies.
	1929	Hoover declares Kellogg-Briand Act in effect.
	1974	United States Supreme Court orders Nixon to surrender tapes.
25 Jul	1941	F. Roosevelt freezes Japanese assets.
26 Jul	1941	F. Roosevelt nationalizes Philippines armed forces.
	1948	Truman bans segregation in the Armed Forces.
	1965	L. Johnson increases troop strength in South Vietnam.
27 Jul	1960	Richard Nixon nominated for President.
	1974	House Judiciary Committee approves two articles of impeachment against President Nixon.
29 Jul	1958	Eisenhower signs bill creating NASA.
	1990	G. H. W. Bush signs Americans with Disabilities Act.
30 Jul	1898	McKinley outlines peace terms to Spain.
	1965	L. Johnson signs Medicare Bill in Independence, MO, while former President Truman observes.
	2002	G. W. Bush signs legislation expanding regulation of U.S. accounting practices.
31 Jul	1793	Washington receives Jefferson's resignation as Secretary of State.
	1855	Pierce removes Andrew Reeder as Kansas governor, replaces him with Wilson Shannon.
	1875	Andrew Johnson dies.
	1948	Truman dedicates Idlewild International Airport in New York.
1 Aug	1946	Truman signs Fullbright Act.[43]
	1956	Eisenhower signs bill to extend Social Security coverage.
2 Aug	1793	Washington requests French government recall Citizen Genet.[44]
	1882	Arthur vetoes the Rivers and Harbors Bill for public works.

Date	Year	Occurrence
	1923	After returning from Alaska, President Harding suffers an attack of ptomaine poisoning, develops pneumonia and dies in San Francisco, CA.
	1927	Coolidge stops efforts to keep him on as President by stating "I choose not to run."
	1939	F. Roosevelt signs Hatch Act.
	1954	Eisenhower signs Housing Act of 1954.
3 Aug	1906	T. Roosevelt appoints W. H. Taft Provisional Governor of Cuba.
	1923	Calvin Coolidge sworn in as President.
	1981	Reagan fires 13,000 air traffic controllers.
5 Aug	1867	A. Johnson requests Stanton's resignation as Secretary of War.
	1912	T. Roosevelt nominated.[45]
	1933	F. Roosevelt establishes National Labor Board by Executive Order.
	1974	Nixon surrenders unedited transcripts of tapes.
6 Aug	1898	McKinley accepts Spain's surrender.
	1945	By order of President Truman, an atomic bomb is dropped on Hiroshima, Japan.
	1965	L. Johnson signs Voting Rights Act.[46]
	1993	Clinton's deficit reduction bill passes Senate.
7 Aug	1794	Washington issues proclamation against Whiskey Rebellion.
	1990	G. H. W. Bush orders troops to Saudi Arabia to counter Kuwait invasion.
8 Aug	1846	Polk asks Congress for 2 million dollars to purchase land from Mexico.
	1893	Cleveland asks for a repeal of the Sherman Silver Purchase Act.
	1968	Nixon receives nomination for President.
	1974	In a televised speech Nixon announces plans to resign.
	1978	Carter signs New York City bailout bill.
9 Aug	1934	F. Roosevelt nationalizes silver at $0.5001 cents per ounce.
	1945	By order of President Truman, an atomic bomb is dropped on Nagasaki, Japan.
	1974	At noon President Nixon's resignation becomes effective. Gerald Ford is sworn in as President.
	1989	G. H. W. Bush signs Savings & Loan Bailout Bill.
10 Aug	1988	Reagan signs legislation to give apologies and reparations to Japanese-Americans for WWII treatment.
	1989	G. H. W. Bush nominates Colin Powell as chairman of the Joint Chiefs of Staff.
11 Aug	1902	T. Roosevelt appoints Oliver Wendell Holmes as Associate Justice of the Supreme Court.
	1939	F. Roosevelt signs Social Security amendment.[47]
12 Aug	1955	Eisenhower signs Fair Labor Standards Act amendment.
	1970	Nixon signs bill making U.S. Post Office an independent government corporation.
14 Aug	1848	Polk signs bill organizing Oregon Territory.

Date	Year	Occurrence
	1935	F. Roosevelt signs Social Security into law.
	1971	Nixon announces 90-day wage, price and rent freeze.
	1980	Carter nominated for 2nd term.
16 Aug	1858	Buchanan sends greetings to Queen Victoria across new Atlantic cable.
17 Aug	1954	Eisenhower warns Communist China against invading Taiwan.
	1988	G. H. W. Bush nominated for President.
19 Aug	1914	Wilson declares the United States to be a neutral party in the conflict in Europe.
	1976	Ford nominated for President.
20 Aug	1866	A. Johnson declares an end to Civil War in Texas.
	1956	Eisenhower nominated for 2nd term.
21 Aug	1957	Eisenhower proposes 2-year nuclear test ban.
	1974	Ford nominates Nelson Rockefeller as Vice President.
22 Aug	1862	Lincoln announces his main objective is "to save the Union, and it is not either to save or to destroy slavery."[48]
	1911	Taft vetoes statehood for Arizona.[49]
	1997	Clinton signs Welfare Reform Bill.
23 Aug	1862	Lincoln's Emancipation Proclamation published.
	1972	Nixon receives nomination for 2nd term.
24 Aug	1814	President Madison and Cabinet witness defeat of U.S. forces at Bladensburg.
	1954	Eisenhower signs Communist Control Act.[50]
	1955	Eisenhower suffers heart attack.
25 Aug	1829	Mexico rejects President Jackson's offer to buy Texas.
	1950	Truman orders Army to seize railroads.
	1958	Law awarding pensions to former U.S. Presidents takes effect.[51]
	1994	Senate passes Clinton's anti-crime package.
26 Aug	1935	F. Roosevelt signs the Public Utilities Act.
	1937	F. Roosevelt signs the Judicial Reform Act.
	1964	L. Johnson nominated for Presidency.
27 Aug	1814	President Madison returns to the ruins of Washington, D.C., after the British looted the city.
28 Aug	1867	A. Johnson annexes Midway Islands.
29 Aug	1962	Kennedy names Arthur Goldberg[52] to replace Felix Frankfurter.
30 Aug	1861	Lincoln countermands order to free Missouri slaves.[53]
	1954	Eisenhower signs the Atomic Energy Bill.
31 Aug	1935	F. Roosevelt signs the Neutrality Act.
	1945	Truman requests Great Britain to admit 100,000 Jews to Palestine.
1 Sep	1983	Reagan condemns Soviet Union attack on KAL flight 007.
2 Sep	1947	Truman flies to Brazil to sign a mutual defense pact.[54]
	1958	Eisenhower signs the National Defense Education Act.[55]
3 Sep	1919	Wilson leaves to tour the country and garner support for the League of Nations.

65. Calender of Presidential Events

Date	Year	Occurrence
5 Sep	1837	In addressing special session of Congress Van Buren endorses Specie as currency.[56]
	1914	Wilson permits the Germans access to U.S. wireless stations.[57]
6 Sep	1901	President William McKinley shot.[58]
	1945	Truman recommends economic recovery plan to Congress.
7 Sep	2003	G. W. Bush asks Congress for additional war funds.
8 Sep	1939	F. Roosevelt proclaims limited national emergency.[59]
	1974	Ford grants Nixon pardon.
9 Sep	1856	Pierce appoints John W. Geary to succeed Wilson Shannon as governor of Kansas.
	1965	L. Johnson signs law creating the Department of Housing and Urban Development.
10 Sep	1833	To his cabinet Jackson announces plans to halt deposits to the Bank of the United States.
11 Sep	1990	G. H. W. Bush addresses joint session of Congress on Kuwait.
13 Sep	1987	100th anniversary of the United States Constitution.
14 Sep	1901	William McKinley dies. T. Roosevelt takes Oath of Office. F. Roosevelt bans shipping to China and Japan.
	1957	Eisenhower meets with Arkansas Gov. Faubus in order to prevent violence and desegregate Arkansas schools.
16 Sep	1940	F. Roosevelt signs Selective Service Act.
	1969	Nixon announces plan to withdraw 35,000 troops from Vietnam.
	1974	Ford grants Presidential Amnesty for Vietnam War draft evaders.
17 Sep	1796	Washington publishes farewell address.[60]
	1978	Carter begins Camp David meetings with Egyptian Prime Minister Sadat and Israeli Prime Minister Begin.
18 Sep	1793	Washington lays cornerstone for new Capitol.
	1900	Minnesota holds first direct Presidential Primary.
19 Sep	1881	President James Garfield dies of gunshot wounds suffered 2 July 1881.
20 Sep	1881	Chester Arthur is sworn in as 21st President.
	2001	G. W. Bush demands surrender of Taliban in Afghanistan.
21 Sep	1949	Truman signs Mutual Defense Assistance Act.
22 Sep	1891	B. Harrison opens 900,000 acres of Indian land to settlers.
	1961	Kennedy signs congressional act establishing the Peace Corps.
	1975	Sara Jane Moore shoots at President Ford.
23 Sep	1833	Jackson fires Sec. of Treasury William J. Duane and replaces him with Roger Taney.
	1952	Nixon delivers "Checkers" speech on nationwide TV.
24 Sep	1794	Washington issues 2nd proclamation against Whiskey Rebellion.
25 Sep	1957	Eisenhower order federal troops to Little Rock, Arkansas, to escort black students to school.

Date	Year	Occurrence
26 Sep	1940	F. Roosevelt declares embargo on scrap metal exports.
27 Sep	1938	F. Roosevelt urges Germany, Great Britain, France and Czecho-slovakia to find a peaceful settlement to the Sudetenland crisis.
28 Sep	1945	Truman issues Executive Order claiming all natural reserves beyond the continental shelf for the federal government.
29 Sep	1792	Washington issues proclamation on Whiskey Tax.
	1919	Wilson suffers stroke.
1 Oct	1953	Eisenhower invokes Taft-Hartley Act to prevent dockworkers strike.
2 Oct	1968	L. Johnson withdraws Abe Fortas as Chief Justice nominee.
	1981	Reagan presents 5 point program to strengthen nation's defense.
3 Oct	1863	Lincoln designates the last Thursday of November as Thanksgiving.
	1913	Wilson calls a special session of Congress to address the tariff issue.
	1965	L. Johnson signs act abolishing immigration quotas.
	1991	Bill Clinton, governor of Arkansas, declares he will run for President in 1992.
5 Oct	1947	Truman is the first U.S. President to speak on television.[61]
7 Oct	1854	Pierce appoints Andrew Reeder as territorial governor in Kansas.
	1942	F. Roosevelt announces plan for United Nations commission for war crimes investigation at end of war.
8 Oct	1869	Franklin Pierce dies.
9 Oct	1959	Eisenhower invokes Taft-Hartley to break steel workers strike.
10 Oct	1913	Wilson opens the Panama Canal.
	1962	Kennedy signs drug bill to safeguard citizens from harmful prescription drugs.
	1973	Vice President Spiro Agnew resigns from office.[62]
11 Oct	1962	Kennedy signs Trade Expansion Bill.
	1985	Reagan tells terrorists, "You can run, but you cannot hide."[63]
12 Oct	1945	Truman confers Medal of Honor on Private Desmond Doss.[64]
	1971	Nixon announces trip to Moscow next year.
13 Oct	1959	In ceremonies in Abilene, Kansas, Eisenhower breaks ground for his Presidential library.
14 Oct	1899	President McKinley becomes the first sitting President to ride in an automobile.[65]
15 Oct	1892	President B. Harrison opens Crow land in Montana to settlers.
	1950	Truman meets with General MacArthur to discuss Korea.
	1966	L. Johnson signs bill creating Department of Transportation.
	1974	Ford signs Campaign Reform Law.
16 Oct	1863	Lincoln names U.S. Grant as General of the Army of the West.
	1901	T. Roosevelt invites Booker Washington to the White House.
	2002	G. W. Bush signs law giving him power to take military action against Iraq.

Date	Year	Occurrence
18 Oct	1939	F. Roosevelt closes U.S. waters to submarines of belligerent nations.
19 Oct	1960	Eisenhower announces Columbia River Pact with Canada.
20 Oct	1964	Herbert Hoover dies.
	1973	Nixon orders Atty. Gen. Elliot Richardson to fire Special Prosecutor Archibald Cox.[66]
	1990	G. H. W. Bush vetoes Civil Rights Act of 1990.[67]
21 Oct	1814	Congress authorizes purchase of Jefferson's library to replace books burned by the British forces.
	1933	F. Roosevelt expands scope of Reconstruction Finance Corporation.[68]
	1964	Herbert Hoover dies.
	1986	Reagan signs budget reduction measure.
22 Oct	1851	Fillmore enjoins U.S. citizens from further military exploits in Mexico.
	1962	Kennedy announces the U.S. has proof of missiles in Cuba.
	1986	Reagan signs sweeping revision of tax code.
23 Oct	1992	G. H. W. Bush announces Vietnam agreement on U.S. forces missing in action.
25 Oct	1983	Reagan orders U.S. Marines into Grenada.
26 Oct	2001	G. W. Bush signs anti-terrorist bill.
27 Oct	1810	Madison annexes W. Florida.
	1993	Clinton unveils national health plan.
28 Oct	1945	Truman becomes 33rd Degree Mason.[69]
30 Oct	1972	Nixon signs Social Security amendment to give additional benefits to the elderly.
31 Oct	1968	L. Johnson ends all bombing in Vietnam.
1 Nov	1861	Lincoln names McClellan General-in-Chief of the Army.
	1950	Two Cuban nationals attempt to assassinate President Truman.[70]
2 Nov	1810	Madison reinstates trade with France.
	1852	Pierce elected President.
	1880	Garfield elected President.
	1920	Harding elected President.
	1948	Truman elected President.
	1976	Carter elected president.
	2004	G. W. Bush re-elected.
3 Nov	1862	Lincoln replaces Gen. McClellan with Gen. Burnside as head of the Army of the Potomac.
	1896	McKinley elected President.
	1908	Taft elected President.
	1936	F. Roosevelt re-elected.
	1964	L. Johnson elected President.
	1966	L. Johnson signs Truth in Packaging Bill.
	1983	Reagan signs bill creating Martin Luther King, Jr. Day.
	1992	Clinton wins Presidency.

Date	*Year*	*Occurrence*
4 Nov	1813	Madison appoints J. Q. Adams as chief negotiator to Great Britain.
	1856	Buchanan wins election as President.
	1884	Cleveland elected President.
	1904	T. Roosevelt wins Presidency.
	1924	Coolidge wins Presidency.
	1939	F. Roosevelt signs Neutrality Act of 1939.
	1952	Eisenhower elected President.
	1980	Reagan elected President.
5 Nov	1811	Madison calls for increased defense.
	1872	Grant re-elected.
	1912	Wilson elected.[71]
	1940	F. Roosevelt elected to 3rd term.
	1997	Clinton re-elected.
	2003	G. W. Bush signs partial abortion bill.
6 Nov	1860	Lincoln elected President.
	1888	Cleveland receives a majority of the popular vote, but B. Harrison wins the electoral vote and the Presidency.
	1900	McKinley re-elected.
	1928	Hoover elected President.
	1956	Eisenhower re-elected.
	1968	Nixon wins Presidential election.
	1984	Reagan elected to 2nd term.
	1990	G. H. W. Bush doubles the Persian Gulf Force.
7 Nov	1848	Taylor elected President.
	1876	Tilden wins Presidential election.
	1916	Wilson re-elected.
	1944	F. Roosevelt elected to 4th term.
	1972	Nixon re-elected.
	1973	Nixon delivers televised address on the energy crisis.
	2000	Due to necessary recounts in Florida, Presidential election is inconclusive.
8 Nov	1864	Lincoln re-elected President.
	1892	Cleveland elected President.
	1931	In annual message to Congress, Hoover requests emergency Reconstruction Finance Corporation.
	1932	FDR elected President.
	1933	F. Roosevelt establishes Civil Works Administration by Executive Order.
	1960	Kennedy elected President.
	1988	G. H. W. Bush elected President.
9 Nov	1906	T. Roosevelt travels to Panama to inspect Canal progress.[72]
12 Nov	1971	Nixon withdraws 45,000 troops from Vietnam.
13 Nov	1987	In a televised speech Reagan addresses the nation on the Iran-Contra Affair.

Date	Year	Occurrence
14 Nov	1971	Nixon institutes flexible wage and price controls.
15 Nov	1958	Eisenhower rejects Soviet proposal for permanent atomic test ban.
	1990	G. H. W. Bush signs Clean Air Act.
	1991	G. H. W. Bush signs a compromise bill on unemployment.
16 Nov	1863	Lincoln delivers his Gettysburg Address.
	1933	F. Roosevelt reestablishes relations with the USSR.
	1973	Nixon signs Alaska Pipeline Bill.
17 Nov	1800	Adams moves into White House.
18 Nov	1886	Chester Arthur dies.
	1952	Truman meets with Eisenhower.
19 Nov	1928	Prior to inauguration, Hoover takes a goodwill trip to South America.
20 Nov	1940	F. Roosevelt establishes the Office of Production Management.
	1952	Eisenhower names John Foster Dulles as Secretary of State.
	1962	The crisis having been resolved, Kennedy ends Naval quarantine of Cuba. By Executive Order Kennedy orders federal agencies to end racial discrimination.
	1967	L. Johnson signs bill creating the National Commission on Product Safety.
21 Nov	1899	Vice President Garret Hobart dies.
	1929	Hoover meets with business and trade leaders.
22 Nov	1875	Vice President Henry Wilson dies.
	1943	F. Roosevelt meets W. Churchill in Cairo for 3 days.
	1963	President John Kennedy is assassinated in Dallas by Lee Harvey Oswald. Lyndon Johnson takes oath as President.
25 Nov	1957	Eisenhower suffers stroke.
	1969	Nixon orders destruction of all germ warfare stockpiles.
26 Nov	1791	Washington holds 1st Cabinet meeting.
	1974	Ford signs Mass Transit Bill.
	1975	Ford announces decision to aid New York City.
27 Nov	1963	L. Johnson assures Congress and the nation that he will continue Kennedy's policies.
28 Nov	1943	F. Roosevelt meets with J. Stalin & W. Churchill in Teheran.
	1972	Nixon begins to reorganize Cabinet.
29 Nov	1963	L. Johnson appoints the Warren Commission to investigate the Kennedy assassination.
	1993	Clinton signs Brady Handgun Bill.
1 Dec	1824	No winner in Presidential election.[73]
	1865	Johnson restores writ of habeas corpus.
	1953	Eisenhower proposes Atoms for Peace in U.N. Address.
	1988	Reagan withholds documents on Iran-Contra matters from Lt. Colonel Oliver North's lawyers.
2 Dec	1806	Jefferson requests ban on slave importation.
	1812	Madison reelected.

Date	*Year*	*Occurrence*
	1817	In first message to Congress, Monroe states Congress has no authority to pass bills on public works programs.
	1823	In annual message to Congress the President presents the Monroe Doctrine.
	1834	Jackson delivers annual message to Congress.
	1840	W. H. Harrison elected President.
	1845	In 1st annual address to Congress, Polk claims Oregon.[74]
	1930	Hoover asks Congress for money for public works.
3 Dec	1800	Presidential election inconclusive.
	1828	Andrew Jackson elected President.
	1833	Jackson makes annual address to Congress.
	1844	In his annual address to the Congress, Tyler requests annexation of Texas.
	1860	In his final address to Congress, Buchanan speaks against secession.
	1868	Grant elected President.
	1901	T. Roosevelt addresses Congress, and declares need to regulate trusts.
	1929	In his annual message to Congress, Hoover declares faith in the economy.
4 Dec	1816	Monroe elected President.
	1839	W. H. Harrison nominated for President by the Whigs.
	1844	Polk elected President.
	1849	Taylor urges Congress to admit California as a state. He also threatens to crush any attempt at secession.
	1857	Buchanan requests troops to calm Mormon disturbances in Utah.
	1918	Wilson sails for Europe for peace talks.
	1942	F. Roosevelt closes Work Projects Administration.
5 Dec	1792	Electoral College elects Washington to 2nd term.
	1804	Jefferson elected to 2nd term.
	1815	In address to Congress, President Madison requests authorization of public works program.
	1831	J. Q. Adams takes seat in Congress, the only former President to do so.
	1832	Jackson re-elected.
	1899	In his annual address to Congress, President McKinley speaks against trusts.
	1952	Eisenhower visits Korea.
6 Dec	1820	Monroe reelected without serious opposition.
	1825	President J. Q. Adams delivers first annual message to Congress.
	1829	President Jackson delivers annual message to Congress.
	1830	In his annual address to Congress, President Jackson attacks the Bank of the United States.

Date	*Year*	*Occurrence*
6 Dec	1836	Van Buren elected President.
	1847	Abraham Lincoln takes seat in House of Representatives.
	1858	In his annual message to Congress Buchanan requests funds to buy Cuba.
	1864	Lincoln appoints Salmon P. Chase as Chief Justice of the United States Supreme Court.
	1887	In annual address to Congress Cleveland requests a reduction in tariffs.
	1904	In his annual address to Congress T. Roosevelt announces the Roosevelt Corollary.[75]
	1973	Gerald Ford is sworn in as Vice President.[76]
7 Dec	1796	Adams elected as President.
	1808	Madison elected.[77]
	1835	In his annual address to Congress, Jackson requests law to prevent the post office from delivering anti-slavery material in the South.
	1915	Wilson requests a standing army of 142,000 and a reserve force of 400,000.
	1991	G. H. W. Bush leads observance of 50th anniversary of Pearl Harbor bombing by Japanese.
8 Dec	1829	Jackson delivers annual message to Congress.
	1931	Hoover asks Congress to establish an emergency Reconstruction Finance Corporation.
	1941	F. Roosevelt delivers "Day of Infamy" speech to Congress.[78]
	1950	Truman bans shipments to Communist China.
	2003	G. W. Bush signs Medicare reform.
9 Dec	1813	Madison calls for embargo against Great Britain.
10 Dec	1832	Jackson warns South Carolina against secession.
12 Dec	1985	Reagan signs the Gramm-Rudman Balanced Budget Bill.
13 Dec.	2000	G. W. Bush declared winner in Presidential election.
	2001	G. W. Bush announces U.S. will withdraw from 1972 Antiballistic Missile Treaty with Russia.
14 Dec	1799	George Washington dies.
16 Dec	1835	W. H. Harrison nominated for President by Anti-Masons.
	1907	T. Roosevelt dispatches "The Great White Fleet" on a world tour.
	1954	Eisenhower names Nelson Rockefeller special assistant on foreign policy.
	1957	Eisenhower leaves for Paris to attend NATO Summit meeting.
18 Dec	1807	Jefferson requests embargo on foreign trade.
	1916	Wilson asks warring powers for their conditions for peace.
	1941	F. Roosevelt creates commission to investigate Pearl Harbor attack.
	1972	Nixon resumes bombing of North Vietnam.
19 Dec	1859	Buchanan opposes slave trade in annual message.

Date	Year	Occurrence
	1941	F. Roosevelt creates the Office of Censorship.[79]
	1974	Rockefeller sworn in as Vice President.
	1998	The House votes on party lines to impeach President Clinton.
20 Dec	1941	F. Roosevelt signs the Draft Act.
	1989	G. H. W. Bush orders troops to Panama to arrest Gen. Manuel Noriega.
21 Dec	1895	Cleveland presents Congress with evidence of Great Britain's intended intrusion into Venezuela.
23 Dec	1913	Wilson presses for reform in banking.
24 Dec	1943	F. Roosevelt announces Eisenhower will be Supreme Commander of European invasion.
25 Dec	1868	Johnson proclaims amnesty for all parties in the Rebellion.
26 Dec	1799	Washington eulogy delivered by Lighthouse Lee.
	1972	Truman dies.
30 Dec	1969	Nixon signs tax reduction bill.
31 Dec	1793	Washington replaces Thomas Jefferson with Edmund Randolph as Secretary of State.
	1860	Buchanan authorizes relief to Fort Sumter.
	1945	Truman dismantles War Labor Board. It is replaced with the Wage Stabilization Board.
	1946	Truman proclaims WWII officially over.

NOTES

1. This was done to stop U.S. citizens from interfering with the Canadian Revolution.

2. Known as the Eisenhower Doctrine, this gives arms to any country requesting aid. It is approved by Congress 7 March 1957.

3. This is the only time a President has had a brother as a Cabinet member.

4. To this date the states had voted on different days, with the Electoral College meeting in early December to elect the President. This act established a national election day as the first Tuesday following the first Monday of November.

5. The committee consisted of 7 Democrats from the Democratically controlled House and 7 Republicans from the Republican controlled Senate. The 15th member was an impartial Republican judge. All votes were 8 Republicans against 7 Democrats.

6. Jackson was unhurt as both pistols misfired.

7. The legislation Truman submitted called for an end of segregation in schools and an end to discrimination in employment.

8. The test took place in 1952 at Eniwetok Atoll in the Pacific.

9. Lincoln met with a delegation from the Confederacy on a ship off Hampton Roads, VA. The South's demands for autonomy deadlocked the talks.

10. In order to avoid a repeat of 1876, this act allows each state to validate its own electoral votes.

11. The 20th Amendment changed the date of inauguration from 4 March to 20 Jan.

12. FDR was not injured, but Mayor Anton Cermak of Chicago died of bullet wounds on 6 March 1933.

13. This act reduced income taxes, surtaxes, and other taxes in order to reduce government at the federal level.

14. This bill would have allowed veterans to borrow against their bonus certificates.

15. This act would be the basis for impeachment action against the President. It denied the President power to remove officials, who had been approved or appointed by Congress, from office.

16. Madison vetoed this bill in the belief that a constitutional amendment was needed for the federal government to involve itself in internal improvements.

17. Called for federal takeover of the Muscle Shoals hydroelectric facility.

18. Under the Roosevelt Corollary, the President acted to quell a revolution and protect life and property.

19. This amendment limits the President to two four-year terms.

20. This allows citizens of Washington, D. C. to vote in Presidential elections.

21. This order applied to federal employees on public work projects.

22. This act allows the President to examine and reorganize federal agencies.

23. Part of the agreement on the 1876 election settlement was that the Republicans end Reconstruction.

24. At a party to celebrate Thomas Jefferson's birthday, the subject of a state's right to nullify an action by the federal government arose. Jackson, supporting the government, lifted his glass and proposed the toast "Our Federal Union — it must, and shall be preserved." Vice President Calhoun replied, "The Union — next to our liberty, the most dear." The issue would continue until the Civil War.

25. Congress granted permission. Huerta was allowing Vera Cruz to be used as a supply port for Germany. U.S. forces seized the port.

26. The World Columbian Exposition commemorated the 400th anniversary of Columbus' voyage to the New World.

27. This raised the minimum hourly wage to $1.15 and then to $1.25 by Sept. 1963.

28. Adams was convinced that James McHenry, his Secretary of War, was involved in a plot to defeat him for reelection.

29. This allowed settlers to acquire up to 160 acres from the government for $1.25 an acre.

30. This is the first time a U.S. President has visited the USSR in peacetime.

31. Roosevelt took this action in anticipation of the U.S. entry into the war.

32. This bill moved the Eastern Indians west. Jackson's goal was for whites to occupy Mississippi.

33. The purpose of this bill was to reduce farm surplus and maintain prices for farmers.

34. Johnson's Reconstruction policy, or restoration as Johnson called it, is very similar to Lincoln's.

35. This treaty established the Oregon border as latitude 40 degrees.

36. While the Union Party is really the Republican Party renamed to attract Democrats, Lincoln is the only President to serve under two party banners.

37. There were allegations that Taylor had been intentionally poisoned. No supporting proof was found.

38. Adams was fearful of the possibility of war.

39. Jefferson took this action in response to the 22 June 1807 incident involving the USS *Leopold-Chesapeake*.

40. The Morrill Act gave federal land to states for establishing agricultural colleges.

41. It had been 45 years since New Mexico was admitted.

42. There are claims that Taylor died of food poisoning.

43. This act created a program for international education exchange.

44. This was brought on by Genet's conduct towards the U.S. in the French war with Great Britain.

45. Teddy bolted the Republican Party and formed the Bull Moose Party.

46. This act empowered the federal government to suspend literacy, knowledge, or character tests for voting.

47. This increased the number of people covered by Social Security.

48. Lincoln was responding to Horace Greeley's editorial "A Prayer of Twenty Million."

49. Arizona's constitution permitted recall of judges. Taft was a man of law and found this objectionable. Arizona removed the provision, and once statehood was granted, reinstated it.

50. This act stripped the Communist Party in the U.S. of immunity and privileges, and subjected the party to penalties under the Internal Security Act.

51. At this point only Herbert Hoover and Harry Truman are alive.

52. Goldberg had been Labor Secretary.

53. Under martial law General Fremont had ordered slaves of secessionists freed.

54. The pact was signed at the Inter-American Defense Conference.

55. Granted government-backed student loans and supported education in the sciences.

56. In the same speech Van Buren condemned state chartered banks.

57. The Germans will use this access to transmit information gathered by spies.

58. While attending a reception at the American Exhibition in Buffalo, N.Y., McKinley is shot by Leon Czolgosz, an anarchist.

59. F. Roosevelt took this action because of Hitler's invasion of Poland. This proclamation made it easier to act in time of emergency.

60. This address is never delivered orally by Washington.

61. Truman spoke on the world food crisis.

62. Agnew had pleaded "No Contest" to charges of tax evasion. This was a result of illegal payoffs received from contractors while he was governor of Maryland.

63. Reagan made this statement after Navy F-14 Tomcats intercepted and forced down a plane with hijackers of the Italian cruise ship *Achille Lauro* aboard.

64. Doss was a conscientious objector who served with distinction as a Medical Corpsman in the Pacific Theater during WWII.

65. McKinley rode in a Stanley Steamer.

66. Cox was investigating Watergate and had refused Nixon's compromise offer of submitting transcripts of private tapes, rather than the tapes themselves. Richardson and his assistant Ruckelshaus resign rather than comply. Cox is then fired by Robert Bork, 3rd in line at the Justice Department. This became known as the Friday Night Massacre, and would lead Congress to begin impeachment proceedings.

67. G. H. W. Bush felt that this act would lead to widespread use of quotas. The Senate failed by one vote to override the veto.

68. The purpose of this agency was to assist on several fronts—including agriculture, housing, banking, and disaster relief—in efforts to overcome the effects of the Depression.

69. Truman is the only U.S. President so honored.

70. Truman was in residence at Blair House while the White House was being renovated. He escaped injury. One of the Cubans, Griselio Torresola, was killed and the other, Oscar Collazo, was wounded. At his trial he received a life sentence.

71. T. Roosevelt and Taft split a majority of the vote. Wilson won with a plurality of the popular vote, but a majority of the electoral vote.

72. This trip marks T. Roosevelt as the first President to travel outside the country while President.

73. Jackson received 99 electoral votes; J. Q. Adams received 84; William Crawford 41; and Henry Clay 37. The election was thrown into the House of Representatives. They were to choose among the top three vote getters. The House voted for J. Q. Adams.

74. In an elaboration of the Monroe Doctrine, Polk warned Russia and other foreign powers against colonizing Oregon. This became known as the Polk Doctrine.

75. In this address T. Roosevelt expanded the Monroe Doctrine.

76. Ford becomes the first appointed Vice President.

77. Jefferson was offered and refused a third term.

78. This followed Japan's attack on Pearl Harbor 7 Dec. 1941. In this speech F. Roosevelt requested Congress to declare that a state of war existed between the United States and Japan.

79. This office was created to control the information vital to war efforts.

66. Presidential Quotes

Presented in order of service.

George Washington

"To be prepared for war is one of the most effectual means of preserving peace."

"As the sword was the last resort for the preservation of our liberties, so it ought to be the first to be laid aside when those liberties are firmly established."

"Government is not reason; it is not eloquence; it is force! Like fire, it is a dangerous servant and a fearful master."

"Few men have virtue to withstand the highest bidder."

John Adams

"A pen is certainly an excellent instrument to fix a man's attention and to inflame his ambition."

"Let every sluice of knowledge be open and set a-flowing."

"By my physical constitution, I am but an ordinary man. The times alone have destined me to fame — and even these have not been able to give me much."

"I pray Heaven to bestow the best of blessing on this house and on all that shall hereafter inhabit it. May none but honest and wise men ever rule under this roof!" (In reference to the White House)

Thomas Jefferson

"The price of freedom is eternal vigilance."

"One man with courage is a majority."

"That government is best which governs the least, because its people discipline themselves."

James Madison

"The truth is that all men having power ought to be mistrusted."

"I believe there are more instances of the abridgement of the freedom of the people by gradual and silent encroachments of those in power than by violent and sudden usurpations."

"The problem to be solved is, not what form of government is perfect, but which of the forms is least imperfect."

James Monroe

"A little flattery will support a man through great fatigue."

"National honor is a national property of the highest value."

"The American continents ... are henceforth not to be considered as subjects for future colonization by any European powers." (Monroe Doctrine)

John Quincy Adams

"Always vote for principle, though you may vote alone, and you may cherish the sweetest reflection that your vote is never lost."

"The art of making love, muffled up in furs, in the open air, with the thermometer at Zero, is a Yankee invention, which requires a Yankee poet to describe."

"May our country be always successful, but whether successful or otherwise, always right."

Andrew Jackson

"I know what I am fit for. I can command a body of men in a rough way; but I am not fit to be President."

"In general, the great can protect themselves, but the poor and humble, require the arm and shield of the law."

"Our Federal Union — it must, and shall be preserved."

Martin Van Buren

"It is easier to do a job right than to explain why you didn't."

"...the less government interferes with private pursuits the better for the general prosperity."

"As to the Presidency, the two happiest days of my life were those of my entrance upon the office and my surrender of it."

William H. Harrison

"All the measure of the Government are directed to the purpose of making the rich richer and the poor poorer."

"But I contend that the strongest of all governments is that which is most free."

"The people are the best guardians of their own rights and it is the duty of their executive to abstain from interfering in or thwarting the sacred exercise of the lawmaking functions of their government."

John Tyler

"Wealth can only be accumulated by the earnings of industry and the savings of frugality."

"If the tide of defamation and abuse shall turn, and my administration come to be praised, future Vice-Presidents may feel some slight encouragement to pursue an independent course."

"Give the President control over the purse ... and I care not what you call him, he is every inch a king."

James K. Polk

"I would keep as much money in the treasury as the safety of the Government required, and no more. I would keep no surplus revenue there to scramble for, either for internal improvements, or for any thing else. I would bring the Government back to what it was intended to be — a plain economical Government."

"With me it is exceptionally true that the Presidency is no bed of roses."

"I am heartily rejoiced that my term is so near its close. I will soon cease to be a servant and will become a sovereign."

Zachary Taylor

"It would be judicious to act with magnanimity towards a prostrate foe."

"The power given by the Constitution to the Executive to interpose his veto is a high conservative power: but in my opinion it should never be exercised except in cases of clear violation of the Constitution, or manifest haste and want of due consideration by Congress."

"The idea that I should become President seems to me too visionary to require a serious answer. It has never entered my head, nor is it likely to enter the head of any other person."

Millard Fillmore

"An honorable defeat is better than a dishonorable victory."

"The man who can look upon a crisis without being willing to offer himself upon the altar of his country is not fit for public trust."

"It is not strange ... to mistake change for progress."

Franklin Pierce

"The storm of frenzy and faction must inevitable dash itself in vain against the unshaken rock of the Constitution."

"In a body (Congress) where there are more than one hundred talking lawyers ... you can make no calculation upon the termination of any debate and frequently the more trifling the subject the more animated and protracted the discussion."

"The revenue of the country levied almost insensibly to the taxpayer, goes on from year to year, increasing beyond either the interests or the prospective wants of the Government."

James Buchanan

"There is nothing stable but Heaven and the Constitution."

"The ballot box is the surest arbiter of disputes among freemen."

To Lincoln: "My dear, sir, if you are as happy on entering the White House as I on leaving, you are a very happy man indeed."

Abraham Lincoln

"The best thing about the future is that it only comes one day at a time."

"Whatever you are, be a good one."

"Things come to those who wait, but only things left by those who hustle."

Andrew Johnson

"There are no good laws but such as repeal other laws."

"The goal is to strive for a poor government but a rich people."

"Honest conviction is my courage; the Constitution is my guide."

Ulysses S. Grant

"My failures have been errors of judgment, not of intent."

"The truth is I am more of a farmer than a soldier.... I never went into the army without regret and never retired without pleasure."

"I have never advocated war except as a means of peace."

Rutherford B. Hayes

"Fighting battles is like courting girls: those who make the most pretensions and are boldest usually win."

"My policy is trust ... peace and put aside the bayonet."

"It is now true that this is God's Country, if equal rights ... a fair start and an equal chance in the race of life are everywhere secured to all."

James A. Garfield

"I have had many troubles in my life, but the worst of them never came."

"A brave man is a man who dares to look the Devil in the face and tell him he is a Devil."

"I would rather believe something and suffer for it, than to slide along into success without opinions."

Chester A. Arthur

"I may be President of the United States, but my private life is nobody's damn business."

"If it were not for the reporters, I would tell you the truth."

"Good ballplayers make good citizens."

Grover Cleveland

"Above all tell the truth."

"A man is known by the company he keeps, and also by the company from which he is kept out."

"It is the responsibility of the citizens to support their government. It is not the responsibility of the government to support its citizens."

Benjamin Harrison

"Lincoln had faith in time, and time has justified his faith."

"Indiscriminate denunciation of the rich is mischievous."

"We Americans have no commission from God to police the world."

William McKinley

"Unlike any other nation, here the people rule, and their will is the supreme law."

"In the time of darkest defeat, victory may be nearest."

"That's all a man can hope for during his lifetime ... to set an example ... and when he is dead to be an inspiration for history."

Teddy Roosevelt

"No man is justified in doing evil in the name of expediency."

"A man who is good enough to shed his blood for his country is good enough to be given a square deal afterward. More than that no man is entitled to, and less than that no man should have."

"I wish to preach not the doctrine of ignoble ease, but the doctrine of the strenuous life."

William H. Taft

"I have come to the conclusion that the major part of the President is to increase the gate receipts of expositions and fairs and bring tourists into the town."

"Politics, when I'm in it, makes me sick."

"Next to liberty, the right of property is the most important individual right guaranteed by the Constitution."

Woodrow Wilson

"We grow great by dreams. All big men are dreamers."

"If you want to make enemies, try to change something."

"It is not men that interest or disturb me primarily; it is ideas. Ideas live; men die."

Warren G. Harding

"My God, this is a hell of a job! I have no trouble with my enemies ... but my damn friends, they're the ones that keep me walking the floor nights."

"Ambition is a commendable attribute without which no man succeeds. Only inconsiderate ambition imperils."

"It is my conviction that the fundamental trouble with the people of the United States is that they have gotten too far away from Almighty God."

Calvin Coolidge

"The business of America is business."

"Four-fifths of all our troubles in this life would disappear if we would only sit down and keep still."

"I have never been hurt by anything I didn't say."

Herbert C. Hoover

"Absolute freedom of the press ... is a founding stone of American liberty."

"War is a losing business."

"True Liberalism is found not in striving to spread bureaucracy but in striving to set bounds to it."

Franklin D. Roosevelt

"Happiness lies in the joy of achievement and the thrill of creative effort."

"The only thing we have to fear is fear itself."

"A good leader can't get too far ahead of his followers."

Harry S Truman

"We need not fear the expression of ideas—we do need to fear their suppression."

"Within the first few months, I discovered that being a President is like riding a tiger. A man has to keep on riding or be swallowed."

"You can not stop the spread of an idea by passing a law against it."

Dwight D. Eisenhower

"It's not the size of the dog in the fight, but the size of the fight in the dog."

"America is best described by one word, freedom."

"I never saw a pessimistic general win a battle."

John F. Kennedy

"Ask not what your country can do for you, ask what you can do for your country."

"If we cannot end now our differences, at least we can help make the world safe for diversity."

"The American, by nature, is optimistic. He is experiential, an inventor, and a builder who builds best when called upon to build greatly."

Lyndon B. Johnson

"You ain't learnin' nothin' when you're talkin.'"

"A President's hardest task is not to do what is right, but to know what is right."

"For this is what America is all about. It is the uncrossed desert and the unclimbed ridge. It is the star that is not reached and the harvest sleeping in the unplowed ground..."

Richard M. Nixon

"I like the job I have, but if I had to live my life over again, I would have ended up a sports writer."

"Any culture which can put a man on the Moon is capable of gathering all the nations of the earth in peace, justice, and concord."

"Once a man has been in politics, once that's been his life, he will always return if the people want him."

"A man who has never lost himself in a cause bigger than himself has missed one of life's mountaintop experiences. Only in losing himself does he find himself."

Gerald R. Ford

"Truth is the glue that holds governments together."

"A government big enough to give you everything you want is a government big enough to take from you everything you have."

"We ... declared our independence 200 years ago, and we are not about to lose it now to paper shufflers and computers."

James E. Carter

"We must adjust to changing times and still hold to unchanging principles."

"The passage of the civil rights act during the 1960's was the greatest thing to happen to the South in my lifetime. It lifted a burden from the whites as well as the blacks."

"The best way to enhance freedom in other lands is to demonstrate here that our democratic system is worthy of emulation."

Ronald W. Reagan

"America is too great for small dreams."

"What I'd really like to do is go down in history as the President who made Americans believe in themselves again."

"Freedom is not the sole prerogative of a chosen few; it is the universal right of all God's children."

George H. W. Bush

"The United States is the best and fairest and most decent nation on the face of the earth."

"I'm a conservative, but I'm not a nut about it."

"Don't try to fine-tune somebody else's view.

William J. Clinton

"There is nothing wrong in America that can't be fixed with what is right in America."

"Politics is about economics. People forget that the New Deal was an economic program. A lot of social good came out of it, but it was an economic program."

"I refuse to be a part of a generation that celebrates the death of communism abroad with the loss of the American Dream at home."

George W. Bush

"If you don't feel something strongly you're not going to achieve it."

"You know what's interesting about Washington? It's the kind of place where second-guessing has become second nature."

"Government can hand out money. But what it cannot do is put hope in our hearts and a sense of purpose in our lives."

---

67. Books by Presidents

Some of our Chief Executives were prolific authors. Kennedy wrote two immensely popular books prior to becoming President. Most wrote memoirs; some wrote on the political scene of their time. Some were published posthumously. All found a ready market for their works.

President	Books
Washington	No known works
Adams	*A Defense of the Constitutions of Government of the United States* (3 vols., 1787–1788); *Discourses on Davila* (1805); *Diary and Autobiography of John Adams*[1] (4 vols., 1960)
Jefferson	*Notes on the State of Virginia* (1785)
Madison	*The Papers of James Madison* (3 vols., 1840)
Monroe	*A View of the Conduct of the Executive in the Foreign Affairs of the United States* (1797)

67. Books by Presidents

President   *Books*

J. Q. Adams   *Dermot MacMorrogh*[2] (1832); *The Lives of James Madison and James Monroe* (1850)
Jackson   No known works
Van Buren   No known works
W. H. Harrison   No known works
Tyler   No known works
Polk   *The Diary of James K. Polk during His Presidency, 1845–to 1849*[3] (4 vols., 1910)
Taylor   No known works
Pierce   No known works
Buchanan   *Mr. Buchanan's Administration on the Eve of the Rebellion* (1896)
Lincoln   No known works
A. Johnson   No known works
Grant   *Personal Memoirs of U.S. Grant* (2 vols., 1885)
Hayes   No known works
Garfield   No known works
Arthur   No known works
Cleveland   *Presidential Problems* (1904); *Fishing and Shooting Sketched* (1906); *Good Citizenship* (1908)
B. Harrison   *This Century of Ours* (1897); *Views of an Ex-President* (1901)
McKinley   *The Tariff in the Days of Henry Clay and Since* (1896)
T. Roosevelt   *The Naval War of 1812* (1882); *Hunting Trip of a Ranchman* (1885); *Life of Thomas Hart Benton* (1887); *Gouverneur Morris* (1888); *Ranch Life and the Hunting Trail* (1888); *The Winning of the West 1769–1807* (1889–1896, 4 vols.) *New York* (1891); *Hero Tales from American History* (1895); *Rough Riders* (1899); *African Game Trails* (1910); *The New Nationalism* (1910); *History as Literature and Other Essays* (1913); *Theodore Roosevelt, An Autobiography* (1913); *Through the Brazilian Wilderness* (1914); *Life Histories of African Game Animals* (1914); *America and the World War* (1915); *Fear God and Take Your Own Part* (1916); *The Foes of Our Own Household* (1917); *National Strength and International Duty* (1917)
Taft   *Four Aspects of Civic Duty* (1909); *Our Chief Magistrate and His Powers* (1916)
Wilson   *Congressional Government: A Study in American Politics* (1885); *The State: Elements of Historical and Practical Politics* (1889); *George Washington* (1893); *An Old Master, and Other Political Essays* (1893); *More Literature and Other Essays* (1896); *A History of the American People* (1902, 5 vols.); *President Wilson's Case for the League of Nations* (1923)
Harding   No known works
Coolidge   *The Autobiography of Calvin Coolidge*
Hoover   *Principles of Mining* (1909); *American Individualism* (1922); *The Challenge to Liberty* (1934); *The Problems of Lasting Peace*[4]

President	Books
	(1944); *The Memoirs of Herbert Hoover* (1951–1952, 3 vols.); *The Ordeal of Wilson* (1958); *An American Epic* (1959–1961, 3 vols.); *On Growing Up* (1962); *Fishing for Fun* (1963)
F. Roosevelt	*The Happy Warrior, Alfred E. Smith* (1928)
Truman	*Year of Decisions* (1955); *Years of Trial and Hope* (1956); *Mr. Citizen* (1960)
Eisenhower	*Crusade in Europe* (1948); The White House *Years: Mandate for Change 1953–1956* (1963); *The White House Years: Waging Peace, 1956–1961* (1965); *At Ease, Stories I Tell to Friends* (1967)
Kennedy	*While England Slept* (1940); *Profiles in Courage* (1956)
L. Johnson	*The Vantage Point, Perspectives of the Presidency, 1963–1969* (1971)
Nixon	*Six Crises* (1962); *RMN, The Memoirs of Richard Nixon* (1978); *The Real War* (1980); *Leaders* (1982); *Real Peach: Strategy for the West* (1984); *No More Vietnams* (1985); *1999: Victory Without War* (1988)
Ford	*Portrait of an Assassin*[5] (1976); *A Time to Heal* (1979)
Carter	*Why Not the Best?* (1976); *Keeping Faith: Memoirs of a President* (1982); *Everything to Gain: Making the Most Out of the Rest of Your Life*[6] (1987); *An Outdoor Journal* (1988); *An Hour Before Daylight: Memoirs of a Rural Boyhood* (2001); *Sharing Good Times* (2004); *Our Endangered Values: America's Moral Crisis* (2005); others
Reagan	*Where's the Rest of Me? The Ronald Reagan Story*[7] (1965); *An American Life: The Autobiography* (1990)
G. H. W. Bush	*Looking Forward: An Autobiography*[8] (1987); *Man of Integrity*[9] (1988)
Clinton	*Putting People First*[10] (1992); *Common Sense Government: Works Better and Costs Less*[11] (1995); *Clinton on Clinton: A Portrait of the President in His Own Words* (1999); *My Life* (2004)
G. W. Bush	*A Charge to Keep*[12] (1999); *Compassionate Conservatism: What It Is, What It Does, and How It Can Transform America*[13] (2000); *We Will Prevail: President George W. Bush on War, Terrorism, and Freedom* (2003); *George W. Bush on God and Country: The President Speaks Out about Faith, Principle, and Patriotism* (2004); *Official George W. Bush Quote Book: The 43rd President on Faith, Freedom, War and More* (2004)

NOTES

1. Compiled by L. H. Butterfield.
2. Subtitled *The Conquest of Ireland: An Historical Tale of the Twelfth Century.* This is a book of poems.
3. Compiled by Milo M. Quaife.
4. Co-author Hugh Gibson.

5. Co-author John Stiles.
6. This was co-authored with wife Rosalynn.
7. Co-author Richard Hubler.
8. Co-author Victor Gold.
9. Co-author Doug Wead.
10. Co-author Al Gore.
11. Co-author Al Gore.
12. Co-author Karen Hughes.
13. Co-author Marvin Olasky.

68. Presidential Historical Sites and Libraries

Presidential libraries started with Hoover. Prior to that the Presidents' places of birth housed their papers and historical artifacts. The following list notes some of the more prominent places to further research our former Chief Executives.

President	*Sites*
John Adams & **John Quincy Adams**	Adams Home[1] 141 Franklin Street Quincy, MA 02169 Phone: 617 773 1177 Web Site: http://www.nps.gov/adam
	Massachusetts Historical Society 1154 Boylston St. Boston, MA 02215 Phone: 617 536 1608
	United First Parish Church[2] 1306 Hancock St. Quincy, MA 02169 Phone: 617 773 1290 Web Site: http://www.ufpc.org Email: ufpc@ufpc.org
Chester A. Arthur	Chester A. Arthur State Historic Site Route 36 Fairfield, VT 05455 Phone: 802 828 3226

President	Sites
James Buchanan	Buchanan Birthplace Historic Site Mercersburg, PA 17236 Phone 717 328 3116 Web Site: http//www.parec.com/state_parks/buchstpk.htm
	Wheatland, Buchanan's Home 1120 Marietta Ave. Lancaster, PA 17603 Phone: 717 392 8721 Web Site: http://www.wheatland.org
G. H. W. Bush	George Bush Library 1000 George Bush Dr. W. College Station, TX 77845 Phone: 979 260 9554 Web Site: http://bushlibrary.tamu.edu Email: library@bush.archives.gov
Jimmy Carter	Jimmy Carter Library 441 Freedom Parkway Atlanta, GA 30307 Phone: 404 331 3942 http://carterlibrary.galileo.peachnet.edu Email: library@carter.archives.gov
	The Carter Center One Copenhill 453 Freedom Pky. Atlanta, GA 30307
	Jimmy Carter National Historic Site 300 North Bond St. Plains, GA 31780 Phone: 229 824 4104 Web Site: http://www.nps.gov/jica Email: JICA_site_supervison@nps.gov
Grover Cleveland	Cleveland Birthplace State Historic Site 207 Bloomfield Ave. Caldwell, NJ 07006 Phone: 973 326 0001
Bill Clinton	Hope "Clinton Loop"[3] Hope Tourist Center Box 596 Hope, AR 71801 Phone: 800 223 4673

President   *Sites*

                              Hot Springs "Clinton Loop"[4]
                              Hot Springs Visitors Bureau
                              Box K
                              Hot Springs, AR 71902
                              Phone: 800 772 2489

Calvin Coolidge   Plymouth Notch–Coolidge State Historic Site
                              P.O. Box 247
                              Plymouth VT 05056
                              Phone: 802 672 3773
                              Web Site: http://www.calvin-coolidge.org

                              Coolidge Memorial Room, Forbes Library
                              20 West Street
                              Northampton, MA 01060
                              Phone: 413 587 1014
                              Web Site: http://www.gazettenet.com/forbeslibrary/
                                 coolidge.html

Dwight Eisenhower   Eisenhower Birthplace State Historic Park
                              208 East Day Street
                              Denison, TX 75020
                              Phone: 903 465 8908

                              Dwight Eisenhower Library
                              200 SE 4th St.
                              Abilene, KS 67410
                              Phone: 785 263 4218
                              Web Site: http://www.eisenhower.utexas.edu
                              Email: library@eisenhower.archives.gov

                              Eisenhower Gettysburg Home
                              97 Taneytown Road
                              Gettysburg, PA
                              Phone: 717 338 9114
                              Web Site: http://www.nps.gov/eise/home.htm
                              Email: eise_site_manager@mps.gov

Millard Fillmore   Fillmore House Museum
                              Shearer Ave.
                              Box 472
                              East Aurora, NY 14052
                              Phone: 716 652 8875

                              Millard Fillmore Log Cabin
                              Fillmore Glen State Park
                              Rte. 38[5]
                              Moravia, NY 13118
                              Phone: 315 497 0130

President	Sites

President   *Sites*

Gerald Ford

Gerald R. Ford Library
1000 Beal Ave.
Ann Arbor, MI 48109
Phone: 734 741 2218
Web Site: http://www.ford.utexas.edu
Email: ford.library@nara.gov

Gerald R. Ford Museum
303 Pearl Street N.W.
Grand Rapids, MI 49504
Phone: 616 451 9263
Web Site: http://www.ford.utexas.edu
Email: information.museum@fordmus.archives.gov

President Ford's Birthsite Gardens
3202 Woolworth Avenue
Omaha, NE 68103
Phone: 402 444 5900
Web Site: http://www.omaha.org/oma/gford.htm

James Garfield

James A. Garfield National Historical Site
8095 Mentor Ave.
Mentor, OH 44060
Phone: 440 255 8722
Web Site: http://www.nps.gov/jaga
Email: jaga_interpretation@nps.gov

Ulysses Grant

Grant's Birthplace at Point Pleasant
P.O. Box 2
New Richmond, OH 45157
Phone: 513 553 4911
Web Site: http://.ohiostory.org/places/grantbir

Grant Schoolhouse[6]
Grant Homestead Association
c/o Stan Purdy
318 W. State Street
Georgetown, OH 45121
Phone: 937 378 4222
Web Site: http//:www.ohiohistory.org/places/grantsch

Ulysses S. Grant National Historic Site
7400 Grant Road
St. Louis, MO 63123
Phone: 314 842 1867 / 314 842 3298
Web Site: http://www.nps.gov/ufsg
Email: USLG-site-manager@nps.gov

Grant's Home State Historic Site
500 Bouthillier Street

President	*Sites*

P.O. Box 333
Galena, IL 61036
Phone: 515 777 0248
Web Site: http://www.state.il.us/HPA/Sites/GalenaCur
rent.htm

Grant National Memorial
New York City, NY
Web Site: www.nps.gov/gegr

Warren Harding   President Harding's Home
380 Mount Vernon Ave.
Marion, OH 43302
Phone: 740 387 9630

Benjamin Harrison   President Benjamin Harrison Home
1230 North Delaware St.
Indianapolis, IN 46202
Phone: 317 631 1898
Web Site: http://www.surf-ici.com/harrison
Email: harrison@surf-ici.com

William H. Harrison   Berkeley Plantation
12602 Harrison Landing Road
Charles City, VA 23030
Phone: 804 529 6018
Web Site: http://www.jamesriverplantations.org/Berke
ley.html

Rutherford B. Hayes   Spiegel Grove, Hayes Presidential Center
1337 Hayes Avenue
Freemont, OH 43420
Phone: 419 332 2081

Herbert Hoover   Herbert Hoover Library
210 Parkside Dr.
P.O. Box 488
West Branch, IA 52358
Phone: 319 643 5825
Web Site: http://hoover.archives.gov
Web Site: library@hoover.archives.gov

Andrew Jackson   Andrew Jackson State Park
196 Andrew Jackson Park Road
Lancaster, SC 29720
Phone: 803 285 3344
Web Site: http://www.travelsc.com/cg-bin/parks/state
parkdetail.cfm?id=3

President	Sites

President

Sites

McKamie Farmhouse[7]
State Rte 75
Waxhaw, NC

The Hermitage
4580 Rachel's Lane
Hermitage, TX 37076
Phone: 615 889 2941
Web Site: http://www.thehermitage.com

Thomas Jefferson

Monticello
Route 53
Box 316
Charlottesville, VA 22902
Phone: 804 984 9800/804 984 9822
Web Site: http://www.monticello.org
Email: publicaffairs@monticello.org

Poplar Forest[8]
P.O. Box 419
Forest, VA 24551
Phone: 804 526 1806
Web Site: http://www.poplarforest.org

Thomas Jefferson Memorial
Ohio Drive
Washington, DC
Phone: 202 426 6841
Web Site: http:www.nps.gov/thje/home.htm

Andrew Johnson

Andrew Johnson National Historic Site
P.O. Box 1088
Greeneville, TN 37744
Phone: 423 638 3551
Web Site: http://www.nps.gov/anjo
Email: ANO_Superintendent@nps.gov

President Andrew Johnson Memorial Museum and
  Library
Gilland Street[9]
Greeneville, TN
Phone: 423 636 7348/800 729 0256 ext 348
Web Site: http://www.tusculum.edu/pages/ajmuesum/
  index.html
Email: clucas@tusculum.edu

Mordecai Historic Park[10]
Wake Forest Road
Raleigh, NC 27601
Phone: 919 834 4844

President	Sites

Lyndon Johnson

Lyndon B. Johnson Library
2313 Red River Street
Austin, TX 78705
Phone: 512 916 5137
Web Site: http://www.lbjlib.utexas.edu
Email: library@johnson.archives.gov

Lyndon B. Johnson National Historical Park
P.O. Box 329
Johnson City,[11] TX 78636
Phone: 830 868 7128
Web Site: http://www.nps.gov/lyjo
Email: LYHO_superintendent@nps.gov

John Kennedy

John F. Kennedy Library
Columbia Point
Boston, MA 02125
Phone: 617 929 4500
Web Site: http://www.jfklibrary.org
Email: library@kennedy.archives.gov

John F. Kennedy National Historic Site
83 Beals Street
Brookline, MA 02446
Phone: 617 566 7937
Web Site: http://www.nps.gov/jofi
Email: FRLA_superintendent@nps.gov

Abraham Lincoln

Abraham Lincoln Birthplace
2995 Lincoln Farm Road
Hodgenville, KY 427148
Phone: 270 358 3137
Web Site: http://www.nps.gov/abli
Email: ABLI_Administration@nps.gov

Lincoln Boyhood National Memorial[12]
P.O. Box 1816
Lincoln City, IN 47552
Phone: 812 937 4541
http://www.nps.gov/libo
Email: LIBO_Superintendent@nps.gov

Lincoln Log Cabin State Historic Site
400 S. Lincoln Highway Road
P.O. Box 100
Lerna, IL 62440
Phone: 217 345 1845
Web Site: http://www.lincolnlogcabin.org
Email: tomandsarah@lincolnlogcabin.org

President   *Sites*

Lincoln's New Salem[13]
R.R. 1 Box 244A
Petersburg, IL 62675
Phone: 217 632 4000
Web Site: http://www.lincolnsnewsalem.com

Lincoln Home National Historic Site
413 South Eighth Street
Springfield, IL 62701
Phone: 217 492 4241 ext 221
Web Site: http://www.nps.gov.liho
Email: LIHO_Superintendent@nps.gov

Lincoln-Herndon Law Offices
6th & Adams Streets
Springfield, IL 62701
Phone 217 525 1825
Web Site: http://www.showcase.netins.net/web/creativ
   e/lincoln/site/law.htm

The Lincoln Family Church
First Presbyterian Church
321 S. 7th Street
Springfield, Il 62701
Phone: 217 528 4311
Web Site: http://showcase.netins.net/web/creative/lin-
   coln/sites/pew/htm

Mary Todd Lincoln Home
578 West Main Street
Lexington, KY
Web Site: http://uky.edu/LCC/HIS/sites/todd.thml
Email: RHoLL00@pop.uky.edu

Ford's Theatre National Historic Site
517 10th St. N. W.
Washington, DC 20034
Phone: 202 426 6924
Web Site: http://www.nps.gov/foth
Email: NACC_FOTH_Interpretation@nps.gov

Lincoln Memorial in National Mall
The National Mall
Washington, DC 20024
Phone: 202 426 6841
Web Site: http://www.nps.gov/linc/home.htm

Lincoln Tomb State Historic Site
Oak Ridge Cemetery
Springfield, IL

President	*Sites*

Phone: 217 782 2717
Web Site: http://showcase.netins.net/web/creative/loc
  oln/sites/tomb.htm

Lincoln Douglas Debate Museum
Coles County Fairgrounds
Corner of "E" Street & Madison Avenue
Charleston, IL
Phone: 217 348 0430
Web Site: http://www.charlestontourism.org/lincoln.
  htm

Abraham Lincoln Library and Museum
U.S. Highway 25 E
Harrogate, TN
Phone: 423 869 6235
Web Site: http://www.lmunet.edu/Museum/main1.htm
Email: almuseum@inetimu.lmunet.edu

William McKinley   McKinley National Memorial and Museum[14]
800 McKinley Monument Drive, NW
Canton, OH 44708
Phone: 330 445 7043

National McKinley Birthplace Memorial
46 N. Main St.
Niles, OH 44446
Phone: 330 652 1704
Web Site: http://www.mckinley.lib.oh.us
Email: mckinley@mcklib.org

McKinley Memorial Library & Museum
40 N. Main St
Niles, OH 44446
Phone: 330 652 1704
Web Site: http://www.mckinley.lib.oh.us
Email: mckinley@mcklib.org

James Madison   Montpelier[15]
11407 Constitution Highway
Montpelier Station, VA 22957
Phone: 540 672 2728
Web Site: http://www.montpelier.org
Email: education@montpelier.org

The James Madison Museum
129 Caroline Street
Orange, VA
Phone: 540 672 1776

President	Sites

James Monroe

Monroe Birthplace
SR 205
Colonial Beach, VA 22443
Web Site: http://www.3n.net/apvannb/monroe/html

James Monroe Museum
908 Charles Street
Fredericksburg, VA 22401
Phone: 540 654 1043

Richard M. Nixon

Richard M. Nixon Library and Birthplace[16]
18001 Yorba Linda Boulevard
Yorba Linda, CA 92686
Phone: 714 993 3393
Web Site: http://www.nixonfoundation.org

Franklin Pierce

The Franklin Pierce Manse
14 Pensacook Street
Concorde, NH 03302
Phone: 603 224 0094

James Knox Polk

Polk Ancestral Home
Box 741
301 W. 7th Street
Columbia, TX 38401
Phone: 704 889 7145
Web Site: http://www.jamespolk.com

James K. Polk Memorial
Box 475
Pineville, NC 28134
Phone: 704 889 7145
Web Site: www.ah.dcr.state.nc.us/sections/hs/polk/polk.
  html

Ronald Wilson Reagan

Ronald Reagan Birthplace
111 Main Street
Tampico, IL 61283
Phone: 815 438 2815

Ronald Reagan Boyhood Home
816 S. Hennepin Avenue
Dixon, IL 61021
Phone: 815 288 3404

The Reagan Ranch
Northwest of Santa Barbara, CA
Web Site: http://www.reaganranch.org

Ronald Reagan Library
40 Presidential Drive

President	*Sites*
	Simi Valley, CA 93065-0600 Phone: 800 410 8354 Web Site: http://www.reagan.utexas.edu Email: library@reagan.nara.gov
Franklin D. Roosevelt	Eleanor Roosevelt National Historic Site 4097 Albany Post Rd Hyde Park, NY 12538 Phone: 845 229 9115 Web Site: http://www.nps,gov/elro Email: ROVA_webmaster@nps.gov
	Home of Franklin D. Roosevelt 519 Albany Post Road Hyde Park, NY 12538 Phone: 845 229 9115 Web Site: http://www.nps.gov/hofr Email: ROVA_webmaster@nps.gov
	Franklin D. Roosevelt Library 4079 Albany Post Road Hyde Park, NY 12538-1999 Phone: 845 229 8114 Web Site: http://www.academic.marist.edu/fdr/ Email: library@roosevelt.nara.gov
	Roosevelt Campobello International Park Executive Secretary P.O. Box 97 Lubec, ME 04652; or Superintendent P.O. Box 9 Welshpool, NB, Canada E0G 3H0 Phone: 506 752 2922 Web Site: http://www.nps.gov/roca Email: info@fdr.net
	Little White House Historic Site Route 1, Box 10 Warm Springs, GA 31830 Phone: 706 655 5870
	FDR Memorial in the National Mall 900 Ohio Drive, SW Washington, DC 20024 Phone: 202 426 6841 or 202 376 6704 Web Site: http://www.nps.gov/frde Email: national_mall@nps.gov

President	*Sites*

Theodore Roosevelt

TR Birthplace National Historic Site
28 East 20th Street
New York, NY 10003
Phone: 212 260 1616
Web Site: http://www.nps.gov/thrb

Sagamore Hill National Historic Site
20 Sagamore Hill Road
Oyster Bay, NY 11771-1809
Phone: 516 922 4788
Web Site: http://www.nps.gov/sahi
Email: sahi_information@nps.gov

TR Inaugural National Historical Site
Ansley Wilcox House
641 Delaware Avenue
Buffalo, NY 14202
Phone: 716 884 0095
Web Site: http://www.nps.gov/thri

William Howard Taft

William Howard Taft National Historic Site
2038 Auburn Avenue
Cincinnati, OH 45219
Phone: 513 684 3262
Web Site: http://www.nps.gov/wiho
Email: WIHO_Superintendent@nps.gov

Zachary Taylor

Montebello
Highway 33, 5 miles west of Gordonsville, VA

Harry Truman

Harry S Truman Library
500 West U.S. Highway 24
Independence, MO 64050-1798
Phone: 816 833 1400
Web Site: http://www.trumanlibrary.org
Email: library@truman.nara.gov

Harry S Truman Home
219 N. Delaware St.
Independence, MO 64050-2804
Phone: 816 254 9929 or 816 254 7199
Web Site: http://www.nps.gov/hstr
Email: HSTR_Superintendent@nps.gov

Truman Farm Home
Grandview, MO
Phone: 816 254 9929 or 816 254 7199
Web Site: http://www.nps.gov/hstr
Email: HSTR-Superintendent@nps.gov

President	*Sites*
John Tyler	Sherwood Forest Plantation 14501 John Tyler Highway (State Rte 5) Charles City, VA Phone: 804 829 5377 Web Site: http://www.sherwoodforest.org Email: ktyler@sherwoodforest.org
Martin Van Buren	Martin Van Buren National Historic Site 1013 Old Post Road P.O. Box 545 Kinderhook, NY 12106-0545 Phone: 518 758 9689 Web Site: http://www.nps.gov/mava Email: mava_info@nps.gov
George Washington	Washington Birthplace National Monument 1732 Popes Creek Road Washington's Birthplace, VA 22443 Phone: 804 224 1732 Web Site: http://www.nps.gov/gewa/index.html Email: james_laray@nps.gov Sulgrave Manor[17] Sulgrave, England Web Site: http://www.stratford.co.uk/sulgrave/sulgrave.html Mount Vernon P.O. Box 110 Mount Vernon, VA 22121 Phone: 703 780 2000 Web Site: http://mountvernon.org E-Mail: mvinfo@mountvernon.org
Woodrow Wilson	Wilson Birthplace and Museum 18–24 Coalter Street Staunton, VA 24401 Phone: 540 885 0897 Woodrow Wilson House Museum 2340 S Street, NW Washington, DC 20008 Phone: 202 387 4062 Web Site: http://www.woodrowwilsonhouse.org Email: faucella@woodrowwilsonhouse.org

NOTES

1. Located in Adams Historical Park, this is also the birthplace of our sixth President, John Quincy Adams.

2. This was the Adamses' family church. Services are still being held here today.

3. This is a tour by car to various Clinton sites in the town of Hope.

4. This is another driving tour.

5. One mile south of Moravia.

6. This is appointment only. Call Selma Brittingham. Address correspondence to Stan Purdy.

7. This is one of the purported birthplaces of Jackson. There aren't as many "Jackson birthplaces" as "Washington slept here" claims, but the race is close.

8. Jefferson's retreat. Well worth the effort to find and visit

9. If you can find Greeneville, Tennessee, this is all the address you will need.

10. Johnson's birthplace.

11. Johnson City is named for the Johnson family. The LBJ Ranch is just outside of Johnson City.

12. This is Lincoln's boyhood home. It is also the birthplace of his mother, Nancy Hanks Lincoln.

13. This is a recreation of New Salem where Lincoln lived as a young man.

14. This memorial is also the final resting place for William and Ida McKinley.

15. Originally named Mt. Pleasant, Montpelier was the Madison family home, and was originally built by the President's father. Madison added two sections to the home.

16. This is the only privately funded Presidential library.

17. This is Washington's ancestral home.